DRYDEN'S CLASSICAL THEORY OF
LITERATURE

DRYDEN'S CLASSICAL THEORY
OF LITERATURE

EDWARD PECHTER

ASSOCIATE PROFESSOR OF ENGLISH
CONCORDIA UNIVERSITY
MONTREAL

CAMBRIDGE UNIVERSITY PRESS

Published by the Syndics of the Cambridge University Press
Bentley House, 200 Euston Road, London NW1 2DB
American Branch: 32 East 57th Street, New York, N.Y. 10022

Library of Congress Catalogue Card Number: 74-80361

ISBN: 0 521 20539 5

First published 1975

Printed in Great Britain by
Alden & Mowbray Ltd
at the Alden Press, Oxford

CONTENTS

TO JOSEPHINE MILES

PREFACE

Since the Introduction says what this book is about, I limit myself here to acknowledgments.

Anyone who writes about Dryden has a solid, continuing tradition of critical discussion to help him. There are four books directly relevant to this one, Huntley's monograph on the *Essay*, Aden's *Dictionary*, Jensen's *Glossary* and Hume's survey. Many books of different kinds consider Dryden's critical theory indirectly or in part, including histories of literary taste, studies of Dryden's drama and studies of his poetry. The most helpful of these have found their way into the text or notes below, as have the most useful (as I think) of the many articles on Dryden.

Volumes of the California edition of Dryden's *Works* have been appearing slowly during the period in which I have been working on this book. My indebtedness to it (especially to Volume 17, *Prose, 1688–1691*, edited by Monk, *et al.*) is substantial, though I haven't changed my critical apparatus to reflect it. Thus, most of my quotations from Dryden's prose are taken from Walter P. Ker's edition, though I've gone to George Watson's more recent edition for material not included in Ker's. I cite page numbers to both editions parenthetically in the text, specifying only Watson's. When I indicate the date for an essay, I have relied upon the chronological table in Aden's *Dictionary*. In punctuating the titles of Dryden's essays there is no clear rule for the use of italics or inverted commas or neither. Rather than facing a series of minor crises in deciding each case, I have chosen to use italics throughout. This seems most consistent with my tendency to view the essays on their own rather than as prefaces to other works. From this tendency follows a further decision which may seem more arbitrary and which is not even strictly correct – namely, to withhold inverted commas from the name of the work prefaced. Thus, for example, not the *Preface to 'Annus Mirabilis'* but the *Preface to Annus Mirabilis*. I find this convenient, and I do not see how any confusion can result.

Moving from books to people: This study had its distant beginnings at the University of California at Berkeley. My thanks there to Paul Alpers and Stanley Fish for encouraging the work, to Alvin Eustis for valuable leads and suggestions, and to Donald Friedman for his continual reminders that sloppy prose meant sloppy thought. I can't list all my colleagues and friends here at Concordia University who listened and talked to me about Dryden over the past few years, but they know who they are. Roger Bird made available to me his manuscript study of Dryden's medieval translations. Eyvind Ronquist read part of the manuscript, eliminating some egregious gaffes and restraining some of my over-ambitious speculations about classicism by means of his much more substantial knowledge. The late Neil Compton and Sid Lamb, who were chairmen here during the years this book was written, both encouraged me more than I had any right to expect. I needed that encouragement, and I miss them both.

Mr G. J. Pocock read the manuscript in its final drafts, and the book is better throughout as a result of his suggestions. A generous grant from the Canada Council for 1970–71 facilitated much of my research. For generous support of a different kind over the past few years, my gratitude goes to Lesley Wynne Pechter.

The dedication simply smiles in passing at debts too many and deep for me to specify.

E. P.

October 1974

INTRODUCTION

Dryden's earliest critical essay was written in 1664, a dedicatory epistle of his first verse play, *The Rival Ladies*. From this date until his death in 1700 Dryden scarcely passed a year without writing a preface, an essay, a discourse, a literary biography – without writing some piece of criticism. If we wanted to include the letters and the prologues and epilogues which often serve a critical function in subordinate ways, the qualifying 'scarcely' would be unnecessary. What results from this long and steady devotion to criticism is a body of work that is, first of all, substantial in the simplest sense, that of quantity. Later critics, Samuel Johnson and Matthew Arnold for examples, built larger bodies of criticism. Moreover, we do not tend to think of Dryden as primarily a critic, as we do of Johnson and Arnold. This is quite proper because the critical endeavor for Dryden was not primary, being always subordinate to the writing of poetry; but if we turn our glance from what followed to what preceded Dryden, the scope of his criticism is singularly impressive. Nothing like it exists in English; and I speak now not only of its substantial size, but of its kind. Many English writers from Elyot to Bacon touch briefly on the place of literature and literary studies, but only as a part of the larger theme of man and his world. Sidney's *Apologie*, generally acknowledged to be the masterpiece of English criticism in the Renaissance, though concerned directly and completely with literature, relegates this concern consistently to the ultimate question of literature's location within a hierarchy of ethical values. As a synthesis of elements in continental and particularly Italian theory, Sidney's *Apologie*, while obviously a rich and vital statement of literary criticism, may be viewed, like the criticism of the writers I have already mentioned, as an aspect of Renaissance humanism. Another tradition of Renaissance criticism, represented by the rhetorical theorists (Wilson, Fraunce, Puttenham, for examples, but the tradition continues until Dryden's own time), is limited in the main to questions of style, and where not so limited, as in the first book of Puttenham's *Arte*, tends to wage its action on the same battlefield as Sidney.

Dryden – to change metaphors and, perhaps, to oversimplify – brought literary criticism out of the church and into the coffee house. In Dryden's criticism, it is possible very nearly for the first time to examine literary works and literary problems on their own terms, free from the felt need consistently to justify literature itself on grounds that are finally religious in nature. To be sure, the concerns of Renaissance criticism find their way into Dryden's criticism. As a serious thinker about literature, he was bound to explore its relation to the larger concerns of life, to locate it, as I have said of Renaissance critics, within a hierarchy of ethical values. But this location is much less explicitly, and certainly not primarily, Dryden's concern. Dryden writes about poems and poetry in specific, from Virgil to Cowley, from Sophocles to Etherege, from the sublime to the under-plot, and always with the inclusion of the works of Dryden himself. He wrote much more criticism than Sidney, but it is the difference in kind rather than in quantity that makes unimaginable the idea of a book on Sidney comparable to John Aden's dictionary, *The Critical Opinions of John Dryden*.[1]

The closest precedent to Dryden in English criticism is Jonson's *Timber, or Discoveries*. As in other respects – his verse style, his dramaturgy – Dryden in his criticism looked back to Jonson. Old and new evolutionary theories both describe accurately the relation between Dryden and Jonson in the history of English criticism. Primarily the new holds; they have common ancestors, Horace especially, in classical antiquity. At the same time Jonson's effort to bring classical ideas and modes of thought into the English tradition justifies his being called a link between Dryden and the classics. However, from *Timber* to Dryden's criticism is still a quantum jump. Though Jonson, in deflecting criticism from its metaphysical concerns, brought it closer to conversation and specificity, he only suggested possibilities which, the exchange between Davenant and Hobbes notwithstanding, were not realized until Dryden. Dryden organized these possibilities into a fully working assumption, a new assumption, that the intelligent discussion and evaluation of literature based upon an understanding of its internal proprieties – 'the rules', if you wish – was a pursuit justifiable in its own terms, that a proper study of mankind was books, not as a means to grace, but as a means to enjoyment. Dryden is, as Johnson called him in a slightly different context, 'the father of English criticism'.[2]

As practitioners of English criticism we have a vested interest in assessing our patrimony, and the essay that follows is an attempt at such an assessment. Only a partial assessment, however; this book is not an 'overview', not an attempt to provide a 'full-scale account' of Dryden's criticism. I am quoting from Robert D. Hume's recent study, *Dryden's Criticism*,[3] which fulfills these ends with such comprehensive sophistication as to leave – I make extravagant use of Dryden's extravagantly admiring comment about Shakespeare – 'no praise for any who come after him'. The following chapters are considerably more limited in scope, and these limitations may be defined with reference to R. S. Crane's influential article, 'On Writing the History of Criticism in England, 1650–1800'. In this article, Crane describes 'the three determinants of the internal character of any critical discourse' the recognition of which makes fair and understanding commentary possible.[4] These are, in paraphrase: 1. the particular problem or complex of problems which the critic wants to resolve; 2. the set of assumptions by which the critic's problem is formulated, which distinguishes it from other problems; and 3. the reasoning devices, the modes of argument by which the critic arrives at his answer. My major interest is in the structure of Dryden's literary theory, the way it is articulated and how its materials are organized and what this organization implies about his literary assumptions – in short, the second of Crane's determinants. Because the structure of Dryden's theory often has itself the effect of a reasoning device, directing and controlling the argument, I find myself frequently concerned with the third of Crane's determinants as well. But the first I tend to ignore almost altogether.

This is a limitation which must be confronted at the outset. In Dryden's case it is an especially questionable omission, because of the famously – the almost notoriously – occasional quality of his critical writing. Nearly all of Dryden's critical pieces are occasional in nature, predicated upon considerations that are immediate and personal – why he has written his work, or how, and why he feels it necessary to explain his methods. They are thus consistently related not only to poetic practice in general, but to the particular poems or plays which they introduce, and often the particular problems that arose in the writing of these poems and plays. About these problems, about the way these problems 'determine' Dryden's criticism, the reader will find little here, except in the last chapter and conclusion. The reason for this limitation is the reason for any limitation – to get a more detailed focus on what I do wish to discuss. Of course there is a point of diminishing returns, but whether this particular point has been exceeded here it is up to the book, not its introduction, to show. Meanwhile, I hope the title of the book and of its first section prevent false expectations: the *structure* of Dryden's *theory*, a particular emphasis on a single aspect, a tendency to abstract the discourse in question from the practical problems that contributed towards its articulation.

What is this structure? In a word, balance, the balance of the golden mean. 'Balanced' is often used to describe Dryden's writing, both poetry and prose, and to describe Augustan literature generally. But the term is often used imprecisely or incorrectly. We hear frequently about the 'antithetical' structure of the poetic line in Dryden and his contemporaries, as if this term were interchangeable with 'balanced'. This is not strictly so. 'Deep' and 'clear', 'gentle' and 'not dull' in Denham's famous line are not antitheses but contraries. They describe different values, both of which the poet admires and seeks. Or closer to home, Dryden's *Essay of Dramatic Poesy*: Dryden's *Essay* is one of the acknowledged classics of literary theory, an essential anthology piece, yet like so many classics its interest and importance for us, even its significance, is not always immediately obvious. Who wins the debate, or is Dryden vacillating and unsure? These questions have dominated interpretations of *An Essay*, but they obscure and misrepresent the

4

poise of its dialogue form. For Dryden in *An Essay* is not trying to reject some alternatives in favor of others, but to describe a variety of literary values, different but not contradictory or antithetical. All of them are legitimate, and the balance of the mean provides a structure of thought flexible enough to contain them all. The mean is classical, Greek in origin, and 'classical' is another critical epithet I've tried to restore to a more exact and meaningful usage. The mean predominates among some writers in antiquity (Aristotle, Plutarch, Horace, Longinus) and other writers around Dryden's time (Jonson, Boileau, Bouhours, Pope). Dryden's *Essay* and indeed his criticism generally should be seen as articulated within this classical tradition. Such a perspective allows us to recognize a far greater clarity and consistency of purpose in Dryden than has usually been granted. It enables us also to become familiar with a traditional mode of examining, ordering and understanding literary experience, vital throughout the Restoration and eighteenth century, and of enduring interest and value.

So much for the structure of Dryden's theory, and now context. By context I mean the cultural and historical circumstances in which the theory was produced. In the *Essay of Dramatic Poesy* Crites asks rhetorically, 'Is it not evident, in these last hundred years...that almost a new Nature has been revealed to us?' It was during the most recent of these years, in the time of Dryden himself, when this revelation became preeminently evident, and though the specific nature of the changes is difficult to define, we can feel justified in accepting the understanding expressed by Dryden himself *in propria persona* throughout his writing that his was a truly new age. Every age is a new age, but some are newer than others in breaking more sharply with the past. One result of such a break is the need to establish a new set of norms that would be responsive to the new taste, the need, in some measure, to reinvent both literature and literary criticism. Dryden is often admired as a civilizing influence, in making the cultural traditions of contemporary Europe and classical antiquity available to English thought and art in ways far more profound than at any earlier time. If Dryden went eagerly to Boileau's Paris and Horace's Rome, the move was dictated in major part by his felt need to explore new and different ideas. And Dryden's responsiveness to the same need justifies our familiar description of him as 'a transitional figure'.

Yet as 'transitional figure' itself suggests, Dryden's novelty is a complicated phenomenon. In 'crossing over' to the new, he came well stocked with much freight, still usable, from the old. This complication characterizes his cultural as well as temporal novelty. Dryden may have civilized his countrymen by making available to them a sophisticated and highly developed foreign tradition, but he didn't just impose it; he incorporated it into a native tradition with its own kinds of sophistication. If he successfully Gallicized English taste, it was because he could Anglicize French thought. In this kind of complication resides the connection between the areas I study in this book, the link between structure and context. Dryden's characteristic structure is, I think, interesting in its looseness, in the way it can contain different ideas and values in a unity without either denying their differences or allowing them to realize their potential contradictoriness. His characteristic transitions themselves imply transitionalness. At once unusually respectful of distinct identities and yet supremely capable of defining an area where they can peacefully coexist, they articulate a body of discourse admirably suited to organize a *variety* of material, old and new, native and foreign. Dryden's style, Samuel Johnson once remarked, lacked 'the formality of a settled style', rather being 'airy, animated, and vigorous'.[5] If it is dynamic, if Dryden's critical style embodies a process of change, this is one measure of its unique adaptability to – or, equally plausible, its determination by – the variously changing contexts within which his criticism was produced.

The organization of this book follows from the interests I outline above. The first three chapters form a single section, an endeavor in explication and description of the structure of Dryden's theory. In the first chapter I range throughout his critical essays in order to examine some of their basic assumptions, techniques and strategies. In the second I analyze the argument as it develops in a single critical piece, *An Essay of Dramatic Poesy*. The third chapter is an attempt to justify 'classical' as a description of Dryden's theory, by showing the affinities in mode between Dryden and classical writers, both ancient and contemporary, especially in the shared balance of the golden mean. The last three chapters broaden the focus to contexts. In the fourth I examine the relations between Corneille's and Dryden's dramatic criticism, with an emphasis upon the vitality of Dryden's ability to adapt and assimilate material borrowed from a different thinker in a different culture. In the fifth chapter I attempt to relate Dryden's theory at once to earlier and later traditions of critical thought in England, to Renaissance and Augustan views, the emphasis again upon Dryden's ability to contain multitudes within a meaningfully coherent structure. The last chapter is somewhat anomalous. Concerned with theory and practice, examining Dryden's criticism in terms of some of the particular problems it wished to resolve, this chapter seeks to go beyond the limitations self-imposed earlier. But it seeks also to make use of the material in earlier chapters in order to suggest how much variety and difference and change Dryden's poetry can comprehend.

PART ONE: STRUCTURE

1

THE STRUCTURE OF DRYDEN'S THEORY

At the center of Dryden's theory of literature is doubleness. What I mean by doubleness is perhaps best explained by illustrations of what I do not mean. Doubleness does not mean the presence of antinomies, antitheses, paradoxes, polarities. All of these suggest such tension between two values or sets of values as precludes sustained coexistence. Both the Manichean heresy and Hegelian dialectic are examples of such structures in that they organize two different forces or ideas or values in ways that embody this kind of tension. In the Manichean heresy conflicting values compete for supremacy, for that state or stasis, however temporary or partial, when one has conquered the other. In Hegelian dialectic there is a similar conflict between mighty opposites, with the difference that thesis and antithesis merge into a new synthesis which becomes immediately a new thesis predicating a new antithesis in a continuing dialectic. Both of these examples describe a situation which is unstable as a result of the competition between equal or nearly equal forces, and which consequently must progress to a new situation. A third example of what I do not mean by Dryden's doubleness is in the relation between good and evil according to traditional Christian doctrine. The situation in this example is much more stable because evil is understood as merely a perversion of good; sin is love misdirected. The stability results from good's subsuming of evil; because good is of a higher order than evil, there can be no ultimate competition between them.

These ways of ordering experience are not helpful in describing the doubleness in Dryden's theory. They impose a kind of order that does not exist; indeed, a kind of order that Dryden wishes to avoid. A case in point of Dryden's doubleness is his admiration for both French drama and English drama. By faithfully observing the unities, the French dramatists, Dryden felt, ensured a close proportion between their plays as works of art and the nature which their plays imitated. For example, if a play took a few hours to perform, the time of its dramatic action should not extend to a period of years. A play that tried to represent years of action in a few hours would be conspicuously artificial. The unities, thus, are associated with the stylistic ideal of perspicuity, the concealment of art. Dryden's most general formula to describe the values he admired in French drama is *a just imitation of nature*. The esthetic values of English drama resided elsewhere, in what Dryden typically calls *a high* or *a lively imitation of nature*. Here the emphasis is not so much on a close proportion between the play and nature as on the elevation and magnitude of the play itself. If French plays depend especially on the judgment, the observing faculty, English plays are primarily the product of the fancy, the elevating faculty. English dramatic action is varied, more complex, and the characters of English drama are larger than life. While French drama is characterized by perspicuity, the particular pleasure of the English stage comes from the audience's sense of the artist as he choreographs his action, unravels his complications in ways too richly complete to be supposed the result of chance.

Dryden's attitude towards French and English drama suggests the nature of his doubleness of view and the inapplicability of the other structures I have described to characterize this doubleness. French and English drama do not correspond to black and white, the mighty opposites of Manicheanism, nor to the poles of Hegelian dialectic. If we picture Dryden's criticism as a dramatic struggle between mutually exclusive values, we are projecting onto his sensibility a psychomachia which, interesting as it might be in itself, is not typical of his mind. He perceives literary qualities in terms of complementaries – both/and; a statement of preference in an exclusive sense, either/or, tends to be the last kind of statement that Dryden wishes to make. There are values in French drama and there are values in English drama, and any responsible theory of literature ought to respond to both sets. The French can learn from English elevation to enlarge the scope of their drama, and the English can learn from French justness to manage their variety better. Dryden's well-known definition of a play in the *Essay of Dramatic Poesy* emphasizes precisely this doubleness: *a just and lively image of human nature.*

His articulation, then, is conjunction rather than disjunction. But if it is conjunction, it is not synthesis. The terms held together by *both* and *and* are never transcended. Fancy and judgment, Dryden tells us, both perform essential functions in the creation of art, but they never merge into any third term. When on rare occasion they are incorporated into a new concept and given a new name, such as imagination or wit, they are not subsumed into a new product, nor do they ever lose their existence as individual concepts referring to distinguishable processes. When Dryden uses wit in an inclusive sense, it is meant to contain the fancy and the judgment in the way that a bag contains apples.

The orthodox Christian view of the relation between good and evil, my third example of what Dryden's doubleness is not, posits a hierarchy for its terms. Good is stronger, better, more virtuous than evil, which is a kind of perversion or deflection or absence of substantial being. This view would seem on the surface to be the most obviously inapplicable to Dryden's theory, since no one would want to suggest that Dryden viewed the French drama or the judgment as perversions of the values of the English drama or of the fancy. But surprisingly, this view, in a watered-down version, is at the basis of much discussion of Dryden's criticism. Though Dryden tends not to emphasize degrees of approval, though he tends to call attention with equal force to the excellencies of both French and English drama, something there is that doesn't love a plane and that creates ladders instead. Thus, for example, we are sometimes told that Dryden *really* liked the English better, or the fancy better. When contrary evidence appears it is used to invoke that venerable bogie of Dryden studies, his inconsistency.

I don't mean to deny that Dryden had his preferences; as he tells his readers in a prefatory note to the *Essay*, 'The drift of the ensuing Discourse was chiefly to vindicate the honour of our English writers, from the censure of those who unjustly prefer the French before them.' (I. 27) But Dryden's 'chiefly' notwithstanding, it seems to me that the *Essay*'s fundamental critical perspective is what I call doubleness – that is, the recognition and definition of two different literary values, or sets of values, and the need, constantly asserted or implied, to respond to both of them. What is more, this doubleness seems to me a reasonably consistent presence throughout Dryden's criticism.

Doubleness is a strange term, and it may be wondered whether the more familiar 'dualism' would not do better. So long as we understand dualism in its strict dictionary sense, it seems to me satisfactory. I am not altogether comfortable with it because it connotes to my mind a thoroughgoing ontology, such as the Platonic dualism of body and soul, and I do not wish to imply that Dryden's thought is systematic in such a way. Then, too, doubleness seems to me advantageous in its very strangeness, which serves as a constant warning against what may be a natural tendency of the mind to relate different ideas in a way that misrepresents Dryden. The two sets of values upon which Dryden's theory is often based certainly are different: French plays are just imitations; English plays are lively imitations. But difference describes a much broader range of relation than antithesis. As Josephine Miles suggests, 'foreign need not necessarily mean hostile or opposed; that is, the alien category need not be contradictory, or contrary, thus setting up paradox or tension by negation; but is rather, simply different, irrelevant until made relevant by context.'[1]

One of the basic assumptions upon which Dryden's criticism is built is faith in 'the rules'. Like most of his contemporaries, Dryden believed in the value of general formulas for the composition and evaluation of poetry. His commitment to them is maintained unequivocally throughout his career, yet along with his more thoughtful contemporaries and successors in France as well as England, he is not an absolute authoritarian. Much of the best recent work on literary theory in the Restoration and eighteenth century has insisted upon its flexibility. Yet I think there is a tendency to construe authoritarianism and flexibility as necessarily hostile elements, each threatening the other's existence. I don't think this is the case, certainly not in Dryden at least, where these elements, conflicting only in potential, exist in fact in harmony. This harmony, I would argue, is an example of the doubleness at the center of Dryden's critical theory.

Flexibility in critical theory during the Restoration and eighteenth century can reveal itself in a variety of manifestations: the recognition of graces beyond the reach of art; of the indefinable (*je ne sais quoi*); of the sublime as distinct from the beautifully regular; the emphasis upon taste along with related interests in sensibility and the psychological association of ideas. All of these are based upon the recognition of individuality and transcendence as coexistent with generality and regularity in the creative and critical process. Many of these emphases are particularly characteristic of theory later than Dryden's, and they are often taken as evidence of the imminent decline in classicism and its replacement by romantic values at the end of the eighteenth century. Yet many of them are insistently present in Dryden's criticism as well. The interrelated notions of indefinable graces, transcendent accomplishments of poetic genius and the Longinian sublime enter Dryden's thought relatively early in his career, through Boileau's translation of *On the Sublime* which was printed with a preface in 1674, a work whose influence is felt with particular intensity in the terms and argument of *The Author's Apology for Heroic Poetry and Poetic Licence* (1677) and, if with less immediate intensity, in later essays as well. Dryden's theory and English criticism in general are often treated as liberated versions of the more strictly authoritarian French theory; it is thus interesting and perhaps chastening to note that the flexibility of *The Author's Apology* is an example of French influence, in particular the influence of Boileau whose credentials as a regularist are impeccable.

I am trying to suggest that flexibility in critical theory during the late seventeenth and eighteenth centuries is not an accidental or particularly localized historical or cultural phenomenon. It may be found in French theory at its height,[2] and in English theory as early as the Restoration;[3] it seems to be an essential aspect of what is usually called 'neoclassicism' in all its various ages and locales. This doesn't deny either that English theory tends to be more free than French, or that English theory tends even more towards freedom as it approaches the middle and end of the eighteenth century. The sense of a development in such an historical approach is not only useful, it is inevitable

– the 'large discourse, looking before and after', the burden of consciousness. Yet it has its dangers; *post hoc* is not *ergo propter hoc*. It may be admitted that a flexible tendency in English neoclassical criticism itself furnished in part the basis for subsequent attacks on English neoclassical criticism, but it does not necessarily follow that such flexibility was inherently an undermining element in the original structure. Rather, it was part of the structure, contributing to its stability. Potentially, perhaps, the belief in graces beyond the reach of art represents a threat to the belief in artistic rules, but until this potential is realized, it need not have been realized.

A case in point, Dryden on the rules and taste. There is a potential dilemma between the demands of regularity and pleasure: A poem may please and be irregular; a poem may be regular and not please. Dryden recognizes and dismisses both these possibilities. Popular taste by itself does not determine poetic value. As he puts it in the *Defence of An Essay* (1668), 'the liking or disliking of the people gives the play the denomination of good or bad, but does not really make or constitute it such'. (1. 120) But Dryden rejects with equal vigor the idea that a literal application of the rules by itself determines poetic value. His decision not to 'discover some rules which I have given to myself in the writing of an opera' is based precisely on the danger of enfranchising those 'little judges, who, not understanding thoroughly, would be sure to fall upon the faults, and not to acknowledge any of the beauties'. (1. 276; 1685) And in the earlier *Author's Apology* Dryden had similarly rejected such 'little judges'. 'I will presume for once to tell them, that the boldest strokes of poetry...are those which most delight the reader.' (1. 183)

What is remarkable about Dryden's rejection of both these extreme positions is his freedom from tension. Dryden's different attitudes *may* be organized in such a way as to posit 'paradox' or 'dilemma', or 'antagonism' or 'collision', requiring one exclusive choice or the other,[4] but in fact they are poised in a tranquil equilibrium. The potentiality for psychomachia is not realized simply because the materials are not felt to be antagonistic. The positive commitment behind these rejections – a commitment to the rules, a commitment to pleasure – are internally consistent, for the rules and pleasure are related as means to ends.[5] This, I believe is clearly the case in two of Dryden's most carefully articulated theoretical expressions of the rules, the *Preface to Troilus and Cressida* (1679) and *A Parallel of Poetry and Painting* (1695), essays widely separated in time but mutually illuminating and corroborative in their positions.

The rules, Dryden says in the *Preface*, are not their own justification. They are 'founded upon good sense, and sound reason, rather than on authority'. (I. 228–9) They are also founded, he tells us in *A Parallel*, upon the practical experience of pleasure in poetry of the past.

There has been found, in the course of many ages, an infinite number of things, the experience of which, has confirmed... usefulness and goodness...This is notoriously true in the...arts; for the way to please being to imitate Nature, both the poets and the painters in ancient times, and in the best ages, have studied her; and from...practice...the rules have been drawn by which we are instructed how to please, and to compass that end which they obtained, by following their example. (II. 134)

Far from being principles inhibitory of pleasure, the rules help to define the pleasurable in order, as he says earlier in the same essay,

that they who before were rather fond...than knowingly admired ...might defend their inclination by their reason; that they might understand those excellencies which they blindly valued. (II. 115)

For a similar reason, the potential conflict between the regular and the transcendent is not realized. Because they were 'invented' – that is, established on the basis of concrete experience, not formulated abstractly – 'by men of transcendent genius' (I. 211) the rules themselves point to those graces beyond their own reach, and because such bold strokes are the most truly pleasurable, they are finally in conformity with the spirit of the rules. Prescriptive generality and concrete experience, thus, are *both* essential, and Dryden adds to his defense of the rules in *A Parallel* the reminder that 'beside the rules which...can be given...to make a perfect judgment of good pictures,...there is further required a long conversation with the best pieces'. (II. 115) These elements in Dryden's theory, rather than constituting antagonistic poles in a dialectic, cooperate in defining and interanimating each other. And in this respect Dryden's position is typical rather than unique with respect to his contemporaries.[6]

Saintsbury has said about Dryden that he 'established...the English fashion of criticizing,...aiming at delight, at truth, at justice, at nature, at poetry, and letting the rules take care of themselves'.[7] This notorious view was offered over fifty years ago, and I don't wish to flog a dead horse. The fact is, though, that this view was common to a whole generation, nearly a whole century, and its ghost still haunts us. The trouble with it is not so much that it underestimates the importance of the rules in Dryden's theory, which of course it does, as that it misrepresents their relation to delight, truth, justice, etc. So long as we describe this as an adversary relation, so long as we conceive taste and the rules to be necessarily antithetical, the supposition at least of Dryden's inconsistency will persist.[8] It may be hoped, however, that Hume's demonstration of the fundamental stability of Dryden's critical principles[9] as well as John C. Sherwood's excellent recent essay on the relation between 'Precept and Practice ni Dryden's Criticism'[10] will help to disestablish such a view once and for all.

I close with one more passage in Dryden, his lengthy discussion of the 'famous anachronism' in Book IV of the *Aeneid* in which Dido and Aeneas are presented as contemporaries. Dryden offers an extended defense of Virgil against the charge that his violation of chronology, in obtruding an element of improbability and untruth between poem and reader, destroys the reader's pleasure. The defense occupies four pages in the *Dedication of the Aeneis* (1697), and it is Dryden at his supposed dullest, arguing an issue that seems today even more than in Saintsbury's day without vitality in itself. Yet it illustrates the same liveliness and open-mindedness of assumption that characterizes Dryden's critical discourse generally.

Dryden's defense is complicated, following four separable – if not rigorously separated – lines. The first two (for the purposes of this discussion) emphasize the transcendent and the pleasurable from outside the perspective of the rules. First of all, Virgil invented the rules but did not make himself a slave to them. He was able to supersede 'mechanic rules...for the same reason that a monarch may dispense with or suspend his own laws'. Second, it is unfair to censure Virgil for a minor indiscretion when Ovid and other poets are commended for major ones, so long as they please; and Book IV of the *Aeneid*, impossible but for the violation of strict chronology, is particularly pleasing, 'one of the greatest beauties of his poem'. The other two lines of defense, on the other hand, are made securely from within the perspective of the rules. The first of these is largely negative. Virgil's indiscretion was minor; it was merely a 'mechanic' or 'cobweb' law that he violated, one 'not altogether fundamental'. ' 'Tis not lawful, indeed, to contradict a point of history which is known to all the world', but this consideration, Dryden supposes, had led Virgil deliberately to choose 'an obscure and a remote era, where...he could invent at pleasure, and not be easily contradicted'. Chronology was meant to avoid obtrusiveness; Virgil, even in breaking the law of chronology, manages to avoid obtrusiveness by virtue of the discretion of his violation. In the final and most important defense, this line of reasoning is transformed into an affirmation. Virgil's fiction, his deviation from chronology, serves finally to guarantee those very literary values – truth, probability, and the end of delight – which the strict regularists would accuse him of placing in jeopardy.

> To give...the original cause of the long wars betwixt Rome and Carthage, to draw truth out of fiction after so probable a manner, with so much beauty, and so much for the honour of his country, was proper only to the divine wit of Maro...If the fictions be delightful (which they always are, if they be natural), if they be of a piece, if the beginning, the middle, and the end be in their due places, and artfully united to each other, such works can never fail of their deserved success.

Virgil's violation of the letter of the law, in other words, turns out to prove his great fidelity to its spirit.

How shall we characterize the assumptions underneath this discussion? The best approach is still perhaps Hoyt C. Trowbridge's in his influential essay, 'The Place of the Rules in Dryden's Criticism'. According to Trowbridge, Dryden believed that

> there is a middle ground between individual taste and arbitrary law, and it is in this area that sound criticism ought to operate... Thus he agrees with Howard that mathematic certainty is unattain-

able in criticism, but he contends that individual fancy is not the only alternative. Rejecting both taste and demonstration, he finds a mean between these extremes in the realm of probable arguments.[11]

Trowbridge's argument that Dryden finds in Probabilism an intellectual tradition mediating absolute scepticism and absolute certainty is a convincing one. I would object only to the conception of the mean as a static 'middle ground' between antitheses that lack value. Though both 'taste' and 'demonstration' are 'extremes' if they ignore each other, they both nonetheless offer legitimate criteria for judging literature, and in this sense Dryden accepts rather than rejects them. Dryden's position *is* the mean, but only in the true dynamic sense of this classical concept (of which much more in a later chapter): a balanced response to different sorts of value. Different, but not antithetical; rather, complementary. Taste is based upon the rules, shaped and educated by them; the rules are based upon taste, the achievements of transcendent genius. A true application of the rules is possible only with reference to their ends – pleasure, delight – and it is taste which registers these ends. Each concept animates the other. Both are qualities needful for proper criticism.

I have been describing a major assumption that informs Dryden's criticism. I turn now to what is probably his most pervasive technique – comparison. Though commentators on Dryden often dwell lovingly on such literary 'characters' as the one of Shakespeare in *An Essay of Dramatic Poesy* or of Chaucer in the *Preface to the Fables*, Dryden is much more of a comparativist than a portrait painter. In fact, in the sense that his critical impulse is nearly always to measure literary values by referring them to other literary values, he may be called an instinctive comparativist. Even the portraits of Shakespeare and Chaucer are excerpted from contexts of comparison (Shakespeare with Jonson, Chaucer with Ovid). Dryden's comparisons extend throughout the range of his critical interests, as I shall try to suggest. Besides writers, he compares genres (drama and epic), poetic faculties (wit in its various aspects – invention, disposition and elocution; fancy and judgment), literary ends (pleasing and instructing) and periods of literary history. Moreover, these frequent and various comparisons tend to have in common an unusually open form, and it is this form which I shall wish to emphasize.

To begin with a simple comparison, the drama with the epic: Which does Dryden prefer? Dryden, of course, shares with his contemporaries a nearly religious veneration for the heroic poem:

Heroic Poetry...has ever been esteemed, and ever will be the greatest work of human nature. (I. 181; 1677)

A HEROIC POEM...is undoubtedly the greatest work which the soul of man is capable to perform. (II. 154; 1697)

These statements, made twenty years apart, are unequivocal assertions of the primacy of the epic among all human accomplishments, let alone all poetic genres, and the essays from which they come, *The Author's Apology* and the *Dedication of the Aeneis*, are given over in large part to sustaining this view. In the course of such sustaining, Dryden makes specifically clear his own preference for the epic to the drama, but in both cases his preference is very moderately stated.

I write not this with the least intention to undervalue the other parts of poetry: for Comedy is both excellently instructive and extremely pleasant; satire lashes vice into reformation, and...I do not dispute the preference of Tragedy; let every man enjoy his taste. (I. 181–2)

The Epic Poem is more for the manners, and Tragedy for the passions...The matter being thus stated, it will appear that both sorts of poetry are of use for their proper ends. The stage is more active; the Epic Poem works at greater leisure, yet is active too, when need requires. (II. 160)

In both these passages there is an eagerness on Dryden's part to avoid what we usually think of as the conclusion inherent in any comparison: the valuing or acceptance of one term by means of an 'undervaluing' or rejection of the other. Though the comparison does work vertically (epic is higher than drama), Dryden gives at least equal emphasis to the horizontal plane. Epic and drama are different genres ('parts', 'sorts'), both of which have their own legitimate ends. The idea of an ascending order of genres, which was established by Virgil and which governed the poetic endeavors of Spenser and Milton, is still subscribed to by Dryden, but so is a typical generic relativism that allows each kind its own claim to existence and refuses to decide between them in any exclusive sense. Comprehensiveness rather than exclusiveness is the critical desideratum, especially if we may judge from *An Essay of Heroic Plays* (1672), where the comparison between drama and epic is given its most sustained expression. *An Essay of Heroic Plays* is a justification of the genre named in the title precisely on the basis of its dual advantage, its combination of at once the scope, elevation and boldness of expression appropriate to the heroic poem and the directness and naturalness of the play, which 'represents to view what the poem only does relate'. (I. 154)

Much of what I am suggesting may become clearer in considering the comparison between Homer and Virgil, a kind of critical set piece to which Dryden turned late in his life.[12] In the *Dedication of the Aeneis* (1697) Dryden distinguishes between the morals of their two heroic poems. In Homer's – Dryden confines his discussion to the *Iliad* – it is to show the value of confederation among princes with common interest. In Virgil's it is to show the necessity of submitting to authority, even if the authority is not wholly legitimate, even if there remain residual republican commitments. In terms of abstract preference Dryden opts for Homer's moral. 'But', he adds, 'let both be fairly stated; and, without contradicting my first opinion, I can show that Virgil's was as useful to the Romans of his age, as Homer's was to the Grecians of his.' (II. 166–7) We have seen generic relativism in connection with drama and epic; here is a kind of cultural relativism.[13] In both cases the effect of the comparison is the same, to define rather than to evaluate. Though there is preference, it is subordinated to a clear sense of the values on both sides. To put it another way, this is a cumulative rather than an eliminative comparison.

Two years earlier in *A Parallel of Poetry and Painting*, Dryden compared Homer and Virgil with regard more to the styles than the morals of their poems.

Of the two ancient epic poets...the invention and design were the particular talents of Homer...: but the *dictio Virgiliana*, the expression of Virgil, his colouring, was incomparably better. (II. 148)

Dryden divides style here into a discussion of three of the parts of rhetoric – invention, design (disposition), elocution – and manages typically to find values in both Homer and Virgil. The question of preference between the poets is now coterminous with a determination of preference between stylistic attributes – invention and disposition on the one hand, elocution on the other. Dryden opts for Virgil and elocution, pointing out that

in poetry, the expression is that which charms the reader, and beautifies the design, which is only the outlines of the fable. 'Tis true, the design must of itself be good; ...but granting the design to be moderately good, it is like an excellent complexion with indifferent features...[making] what was before but passable appear beautiful... In that [i.e., elocution] I have always endeavoured to copy [Virgil]. (II. 148)

But even here, in emphasizing elocution, Dryden recognizes the need for the design to be good, and he offers Virgil as the model only for elocution.

When Dryden returns to the comparison five years later in the *Preface to the Fables* (1700), although his emphasis changes to the Homeric values, he is perfectly consistent with the statement made in *A Parallel*.

If invention be the first virtue of an epic poet, then the Latin poem can only be allowed the second place...The words are the colouring of the work, which, in the order of nature, is last to be considered. The design, the disposition, the manners, and the thoughts, are all before it: where any of those are wanting or imperfect, so much wants or is imperfect in the imitation of human life, which is in the very definition of a poem. Words, indeed, like glaring colours, are the first beauties that arise and strike the sight; but, if the draught be false or lame, the figures ill-disposed, the manners obscure or inconsistent, or the thoughts unnatural, then the finest colours are but daubing, the piece is a beautiful monster at the best. (II. 252–3)

In praising Virgil's elocution, Dryden had admitted the need for invention and design. Here, in praising Homer's invention and design, he recognizes that the colors are the first beauties that arise and strike the sight, that they must of necessity be part of any successful poem. The *if* followed by the protasis in the subjunctive ('if invention be the first virtue of an epic poet') 'implies that the speaker guards himself against endorsing the truth of the statement'. (*OED*) I suggest that Dryden avoids affirming invention to be the first virtue because it would deny the reasonableness of the other view which he had emphasized in the earlier essay, and to which he still wishes to keep himself open. The clause, in other words, suggests that the view that *elocution* might be the first virtue of an epic poet is not necessarily illegitimate. (An additional complication inheres in Dryden's use of 'first'. Is the primacy in value or simply in chronology? Phrases later in the quotation – '*last* to be considered' and '*first* beauties that arise' – seem to offer conflicting evidence, but I believe that one can make sense of the statement.) This comparison, perhaps even more clearly than the others we have seen, avoids the expression of exclusive preference. By means of a kind of psychological relativism analogous to the generic and historical relativism we have already noted, Dryden's comparison concludes by calling attention to values in both Homer and Virgil and, by implication, the values of invention and design and of elocution, to all of which, it is strongly suggested, literary theory ought to be responsive. 'That which makes them excell in their several ways is, that each of them has followed his own natural inclination, as well in forming the design, as in the execution of it.' (II. 253)

If the comparison between Homer and Virgil develops into a comparative description of different aspects of their poems, so conversely the famous tripartite description of poetic imagination in the *Preface to Annus Mirabilis* (1666) develops into a comparison between two different writers. The three parts of Dryden's description are very similar to the terms we have already seen. The first and third are the same, invention and elocution; the second, not specifically nominated design, seems though to be a more detailed and complicated approximation of it; 'the second is fancy, or the variation, deriving, or moulding, of that thought, as the judgment represents it proper to the subject'. (I. 15) At this point Dryden turns to a comparison between exemplary poets:

For the first two of these, Ovid is famous amongst poets; for the latter, Virgil. Ovid images more often the movements and affections of the mind, either combating between two contrary passions, or extremely discomposed by one. His words therefore are the least part of his care; for he pictures nature in disorder, with which the study and choice of words is inconsistent. This is the proper wit of dialogue or discourse, and consequently of the Drama, where all that is said is supposed to be the effect of sudden thought; which, though it excludes not the quickness of wit in repartees, yet admits not a too curious election of words, too frequent allusions, or use of tropes, or in fine, anything that shows remoteness of thought, or labour in the writer. On the other side, Virgil speaks not so often to us in the person of another, like Ovid, but in his own: he relates almost all things as from himself, and thereby gains more liberty than the other, to express his thoughts with all the graces of elocution, to write more figuratively, and to confess as well the labour as the force of his imagination...We see the objects he presents us with in their native figures, in their proper motions; but we so see them, as our own eyes could never have beheld them so beautiful in themselves. We see the soul of the poet, like that universal one of which he speaks, informing and moving through all his pictures. (I. 15–16)

The subordination of evaluation to other comparative aims is even more evident in this comparison, for no clear preference is discernible. The effect is not primarily to offer *either* Ovid *or* Virgil as a model for imitation (though of course Dryden admires Virgil more). It is rather to offer *both* Ovid *and* Virgil, each with his own particular excellencies in aspects of the poetic imagination, each with his own 'proper wit', in each of whom the poet may find material to learn, depending upon the kind of poem he wishes to write.

The description of imagination in the *Preface to Annus Mirabilis* is the most technically ambitious in Dryden's criticism. As Ker notes, 'He never again committed himself to anything so nearly resembling philosophical analysis.' (I. xxxiv) It is not so much the use of technical terms as the explicit insistence upon two distinct literary criteria which makes the definition unique. He describes 'the proper wit of an Heroic or Historical Poem' as 'some *lively and apt* description...such...that it sets before your eyes the absent object *as perfectly, and more delightfully* than nature'. (II. 14, 15; my emphasis) On the one hand Dryden says that the description should be apt and perfect, the attributes of what he elsewhere calls a faithful or just imitation of nature. On the other hand he says that the description should be lively and more delightful or, to use the terms of *An Essay of Dramatic Poesy* written probably in the same year as the *Preface*, 'Nature wrought up to an higher pitch'. (I. 100) Yet the description in the *Preface* is not, I believe, fundamentally different from other considerations of wit in Dryden's criticism – only more detailed; for the same felt need to respond to two different aspects of wit is at least implied in Dryden's later descriptions.

For example, in the *Preface to An Evening's Love* (1671), Dryden says that 'Ben Johnson's plays were pleasant:...but that pleasantness was not properly wit, or the sharpness of conceit, but the natural imitation of folly'. (I. 138–9) 'Sharpness of conceit' indicates the emphasis upon liveliness as distinct from the apt and perfect description of 'natural imitation'; but this is an emphasis only. He is willing not to press this emphasis in writing about Jonson a year later in the *Defence of the Epilogue* that,

the most judicious of poets, he always writ properly, and as the character required; and I will not contest farther with my friends who call that wit: it being very certain, that even folly itself, well represented, is wit in a larger signification; and that there is fancy, as well as judgment, in it, though not so much or noble. (I. 172)

By the time of *The Author's Apology* (1677) there is a new emphasis, not on liveliness but on aptness. 'Wit...is a propriety of thoughts and words; or, in other terms, thoughts and words elegantly adapted to the subject.' (I. 190) But again, this is a change in emphasis only. Dryden is still being responsive to the aspect of liveliness, here rendered as elegance.[14] In the relatively late *Dedication of the Examen Poeticum* (1692) Dryden's discussion of wit takes the form once again of a comparison between poets – Ovid and, among others, Virgil. 'If wit be pleasantry, he [Ovid] has it to excess; but if it be propriety, Lucretius, Horace, and, above all, Virgil are his superiors.' (II. 9) The implied doubt of the if-subjunctive constructions illustrates once again Dryden's open-mindedness. Wit may and should be seen as residing in both pleasantry and in propriety. Dryden's comparison does not reject one poet or the other. It functions rather as a description of different kinds of legitimate poetic value.

One set of terms available to us from Dryden's criticism to describe these different literary values, or to name the poetic faculties that realize them, is judgment and fancy. Judgment accomplishes aptness, perfectness, accurate representation – a just imitation. Fancy accomplishes liveliness, elegance – in other words, works nature up to an higher pitch. In the first paragraph of Dryden's first critical essay, he describes the judgment and the fancy as interdependent entities combining in the process by which the raw material of nature is transformed into the substance of art. So too, as we have seen, the two faculties are comprehended in the second part of the three-part description of wit in the *Preface to Annus Mirabilis* ('fancy, or the variation...of that thought, as the judgment represents it...'), and in the 'larger signification' of wit employed in the *Defence of the Epilogue* that allowed Jonson to possess it ('there is fancy, as well as judgment, in it'). It is the comprehensive nature of wit, its inclusion of both fancy and judgment, that Dryden insists upon throughout. There is a similar comprehensiveness in Pope's famously puzzling couplets from *An Essay on Criticism*.

> Some, to whom Heav'n in Wit has been profuse,
> Want as much more, to turn it to its use;
> For *Wit* and *Judgment* often are at strife,
> Tho' meant each other's Aid, like Man and Wife. (I. 80–3)

Pope left these lines unchanged, ignoring Dennis's suggestions that he elsewhere followed, apparently to insist upon the seeming paradox. Edward Niles Hooker comments upon the passage that Pope 'saw that wit...and judgment in the artist are but two aspects of a single way of thinking', and he is fully justified in citing Dryden's criticism as anticipatory of Pope's.[15] In neither Pope nor Dryden are the two faculties ever integrated or merged into a new term. They remain separable, different, even potentially in conflict 'like man and wife', but married finally nonetheless, and happily so. Both Dryden and Pope insist that the process of writing poetry, like the process of literary criticism, is – or at least should be – single and whole, comprehending all its constituent discrete faculties in a peaceful balance, though not dissolving them.

I would like to touch finally upon the most extended of all Dryden's comparisons, the one between Horace and Juvenal in the *Discourse Concerning the Original and Progress of Satire* (1692; actually it is a three-part comparison, including Persius whom Dryden typically concludes to be 'not equal, in the main, to... Juvenal or Horace, and yet in some things to be preferred to both of them'; II. 70). This comparison comes to a multiple conclusion. Horace is a better satirist because his genial mode of correcting vice is a more effective agent of instruction than Juvenal's angry declamatory mode. However, Dryden characteristically avoids any absolute exclusiveness. He enters upon an extended historical analysis to show – as we have earlier seen him do in connection with Homer's and Virgil's morals – that the mode of 'Juvenal was as proper for his times'. (II. 91) Moreover, Dryden's careful distribution of awards on the basis of the ends of poetry, pleasure and instruction, further complicates his conclusion. If Horace is a more instructive satirist, Juvenal is a more pleasing poet, primarily because of his higher style. In yet an additional complication, Dryden points out that Juvenal's superiority here is only a matter of emphasis. 'I am profited by both, I am pleased with both; but I owe more to Juvenal for my pleasure.' (II. 82) Dryden does finally state his preference – 'Juvenal has railed more wittily than Horace has rallied.' (II. 95)[16] – but even after all this qualification Dryden feels it necessary to insert an extensive quotation from Dacier, one of Horace's supporters, 'to show I am impartial'. (II. 96–7)

All of Dryden's comparisons are self-conscious in the sense that he is always aware of what he is doing. But, as we might expect, the comparison of Horace with Juvenal, the most carefully developed and sustained of his comparisons, is characterized by a special intensity of self-awareness. It is again, like the comparison of Homer with Virgil, a kind of critical set piece. Dryden himself lists the predecessors: Rigaltius, Heinsius, Dacier, the elder Scaliger, Casaubon. Each of these commentators has his axe to grind, his partiality to one or the other of the satirists, and this is Dryden's objection to them. They make literary criticism into a kind of Roman 'game...of the Circus', (II. 68) with a victor and a vanquished.

It had been much fairer, if the modern critics, who have embarked in the quarrels of their favourite authors, had rather given to each his proper due; without taking from another's heap, to raise their own. There is praise enough for each of them in particular, without encroaching on his fellows, and detracting from them, or enriching themselves with the spoils of others. (II. 69)[17]

Dryden for his part labors 'to divest myself of partiality or prejudice'. (II. 69)

A dispute has always been, and ever will continue, betwixt the favourers of the two poets. *Non nostrum est tantas componere lites.* I shall only venture to give my own opinion, and leave it for better judges to determine. (II. 79)

The preferential choice of such partial critics at least implies a kind of exclusiveness; litigations, like Roman Circuses, must have losers in order to determine winners. As a figure for the true method of critical comparison, Dryden leaves the law court and the Colosseum for the Sicilian setting of the heroic games in *Aeneid* v,

where Aeneas proposes the rewards of the foot-race to the three first who should reach the goal...Let those three ancients be preferred to all the moderns, as first arriving at the goal; let them all be crowned, as victors, with the wreath that properly belongs to satire. (II. 98)

In the crowning of all as victors, the values on all sides are recognized in the theoretical ideal of comprehensiveness.

It may seem like over-solemn critical cant to talk about 'the structure of Dryden's theory' in the face of the immediate experience of reading Dryden's critical essays; the phrase implies a philosophical rigor that seems to be denied by the occasional nature of the essays, and indeed by every typical aspect of Dryden's critical strategy. Late pieces such as the *Discourse Concerning...Satire, A Parallel of Poetry and Painting* and the *Dedication of the Aeneis* tend to be longer and more weighted with sustained, explicit theory, but they do not really contradict the impression of easy-going empiricism that is furnished generally by Dryden's prefaces. Jonson, Corneille and even Montaigne may have contributed towards defining the form of the critical essay in Dryden's mind,[18] but none of them has much of the tone that is Dryden's special mark – casual, witty, above all conversational, as Dryden conceived the conversational norm of style, combining elegance with naturalness.

Of course we know that this isn't conversation, that no one could talk so well, and certainly not Dryden himself if we can trust his own estimate.[19] Yet the essays are so successful in achieving their effect of artlessness that, even with our understanding that this must be a contrived effect, we are inclined more to express appreciation of it than to describe the process by which it is realized. Perhaps this is why we have been treated to such genial appreciations, variations on the formula of conversational ease, as Walter Ker's praise for 'the grace of Dryden's free elocution...Dryden's sentences are like sentences of good conversation, in which it is not necessary that every point should be deliberated. They run on easily...' (I. xxvi-xxvii) Perhaps this too explains Mark Van Doren's comment in the most recent edition of his study of Dryden.

> If I should ever write another book about Dryden it would be about his prose, which I more and more admire. I take it to be the best English prose, unless Shakespeare's is, and it would give me high pleasure to praise it. But I shall not write such a book, believing as I do that no need for it exists. All the world agrees that Dryden was indeed a master of 'the other harmony'.[20]

No doubt everyone does like Dryden's prose, but it can't hurt to ask why. In the following pages I risk some analysis. I try to suggest how Dryden's effects, his occasional and conversational qualities in particular, are realized; even to suggest that these qualities, rather than invalidating attempts to define a theoretical structure in Dryden's work, may be seen as themselves consequences of such a structure.

The following is a passage from the *Dedication of the Aeneis* in which Dryden defends the triplet in his translation of Virgil's poem:

> *When I mentioned the Pindaric line, I should have added that I take another licence in my verses*: for I frequently make use of triplet rhymes, and for the same reason, because they bound the sense. And therefore I generally join these two licences together, and make the last verse of the triplet a Pindaric: for, besides the majesty which it gives, it confines the sense within the barriers of three lines, which would languish if it were lengthened into four. Spenser is my example for both these privileges of English verses; and Chapman has followed him in his translation of Homer. Mr. Cowley has given into them after both; and all succeeding writers after him. I regard them now as the *Magna Charta* of heroic poetry, and am too much an Englishman to lose what my ancestors have gained for me. Let the French and Italians value themselves on their regularity; strength and elevation are our standard. *I said before, and I repeat it*, that the affected purity of the French has unsinewed their heroic verse. The

language of an epic poem is almost wholly figurative: yet they are so fearful of a metaphor, that no example of Virgil can encourage them to be bold with safety...*Not that* I would discourage that purity of diction in which he excels all other poets. But he knows how far to extend his franchises, and advances to the verge, without venturing a foot beyond it. *On the other side*, without being injurious to the memory of our English Pindar, I will presume to say, that his metaphors are sometimes too violent, and his language is not always pure. *But at the same time* I must excuse him; for through the iniquity of the times he was forced to travel, at an age when, instead of learning foreign languages, he should have studied the beauties of his mother tongue, which, like all other speeches, is to be cultivated early, or we shall never write it with any kind of elegance...

There is another thing in which I have presumed to deviate from him and Spenser. They both make hemistichs...(II. 228–30; my emphases)

The passage is a typical statement of Dryden's theory; it insists upon a balanced response to two separate criteria, upon the mean. The extremes define the mean negatively: the excessive boldness of Cowley that is 'sometimes too violent', the deficient boldness or 'affected purity' of the French that 'has unsinewed their heroic verse'. The mean is defined positively by Virgil's practice. 'Bold with safety', he 'advances to the verge, without venturing a foot beyond it'. The triplet culminating in an Alexandrine exemplifies the mean, both bold and pure. 'Besides the majesty which it gives, it confines the sense.'

Why does my paraphrase sound so different from Dryden's statement? (I ignore differences in skill or talent.) It is not merely that I have stripped the flesh to the bone; more important, I have changed the structure itself. I have mainly organized my paraphrase from the top down, from the theoretical abstraction, 'a balanced response to two separate criteria', to the particular practices, or Dryden's opinions of the practices, which constitute the abstraction. Dryden, though, organizes from the bottom up, tends even perhaps to stay on the bottom. He conveys his particular opinions – of Cowley, of the French, of Virgil – without explicitly establishing any containing unity of theory. This is true not just about the paragraph, but about the larger discussion of which it is part. Dryden might have gathered his discussions of Alexandrine, triplet and half-line, quite similar in tone and meaning, under the umbrella of a unifying abstraction: 'Because I believe in a balance of both boldness and purity, I have used Alexandrines and triplets, but not half-lines. To begin with the Alexandrine...'

If he had done so, Dryden could have avoided the repetitions ('they bound the sense', 'it confines the sense'; 'I said before, and I repeat it') and those tell-tale signs in the transitions, which examiners of first-year undergraduate work know well, of a 'failure to develop' a coherent logical structure: 'When I mentioned the Pindaric line, I should have added, that I take *another* license...'; 'There is *another* thing in which I have presumed to deviate...' Yet the instinct to reach for the red pencil is never felt, because the passage is not a failure to develop – not, that is, an unsuccessful attempt; Dryden is not trying for logical development in the usual sense. His transitions do insist that the reader recognize the relation between the parts of his statement: 'Not that', 'But he knows', 'On the other side', 'But at the same time'. These transitions, though, do not contribute to any development of argument; they inform the reader merely that Dryden is moving to a different, to *another* kind of practice and stylistic criterion. The particular preferences are kept separated, like the syntactical units in which they are expressed. Irène Simon notes this as 'a stylistic device which... recurs repeatedly in Dryden: a pause before the connective'.[21] As Samuel Johnson put it, Dryden's prefaces 'have not the formality of a settled style, in which the first half of the sentence betrays the other. The clauses are never balanced, nor the periods modelled'.[22] Because the parts of Dryden's potentially complex sentences are simple wholes, two separate sentences, no precise relation between them is forced upon the reader's attention. 'Another', a most latitudinarian transition, is one crucial to Dryden's style.

Even more important than the loose relation between the parts is the loose relation between the parts and the whole. The whole, the theoretical concept of the mean, is in a sense the significance of the passage, but its presence is not strongly rendered. Unless we are reading with some care we may not notice it. It is never mentioned as such, as a theoretical concept; its most forceful expression takes the form of a mimetic image of a particular practice: 'he advances to the verge...'. We tend to take this as a description of Virgil's style, on a plane with descriptions of others' styles, not as the statement of a theoretical criterion governing the whole discussion. The fact is that, unless the passage is reorganized as I have done above, the statement is *not* the governing abstraction, because Dryden's particular opinions are not insistently related to it. For example, we are made to understand that Cowley is commendably bold and, much later, that Cowley is sometimes unfortunately over-bold and lacking in purity. However, because of the syntactical separation of the statements, emphasized by the relatively large intervening space on the page or the relatively long intervening time in the reading, we are not likely to refer these two perceptions to any 'higher' level of discourse that might contain them: a balance of boldness and purity.

Johnson's statement that Dryden's 'clauses are never balanced, nor the periods modelled' is an accurate description, yet oddly so considering how crucial the concept of balance is to Dryden. The potentials for balanced statement are abundant in the passage about triplets, and a gifted stylist could no doubt re-write it to get an effect similar to Johnson's own famous *tour-de-force* 'parallel' of Dryden and Pope.[23] Yet, as Wimsatt shows in his study of Johnson's prose, stylistic balance is conspicuous only when two or more terms are referred to a third, united somehow by context.[24] Such a context might be established by a complex syntactical structure and by over-arching generalization; Dryden's simple syntax and empiricism de-emphasize the context and thus prevent the balance from being realized. This empiricism I take to be crucial, though it is perhaps the wrong word if it is taken to deny altogether the importance of rule or principle. I do not mean to contradict my earlier discussion of the status of the rules in Dryden's theory; both practice and principle are equally important to Dryden, but 'use' tends to be chronologically, if not ontologically, prior to 'reason' in the way Dryden perceives literary experience:

When I mentioned the Pindaric line, I should have added, that I take another licence in my verses: for I frequently *make use* of triplet rhymes, *and for the same reason,* . . .

To put it another way, Dryden does not so much illustrate a theoretical prescription by means of particular preferences; rather more he lists particular preferences that may be seen as

33

component elements of a prescription. Or, yet once more: His style makes us aware primarily of parts which may be balanced; secondarily of the balancing of these parts; only thirdly of the 'settled' balance of the parts.

These paragraphs have been hard to read, but I think they help in naming some of those qualities that make Dryden easy to read. The occasional quality of his critical essays is the natural consequence of a sensibility that perceives literary values primarily in terms of concrete experience. The conversational quality of his style may be seen in part as following from this; because these concrete experiences are not insistently interrelated by sentence structure or abstraction, the reader perceives them *seriatim*, as separate events, like the sequence of ideas in an unplanned conversation 'in which it is not necessary that every point should be deliberated', or perhaps like the couplets in some contemporary poems. One is rarely asked to relate a part, a syntactical unit, to any but the immediately preceding one. Thus, when Dryden begins his next paragraph by discussing 'another thing in which I have presumed to deviate from' Cowley, no reader is likely to object that the earlier paragraph had begun with an example of Dryden's *following* Cowley. The fact is, one doesn't remember; that the last part of the preceding paragraph is a criticism of Cowley is sufficient for a smooth transition.

It seems to me that these smooth transitions are essential to Dryden's tone. His *anothers* – and all those emphasized transitions have the effect of *another* – strike just the right balance between two conspicuous extremes. On the one hand, by relating the ideas only loosely, they avoid the kind of jerkiness that characterizes rigid subordination and antithesis, the hypotactic jerkiness that Wimsatt notes in the style of Johnson's prose or one of Pope's typical couplets.[25] On the other hand, Dryden avoids the other extreme of paratactic jerkiness, in which the structure is so loose as to seem no structure at all, a collection not simply of separated but of totally disconnected and thus isolated items; as examples, some of Pound's adaptations from the Chinese, the opening page of Joyce's *Portrait* or practically any page in *The Autobiography of Alice B. Toklas*. Dryden's style, then, is neither hypotactic nor paratactic, or rather, like all styles, it is both, but both in such a balanced proportion as to strike us as neither. Again, the *anothers* are essential, for in their loose but clear articulation, they guarantee the easy flow, informing us of our progress to a *different* aspect of the *same* phenomenon. On the poise of these *anothers*, Dryden's style is artlessly balanced – artless in the good sense, according to 'that maxim of all professions', as Crites puts it in *An Essay of Dramatic Poesy*, '*Ars est celare artem*'. (I. 92) This poise is what I have been trying to describe as the structure of Dryden's literary theory.

2

THE ARGUMENT OF DRYDEN'S *ESSAY*

In the past chapter I have been ranging throughout Dryden's essays in order to describe significant recurring assumptions, techniques and strategies that may be said to constitute a consistent structure. I turn now to examine a single piece of criticism, *An Essay of Dramatic Poesy* (1665). I choose the *Essay* primarily because of its form. As a dialogue or series of dialogues, it provides us with an opportunity to examine the sustained development of an argument along the lines I traced out earlier. My contention is that the positions represented by the various speakers act more to complement than to defeat each other.[1] For this reason I tend to feel that the identifications of the speakers as actual persons, first suggested by Malone in 1800 and subsequently much debated, have had certain unfortunate consequences.[2] Too much insistence upon the actual context of contemporary debate, such as the continuing exchange between Dryden and Howard,[3] coupled with the identification of these figures (Howard is Crites, Dryden is Neander), inevitably establishes preconceived notions of adversaries and finality in the mind of any reader who attempts to understand the *Essay*'s larger structure: Neander and truth triumph over Crites and error.

Dryden himself provides an alternative approach in the *Dedicatory Epistle of the Essay*, probably written in 1667. The *Essay*, he says, was written in a 'rude and undigested manner... wherein all I have said is problematical'. (1. 23) With acknowledgments duly made to the almost compulsory dedicatory modesty, I think we do well substantially to accept Dryden's suggestions here. For one thing, it seems consistent with the

36

scepticism that Bredvold, Harth and others have shown to characterize Dryden's temperament generally.[4] For another, more important, it seems consistent with the facts of the *Essay*. While it is true that Crites's position seems to be the weakest, he is hardly a strawman set up to be torn down. In many cases his positions anticipate those of Neander himself, and most important, his theoretical bases are accepted by every other speaker. In the face of this, the simple schematic identifications of the characters and their positions as good and bad, right and wrong, break down completely. The dialogues are just not structured in order to form a judgment. At the same time, the dialogues do articulate significantly different positions which are never made to merge into a synthesis. 'Neither do I take upon me to reconcile, but to relate them,' as Dryden suggests, again in the *Dedicatory Epistle*. (i. 27) There is a delicately poised balance not just between Crites and Neander but among all the speakers in the *Essay*. Sometimes they can share theoretical assumptions while differing in specific judgments, as Crites and Neander do on rhyme. Inversely, they can differ in assumptions and agree in particular opinions, as Lisideius and Neander do in preferring modern to ancient drama. It is by means of such developing complexity of relationship that the theory in the work as a whole is given expression.

The introductory material preceding the dialogues themselves suggests what is to follow. All the speakers agree substantially with Lisideius's 'rude notion' of what a play ought to be: 'A just and lively image of human nature, representing its passions and humours, and the changes of fortune to which it is subject, for the delight and instruction of mankind.' (i. 36) This agreement establishes a common ground, even helps to describe it with its conjunctive pairs (just and lively, delight and instruction), yet Crites's immediate objection 'that it was only *a genere et fine*' promises divergences within the shared framework. All the speakers also share a contemptuous disapproval of two unnamed contemporary poets. The passage describing these poets is sufficiently interesting to quote in full. Crites speaks first:

'I ask you, if one of them does not perpetually pay us with clenches upon words, and a certain clownish kind of raillery? if now and then he does not offer at a catachresis or Clevelandism, wresting and torturing a word into another meaning: in fine, if he be not one of those whom the French would call *un mauvais buffon*; one that is so much a well-willer to the satire, that he spares no man; and though he cannot strike a blow to hurt any, yet ought to be punished for the malice of the action,...' 'You have described him,' said Crites, 'so exactly, that I am afraid to come after you with my other extremity of poetry. He is one of those who, having had some advantage of education and converse, knows better than the other what a poet should be, but puts it into practice more unluckily than any man; his style and matter are everywhere alike: he is the most calm, peaceable writer you ever read: he never disquiets your passions with the least concernment, but still leaves you in as even a temper as he found you; he is a very Leveller in poetry: he helps out his numbers with *For to*, and *Unto*, and all the petty expletives he can find, till he drags them to the end of another line; while the sense is left tired half way behind it: he doubly starves all his verses, first for want of thought, and then of expression; his poetry neither has wit in it, nor seems to have it; ...He affects plainness, to cover his want of imagination: when he writes the serious way, the highest flight of his fancy is some miserable antithesis, or seeming contradiction; and in the comic he is still reaching at some thin conceit, the ghost of a jest, and that too flies before him, never to be caught; these swallows...on the Thames are the just resemblance of his wit: you may observe how near the water they stoop, how many proffers they make to dip, and yet how seldom they touch it; and when they do, 'tis but the surface: they skim over it but to catch a gnat, and then mount into the air and leave it.' (I. 31–2)

The two figures have been identified as Robert Wild and, less certainly, Richard Flecknoe, and I shall be using these names in order to simplify discussion. The passage, however, does far more than simply allow Dryden to get in his digs at contemporary poets. It is a foretaste of the complexity of argumentation to follow.

First of all we can note that Wild and Flecknoe are extremes ('my other extremity') each of which illuminates the other's failures. Wild, with his violent metaphors and his puns, is too conspicuously artificial in his style, 'offer[ing] at a catachresis ..., wresting and torturing a word into another meaning.' Flecknoe, on the other hand, is stylistically too low, 'a very Leveller in poetry: he creeps'. When taken together these two extremes anticipate by contrast and negation a comprehensive notion of proper wit which the *Essay* as a whole may be said to define. Wild, liveliness in excess, is an emblem of the danger in lacking judgment, but the example of Flecknoe, the other extreme, tells us that there is a legitimate and necessary kind of elevation and artifice, later located in detail in the Moderns, the English and rhyme. Flecknoe, justness in excess, emblemizes the danger of deficient imagination, but Wild's bad example warns us that the regularity and perspicuity that are associated with the judgment are themselves essential, and their claim will later be stated affirmatively and in detail in the *Essay* by the speakers for the Ancients, the French and blank verse.

Yet we mustn't push this formal scheme too far. Since Flecknoe is too low, we might, and not without reason, want to call Wild too high; yet Wild himself is low ('clownish kind of raillery', '*un mauvais buffon*'). Since Wild is too conspicuous, we might want to call Flecknoe not conspicuous enough, and there is truth here too, but the final simile tells us that Flecknoe himself is too conspicuous (compare 'reaching at' in the final simile to 'offer at' applied earlier to Wild). If the crucial issue is true wit as a proper balance between fancy and judgment, we have to say that both poets are deficient in both qualities, because it is impossible to have either without the other. Finally, and rather oddly, both of these extremes are nearly the same in their failures. The passage as a whole has a rhetorical thrust very similar to the couplet I quoted earlier from Pope –

> Some, to whom Heav'n in Wit has been profuse,
> Want as much more, to turn it to its use –

and one borders on despair at the limits of interpretive formulas in representing the statement fully. I trust this difficulty justifies the painstaking detail with which I examine the language of the *Essay* in what follows.

One final point. The *Essay*'s unique suitability for my purposes is also simply its uniqueness in Dryden's criticism as a whole. It is the one work not written *in propria persona*. It is also exceptionally, if not uniquely, removed from the immediacies of poetic practice, having been written at Charlton in Wiltshire where Dryden had fled – to use a *Mac Flecknovian* zeugma – both the plague and the Restoration theater. Though rooted in contemporary critical debates like the rhyme controversy, the Sorbière-Sprat controversy, and perhaps even contemporary politics,[5] it is the one complete critical work of Dryden that is not in any measure directed towards defending or describing one of his poetic productions. For these reasons, the *Essay* can hardly be called a representative work, yet I will try to suggest at the end of this chapter that it may indeed be useful as implying a framework within which many of the other essays can be understood, in defining a set of problems and a way of dealing with these problems to which Dryden has frequent recourse later on.[6] This, however, will be only a tentative suggestion, and I have banished into the footnotes references to similar statements in other essays, except where they are intended to clarify positions in the *Essay* itself. My purpose remains fixed on the *Essay*; it will be enough if I can do justice to its manner of argument and development. Towards this end, I organize my discussion into three sections according to Dryden's own familiar sequence of dialogues – Ancients and Moderns, French and English, blank verse and rhyme.

Crites begins his argument for the Ancients with a comparison between contemporary and classical times. 'Every age,' he says, 'has a kind of universal genius, which inclines those that live in it to some particular studies.' (I. 36) The ages of classical drama were such as to encourage great works, whereas 'in these last hundred years...almost a new Nature has been revealed to us'. (I. 36–7) If classical antiquity was characterized by 'the more than common emulation...of writing well', in the current age 'the rewards of honour are taken away', (I. 37) and Crites uses this, along with the disruption of Nature, in his argument for the Ancients:

Those Ancients have been faithful imitators and wise observers of that Nature which is so torn and ill represented in our plays; they have handed down to us a perfect resemblance of her; which we, like ill copiers, neglecting to look on, have rendered monstrous and disfigured. (I. 38)

This comparison serves to introduce the 'famous rules', the three unities, upon which Crites's argument will be based, for the unities are means to the end of faithful imitation, a just proportion between the poetic work and its source, between art and nature:

The Unity of Time they comprehend in twenty-four hours, the com-

40

pass of a natural day, or as near as it can be contrived; and the reason of it is obvious to every one, – that the time of the feigned action, or fable of the play, should be *proportioned as near as can be* to the duration of that time in which it is represented: since therefore, all plays are acted on the theatre in a space of time much within the compass of twenty-four hours, that play is to be thought the *nearest imitation of nature*, whose plot or action is confined within that time; ...For the second Unity, which is that of Place, the Ancients meant by it, that the scene ought to be continued through the play, in the same place where it was laid in the beginning: for the stage on which it is represented being but one and the same place, it is *unnatural* to conceive it many...As for the third Unity, which is that of Action, the Ancients meant no other by it than what the logicians do by their *finis*, the end or scope of any action;...the poet is to aim at one great and complete action, to the carrying on of which all things in his play, even the very obstacles, are to be subservient; and the reason of this is as evident as any of the former.[7] (I. 39–41; my emphases)

This emphasis upon a close proportion has been subject to a certain fundamental misunderstanding. It may be supposed to indicate scepticism concerning the workability of dramatic illusion; as if, doubting the ability of an audience to accept theatrical conventions, Crites offers the unities as a means to convince it that it is present at a real action. Essentially this is the way Howard took Crites's (and Dryden's) position in his own day.[8] Yet in a part of the passage above which I omitted, Crites, talking about unity of place, specifies that he does 'not deny but...the fancy...will contribute to its own deceit', (I. 40) and in the third dialogue, he is even more explicit: 'We know we are to be deceived, and we desire to be so'. (I. 92) Writing *in propria persona* in the *Defence of An Essay*, Dryden wrongly attributes to Howard and then rejects the kind of unqualifiedly naturalistic theory that Howard had wrongly attributed to him. (I. 114) Although there are occasional instances when Dryden's emphasis upon a just imitation does in fact seem to constitute a doubt concerning dramatic illusion, the overwhelming number of cases contradicts this conclusion.[9] Indeed, to judge from the *Dedication of the Spanish Friar* (1681), Dryden's attitude towards dramatic illusion is the reverse of doubt. In this essay Dryden points out angrily, almost in disgust, how everything about the spectacle of drama contributes to cast a mist upon the...understanding...; not unlike the cunning of a juggler, who is always staring us in the face, and overwhelming us with gibberish, only that he may gain the opportunity of making the cleaner conveyance of his trick. But these false beauties of the stage are no more lasting than a rainbow. (I. 245)

No doubt dramatic illusion 'works'; it works only too well. If we may draw inferences about the earlier position from the later, we might suggest that Crites's emphasis on the unities is meant primarily not to foster belief, but to guard against the imposition of too facile a belief.

In any case, what we can say with certainty is that Crites's emphasis upon faithful imitation, upon close proportion, represents a commitment to the faculty of judgment ('a *just* and lively image'), the observing faculty.[10] The just, precise observation of nature guarantees perspicuity, a transparent artistic surface through which the subject, nature, passes without refraction or distortion. This smoothness of esthetic surface, parodied in the style of Flecknoe ('the most calm, peaceable writer you ever read'), finds its legitimate dramatic equivalent in *liaison des scènes*, 'the continuity or joining of the scenes', a corollary of unity of place, for which Crites praises Corneille: ' 'Tis a good mark of a well-contrived play, when all the persons are known to each other, and every one of them has some affairs with all the rest'. (I. 40) *Liaison* avoids an obtrusive sense of the artist's manipulation of his materials, and unity of time serves the same function. The Ancients, by

beginning...their plays, falling close into that part of the story which they intend for the action or principal object of it, leaving the former part to be delivered by narration...set the audience, as it were, at the post where the race is to be concluded; and, *saving them the tedious expectation of seeing the poet set out and ride the beginning of the course,* you behold him not till he is in sight of the goal and just upon you. (I. 39; my emphasis)

And in the same sense again, unity of action spares the audience the distracting sense of 'two actions, equally *laboured and driven on by the writer*' in favor of the 'one complete action which leaves the mind of the audience in a full repose'.[11] (I. 41; my emphasis)

As I have tried to suggest, Crites's position is not eccentric. It is perfectly consistent with statements made by Dryden himself throughout his criticism – that truth, nature undistorted by any obtrusive sense of artistic manipulation, must be the basis of all art.[12] It is significant in this respect that Eugenius's first response to Crites is one of agreement:

I deny not what you urge of arts and sciences, that they have flourished in some ages more than others; but your instance in philosophy makes for me: for if natural causes be more known now than in the time of Aristotle, because more studied, it follows that poesy and other arts may, with the same pains, arrive still nearer to perfection. (I. 44)

This first response governs the tone of Eugenius's entire statement. Eugenius by no means offers a systematic refutation of Crites's principles. He is concerned only in passing with the unities, and he does not actually confront Crites in any direct theoretical way; his point is merely that it is historically inaccurate to attribute the formulation of the unities as rules to the Ancients, and that in fact they often neglected them. In the same way, Eugenius points out that the Greeks knew little about the division into acts, a structuring device which Crites had approved of on grounds similar to his argument for the unities. As to the *liaison des scènes*, again Eugenius accepts Crites's position, content largely to point out how the Ancients themselves occasionally failed in this regard, citing two instances from Terence of soliloquies which do not follow smoothly from the preceding action. Yet his very terms of disapproval – one monologue is 'very *inartificial*', the second an '*unnatural* way of narration' (I. 49 and I. 50) – suggest the same desire for close proportion between art and nature and the same eagerness to avoid any potentially distortive artistic presence as had characterized Crites's own position. Facts rather than principles are at issue. To put it another way, Eugenius faults Crites as a literary historian, not as a literary theorist.

But Eugenius goes further than this. There are undertones throughout his argument that tend to suggest a genuine theoretical confrontation with Crites's position. In the case of *liaison*, though Eugenius is forced to grant the superiority of the Ancients, he suggests that their victory is at the expense of variety of plot and richness of character. 'The plots of their plays being narrow, and the persons few, one of their acts was written in a less compass than one of our well-wrought scenes.' (I. 49) For a moment Eugenius suggests that there is something more to art than was dreamed of in Crites's philosophy; but this is only a moment, and he quickly reverts again to criticizing Crites's argument by appealing to Crites's own values. 'And yet they are deficient even in this', that is, *liaison*. (I. 49) Eugenius's discussion of tragicomedy is similarly suggestive. Though he offers no theoretical support for his position, he feels that it is to the disadvantage of the Ancients that 'the sock and buskin were not worn by the same poet'. But immediately the thrust is changed: 'Having then so much more care to excel in one kind, very little is to be pardoned them, if they miscarried in it.' (I. 50) What might have been a change of terms implying a want of variety in the Ancients turns out finally to be an acceptance and even more rigorous application of the same terms.

In one instance only do these undertones of theoretical disagreement become explicit for more than a passing moment. Again the issue is variety of action, a crucial issue throughout the *Essay*. Eugenius attributes dullness to Greek tragedy, in which the familiar legendary material is told to death, with the result that the audience

sat with a yawning kind of expectation,...till their appetites were cloyed with the same dish, and, the novelty being gone, the pleasure vanished; so that one main end of Dramatic Poesy in its definition, which was to cause delight, was of consequence destroyed. (I. 47)

He makes a similar charge that Roman comedies, with their familiar twists and surprises and conventional stock figures, are unsatisfactory.

These are plots built after the Italian mode of houses; you see through them all at once: the characters are indeed the imitations of Nature, but so narrow, as if they had imitated only an eye or an hand, and did not dare to venture on the lines of a face, or the proportion of a body. (I. 47–8)

Elder Olsen has recently suggested that two different kinds of literary theory here confront one another. For Crites,

poetic probability is...absolutely determined by natural probability; the argument is from what is unitary or probable in nature to what must be unitary or probable in art. Eugenius...argues in precisely the opposite fashion, determining the subject matter of poetry from the effect; it is not what is probable or necessary in nature which determines poetic probability, but what will impress the audience as probable or necessary.[13]

In other words Crites bases his reference upon the relation between the artifact and nature, Eugenius on the relation between the artifact and its audience; Crites approves of unity of action as a just imitation, Eugenius approves of a more various action as pleasing.

There is much truth in this scheme, but the details of the text tend to render it less than wholly adequate. True, 'mimetic' and 'pragmatic' concerns (to use M. H. Abrams's familiar terms) are *emphasized* by Crites and Neander respectively, but they are not rigorously disjoined from one another. Eugenius, though he may emphasize the effect, is concerned with the mimetic question as well, as his frequent adoptions of Crites's theoretical bases make clear. And moreover, Crites was himself concerned with the poem's effect. His argument for the unities had been based in major part upon pleasure, or rather upon the avoidance of an audience's displeasure in an obtrusively irregular work ('saving them the tedious expectation', 'equally laboured and driven on'). In terms specifically of unity of action he had pointed out that 'but one...complete action...leaves the mind of the audience in a full repose', and moreover, he is even very close in substance to Eugenius's position in his immediate addition that 'this cannot be brought to pass but by many other imperfect actions, which conduce to it, and hold the audience in a delightful suspense of what will be'. (I. 41) It is a denial of the *Essay*'s complexity to transform such delicate shifts of emphasis into 'absolute' schemes of 'precise opposition'. One tends to feel that the mimetic and pragmatic questions are finally too interdependent for such rigorous separation, a feeling for which there is ample supporting evidence throughout the rest of Dryden's criticism.[14]

Only in Eugenius's very interesting and suggestive metaphor – 'indeed the imitations of Nature, but so narrow...' – does the theory itself undergo a kind of change. The implied idea of a broad imitation allows Eugenius to insist more emphatically than Crites upon varied plots and rich characters in order to produce effectively engaging poetry. At the same time, the metaphor does not deny the value of artlessness in the good sense, an undistorted representation. The ambiguous reference of 'but so narrow' allows the formula to signify the desirability of *imitation of broad nature* at least as plausibly as *a broad imitation of nature*. If this is the case, the poet's task would be not to enlarge nature but simply to select its higher manifestations, kings instead of clowns, and Crites's principle of a just imitation would be in no way altered. It is within this context that we should understand the author's entrance at the end of the first dialogue to announce the results. 'This moderation of Crites, as it was pleasing to all the company, so it put an end to that dispute; which Eugenius, who seemed to have the better of the argument, would urge no further.' (I. 55) Eugenius's victory here is rendered only as a possibility within a subordinate clause. This is more than just gentlemanly *honnêteté*; it should serve to warn us that the dialogue has not been organized primarily to establish a clear superiority, and further, perhaps, that the concept of superiority is being used in a specialized sense. Eugenius doesn't defeat Crites, doesn't contradict his premises, only adds to them, develops them by subtle shifts of emphasis. 'Better', then, seems to mean primarily 'more', an ability to recognize richer variety within a shared framework. The major value expressed by the first dialogue in general, thus, is comprehensiveness.

It seems to me that the first two dialogues are related as the parts of the first. That is, the second tends to re-explore the same general considerations, further describing emphases and examining further nuances. 'Further' in both senses – to a greater extent and additionally. The second dialogue tends to repeat, but also to make more clear. Lisideius's position is a case in point. His reasons for preferring the French are similar to Crites's reasons for preferring the Ancients – the unities. 'Of all nations the French have best observed them.' (I. 57) And in his praise of the French for their unified action, Lisideius provides perhaps the clearest exposition in the entire *Essay* of the value of regularity; it avoids that distorting, pleasure-destroying artistic presence that he finds in the English, where 'we see two distinct webs in a play, like those in ill-wrought stuffs; and two actions, that is, two plays, carried on together, to the confounding of the audience'. (I. 57) The French in particular avoid the unnatural mixture of tragicomedy and in general 'do not *embarrass, or cumber* themselves with too much plot... by pursuing close one argument, which is not cloyed with many turns'. (1. 60; my emphasis; we have met with *cloyed* before, but in an opposite context – 'cloyed with the same dish'.) They scrupulously follow *liaison des scènes*, 'which, if observed, must needs render all the events in a play more natural; for there you see the probability of every accident, in the cause that produced it'. (1. 66) When Crites returns to argue again for a just imitation in the third dialogue, he will specify the single criterion which perhaps best sums up the position which he and Lisideius emphasize: 'that maxim of all professions, *Ars est celare artem*, that it is the greatest perfection of art to keep itself undiscovered'. (1. 92)

However, it would be a simplification to suggest that Lisideius is merely transplanting the roots of Crites's argument to a new soil. While he does substantially adopt Crites's position, in the course of his discussion he modifies and qualifies it in ways suggesting that he had indeed been listening to the preceding dialogue; not simply to Crites's side, but to Eugenius's as well. Though he defends the scrupulousness of the French in designing plot and portraying character, it is always with an additional insistence that such scrupulousness does not exclude richness and variety. Thus when he rejects what he considers to be the absurd and unnatural mixture of genres in English tragicomedy in favor of regular French plots, he is quick to add that 'the French affords you as much variety on the same day, but they do it not so unseasonably or *mal à propos* as we'. (1. 58) In the same way Lisideius approves of the French practice of making one character predominate in, and thus unify, the design. But lest he be open to a charge similar to Eugenius's against stock Roman types, he denies 'that in exalting one character the rest are neglected'. (1. 61) Crites's argument had contained similar qualifications, but Lisideius makes them more explicit.

If we examine in some detail one of Lisideius's sustained arguments, we can get some indication of the greater complexity in this second dialogue. Lisideius praises the French plots because they 'are always grounded upon some known history'. The argument continues:

And in that they have so imitated the Ancients, that they have surpassed them. For the Ancients, as was observed before, took for the foundation of their plays some poetical fiction, such as under that consideration could move but little concernment in the audience, because they already knew the event of it. *But* the French goes farther: ...He so interweaves truth with probable fiction, that he puts a pleasing fallacy upon us; mends the intrigues of fate, and dispenses with the severity of history, to reward that virtue which has been rendered to us there unfortunate...*Even then* we are willing to be deceived, and the poet, if he contrives it with the appearance of truth, has all the audience of his party; at least during the time the play is acting: so naturally we are kind to virtue, when our own interest is not in question, that we take it up as the general concernment of mankind. *On the other side*, if you consider the historical plays of Shakespeare, they are rather so many chronicles of kings, or the business many times of thirty or forty years, cramped into a representation of two hours and an half; which is not to imitate or paint Nature, but rather to draw her in miniature, to take her in little; to look upon her through the wrong end of a perspective, and receive her images not only much less, but infinitely more imperfect than the life: this, instead of making a play delightful, renders it ridiculous: ...For the spirit of man cannot be satisfied but with truth, or at least verisimility. (I. 58–9; my emphases)

The argument is predicated originally upon the value of historical accuracy embodied in French drama. Later references in the argument to 'a pleasing fallacy', the will 'to be deceived' and the 'forty years, cramped into...two hours and an half' return us unmistakably to the framework of Crites's discussion of the unities of time and place. The same theoretical issues are at stake; by observing historical accuracy – or rather, by avoiding conspicuous historical inaccuracy – the play does not call attention to itself as artifact. But this is only the starting point for Lisideius; he immediately changes his perspective. Remembering Eugenius's criticism of Greek tragedy, he admits that strict historical accuracy, unqualified, would 'move but little concernment in the audience', and he in fact approves of the poetic transmutation of historical experience made by the French poets in order to render poetic justice. At this point the argument begins to shift back to its original perspective. Though permitting and even commending fiction, Lisideius insists that it be a 'probable fiction', a deception contrived 'with the appearance of truth'. His approval of the artistic transmutation involved in rendering poetic justice – and thus distorting history, truth and nature – is justified precisely by an appeal to nature: 'so naturally we are kind to virtue'. The meaning of nature is here silently shifted from its perhaps more usual signification of a predominantly external reality (as in 'a new Nature has been revealed to us') to a specifically human response (as in 'a just and lively image of human nature'), an unchanging generic norm shared by the audience as indeed by all men, 'the general concernments of mankind'.

Mary Thale has pointed out that this last shift allows Dryden to contain potentially conflicting elements harmoniously within the structure of a single formula.[15] In fact this is true about all the shifts of perspective in Lisideius's argument, for, like the transitions I discussed at the end of the last chapter, Lisideius's *but* and *even then* and *on the other side* have the typical effect of Dryden's *anothers*, relating loosely, guaranteeing a smooth flow even as they indicate a change of direction in the argument. This is the effect also of Lisideius's metaphor towards the end of the passage – 'which is not to imitate or paint Nature, but rather to draw her in miniature...' One is reminded of Eugenius's metaphor earlier, 'indeed the imitations of Nature, but so narrow...';[16] or one can look ahead to another metaphor used by Lisideius himself in a fascinating passage which I shall not analyze: 'There are many actions which can never be imitated to a just height.' (I. 63) 'Just height', like Pope's couplet on wit and judgment, like Dryden's own description of Virgil in *A Parallel*, that he 'had judgment enough to know daring was necessary' (II. 152) – all these, because of their compression, seem to verge on paradox, but they are not paradoxical. Rather, they make use of the flexibility of figurative discourse to allow different literary values to coexist within the framework of a single formula. And in this sense, the statement of the *Essay* as a whole might be called metaphorical.

I turn now to Neander's response, arguing for the English. If Lisideius extends and complicates Crites, Neander extends and complicates Eugenius. As Eugenius had begun his response by accepting Crites's assumptions about the 'new Nature', so here Neander is perfectly willing to admit agreement on most issues with his predecessor and supposed opponent. 'I shall grant Lisideius, without much dispute, a great part of what he has urged against us.' (I. 63) He concedes the French their regularity, their decorum, their exactness, and then begins his claim for the English.

Yet, after all, I am of opinion that neither our faults nor their virtues are considerable enough to place them above us. For the lively imitation of Nature being in the definition of a play, those which best fulfil that law ought to be esteemed superior to the others. 'Tis true, those beauties of the French poesy are such as will raise perfection higher where it is, but are not sufficient to give it where it is not: they are indeed the beauties of a statue, but not of a man, because not animated with the soul of Poesy. (I. 67)

Here again, key figures – 'a lively imitation', 'a statue,...not a man'. By means of these, Neander can go further than Eugenius did. Variety and richness, he tells us, are not merely values which the rules must not exclude but, more positively, the *sine qua non* of poetic art; the vital substance of poetry, thus, resides in values for which the rules are insufficient guides. At the same time, he hardly denies the rules' validity, at least as ancillary ('raise it where it is'), and chiefly it is the last metaphor that gives him enough room to accomplish this. The rules throughout the *Essay* have been used to defend the idea of a play as the undistorted representation of nature rather than the falsely artificial construct. But Neander's metaphor makes the regular (or, from his perspective, excessively regular) French play into the artificial construct, the statue, and the lively and varied English play into the natural image, the man. (Again, there is an implied shift in nature here.) The metaphor, though more bold and positive in its emphasis upon heightening, serves to extend perhaps but not to contradict any of the previous discussion. It changes an emphasis and thus changes the particular application of the earlier speaker's argument, but it does this by appealing to the same theoretical assumptions which had underlain that argument.

In a similar way Neander relies heavily on Lisideius's assumptions in defending the variety of action in English plays. Lisideius had based his attack on English tragicomedy upon the values of a just imitation ('two distinct webs...confounding... the audience'). Neander does not turn initially from the judgment to appeal to the fancy, the elevating faculty. His defense of tragicomedy simply takes a broader view of what may be comprehended by the senses and logic and, by fairly clear implication, by that faculty which observes contraries, the judgment itself:

> Why should he imagine the soul of man more heavy than his senses? Does not the eye pass from an unpleasant object to a pleasant in a much shorter time than is required to do this [i.e., shift from a tragic to a comic scene]? and does not the unpleasantness of the first commend the beauty of the latter? The old rule of logic might have convinced him, that contraries, when placed near, set off each other. (1. 69–70)

And by the same token, his initial response to the charge that English tragicomedy is unnatural is to enlarge the concept of the natural.

> The orb of the fixed stars, and those of the planets, though they have motions of their own, are whirled about by the motion of the *Primum Mobile*, in which they are contained. That similitude expresses much of the English stage; for if contrary motions may be found in nature to agree; if a planet can go east and west at the same time, one way by virtue of his own motion, the other way by the force of the First Mover, it will not be difficult to imagine how the underplot, which is only different, not contrary to the great design, may naturally be conducted along with it. (1. 70–1)

Mary Thale missed this particular shift in the significance of nature, but its effect is the same as the others she has described. Nearly thirty years later in the *Discourse Concerning...Satire* (1692), Dryden would again defend the naturalness of tragicomedy, this time by means of an extended analogy to the Copernican system. (II. 102) The effect, though, is the same as in this passage from the *Essay*, to show us variety and unity as mutually sustaining rather than mutually exclusive concepts – an especially remarkable instance of the adaptability of Dryden's theory.

When Neander finally turns from defense in order to propose the positive advantages of the English, he is scrupulous to leave Lisideius's assumptions intact. He simply shifts emphases, reverses Lisideius's subordinations. 'Our variety, *if well ordered*, will afford a greater pleasure.'[17] (1. 71; my emphasis) The greater variety that Neander opts for inevitably results in a more conspicuous artistic presence, but Neander doesn't forget Crites's and Lisideius's view that this might 'cumber', 'embarrass' and 'dissatisfy'; he merely relegates it to a subordinate clause.

'Tis evident that the more the persons are, the greater will be the variety of the plot. *If then the parts are managed so regularly,...and...become not a perplexed and confused mass of accidents*, you will find it infinitely pleasing to be led in a labyrinth of design, where you see some of your way before you, yet discern not the end till you arrive at it. (I. 73; my emphasis)

Again, his purpose is to add, not detract, to complement, not defeat – a purpose admirably summarized in one of his last statements: 'We have many plays of ours as regular as any of theirs, *and which, besides*, have more variety of plot and characters'. (II. 78; my emphasis)

Let me suggest what will no doubt seem to be a preposterous analogy: Reading Dryden's *Essay* is like reading Eliot's *Four Quartets*, in some ways anyway. Dryden's sprightly tone is vastly different from Eliot's; but in the dependence for its development on repetition, on very fine shifts in emphasis and on figurative language, the *Essay* is in its own way meditative and poetic. The end of all the exploration is to arrive at the point of departure and know the place for the first time. This brings me to the end of Dryden's exploration in the *Essay*, the third dialogue, concerned with the suitability of rhymed verse to the drama. The issue is not very interesting in itself, but Ancients-and-Moderns and French-and-English don't seem any more obviously engaging, and I find it hard to explain this last dialogue's relative unpopularity. In any case, considering it in isolation is unfair both to it and the *Essay* as a whole, for its purpose is clearly integrated with what has preceded. This dialogue comes to the same multiplicity of conclusions. Use rhyme, Neander says, because it elevates, but therefore only or especially in tragedy, and in any case only if you make it natural – which is what Crites wanted in the first place. That is, the dialogue tells us, *and* make it natural – just as well as lively. The last dialogue, in other words, serves to explore the same theoretical issues as the previous two, and in the same way. It doesn't change the level of discourse; if it carries more weight, this is simply the weight of what has preceded. In a work emphasizing comprehensiveness throughout, the last statement tends to be comprehensive above all. Nothing is revealed that hadn't been at least implied earlier; conclusions, however, are rendered more explicit.

Typically, the discussion begins from Crites's perspective, in fact with the words of Crites himself:

Rhyme is unnatural in a play, because dialogue there is presented as the effect of sudden thought: for a play is the imitation of Nature; and since no man without premeditation speaks in rhyme, neither ought he to do it on the stage. This hinders not but the fancy may be there elevated to an higher pitch of thought than it is in ordinary discourse; for there is a probability that men of excellent and quick parts may speak noble things *ex tempore*: but those thoughts are never fettered with the numbers or sound of verse without study, and therefore it cannot be but unnatural to present the most free way of speaking in that which is the most constrained. For this reason, says Aristotle, 'tis best to write tragedy in that kind of verse which is the least such, or which is nearest prose: and this amongst the Ancients was the iambic, and with us is blank verse, or the measure of the verse kept exactly without rhyme. (1. 91)

And as to rhymed repartee, the *experimentum crucis*, Crites asks,

Now what is more unreasonable than to imagine that a man should not only light upon the wit, but the rhyme too, upon the sudden?... it will appear that your actors hold intelligence together; that they perform their tricks like fortune-tellers, by confederacy. The hand of art will be too visible in it, against that maxim of all professions, *Ars est celare artem*, that it is the greatest perfection of art to keep itself undiscovered. Nor will it serve you to object, that however you manage it, 'tis still known to be a play; and, consequently, the dialogue of two persons understood to be the labour of one poet. For a play is still an imitation of Nature; we know we are to be deceived, and we desire to be so; but no man was ever deceived but with a probability of truth; for who will suffer a gross lie to be fastened on him?...since the mind of man does naturally tend to, and seek after truth; and therefore the nearer any thing comes to the imitation of it, the more it pleases. (1. 92–3)

These arguments should be sufficiently familiar to justify only a bare summary: *Granted*, 1. we do not want a literal identity between source and artifact, we want elevation by means of the fancy, deceit is both necessary and desirable; *still*, 2. there ought to be a close proportion between source and artifact, that is in this case, blank verse; *because*, 3. anything more obtrusively conspicuous by way of artistic manipulation will destroy the audience's pleasure.

Neander, of course, accepts Crites's first assumption completely. His response is directed only to the second two points. Typically, he does not try to invalidate Crites's claim for naturalness, for a just proportion. Indeed, much of his argument is that rhyme itself can be made natural. He urges 'an election of apt words, a right disposing of them. For the due choice of your words expresses your sense naturally, and the due placing them adapts the rhyme to it.' (i. 95) He also recommends 'breaks in a hemistich, or running the sense into another line, thereby making art and order appear as loose and free as Nature'. (i. 97) The smoothness that Neander recommends here – the true perspicuity parodied in the style of Flecknoe, the 'other extremity' – serves the equivalent purpose in stylistic terms to *liaison des scènes* in terms of dramatic convention and is predicated upon the same value of concealing art. Where the two speakers tend to differ is largely in emphasis; as an example, Neander's defense of rhyme's particular suitability to tragedy:

I answer you...by distinguishing betwixt what is nearest to the nature of Comedy, which is the imitation of common persons and ordinary speaking, and what is nearest the nature of a serious play: this last is indeed the representation of Nature, but 'tis Nature wrought up to an higher pitch. The plot, the characters, the wit, the passions, the descriptions, are all exalted above the level of common converse, as high as the imagination of the poet can carry them, with proportion to verisimility. (i. 101–2)

Neander's statement here deviates from Crites's only in its subordination. Crites's emphasis upon a just imitation had not precluded an elevation by means of fancy, the need for deception. Neander's emphasis upon exaltation, Nature wrought up to an higher pitch, does not preclude a response to the demand for verisimilitude. Both arguments center on imitation as a proportionate relation between the source, nature, and the poetic construct, art. It is simply that Neander is inclined to be more generous in the proportional ratio, at least in the case of tragedy.[18]

Only in connection with the third point, the audience's pleasure, does Neander depart significantly from Crites's position, and he does so typically by means of a metaphor.

Verse, 'tis true, is not the effect of sudden thought; but this hinders not that sudden thought may be represented in verse, since those thoughts are such as must be higher than Nature can raise them without premeditation, especially to the continuance of them, even out of verse; and consequently you cannot imagine them to have been sudden either in the poet or in the actors. A play, as I have said, to be like Nature, is to be set above it; as statues which are placed on high are made greater than the life, that they may descend to the sight in their just proportion. (I. 102)

This particular figure may be seen as the culmination of a series of such figures crucial to the *Essay*'s development. Most recently, Neander himself had preferred the man, English variety, to the statue, French regularity. That he opts now for the statue, rhyme, and not the man, blank verse, is only an apparent inconsistency, for the statue looks to the audience more like the man than the man does himself. The figure elaborates also upon the earlier 'imitated to a just height', and I think shows even more conclusively how the potentialities for paradox are not realized. There is not, as Dean Tolle Mace suggests, 'an antagonism between psychological "truth" and external objective "truth"'.[19] Rather, the two truths cooperate and interanimate each other. Neander's position calls for a heightening and enlarging, by means of the fancy, in the process of imitation. This heightening and enlargement is justified on pragmatic grounds in terms of the audience's response – Mace's 'psychological "truth"'. However, the demand for the psychological truth of the artifact moves in turn back to the mimetic issue, to which it is by no means antagonistic. Crites had said that the closer the imitation, the more pleasing it will be; Neander's change is to the following effect: the closer the imitation *seems to be to the audience*, the more pleasing it will be. What pleases the audience is exactly the *sense* of a faithful imitation, which sense is secured by a heightening and enlargement of imitation. The elevation of fancy guarantees the appearance of a just proportion. The metaphor is the final and most explicit statement of the interdependence of these two concepts, and interdependence upon which the theory in the *Essay* has been based from the first.

Neander makes more explicit also the kind of artistic presence that the *Essay* as a whole with, it must be insisted, the help of all four speakers, has been seeking to define. Crites and Lisideius themselves, though objecting emphatically to an overly conspicuous presence, do not propose an alternative of literal artlessness. This would be either nature *tout court*, or Flecknoe, the very leveller in poetry, the imagination-less, who, we remember, is himself too conspicuous ('you see how many proffers they make to dip'). The true alternative is the proper sense of the artist as described by Neander:

But you tell us, this...looks more like the design of two, than the answer of one. Supposing we acknowledge it: how comes this confederacy to be more displeasing to you, than in a dance which is well contrived? You see there the united design of many persons to make up one figure: after they have separated themselves in many petty divisions, they rejoin one by one into a gross: the confederacy is plain amongst them, for chance could never produce any thing so beautiful; and yet there is nothing in it, that shocks your sight. I acknowledge the hand of art appears in repartee, as of necessity it must in all kinds of verse. But there is also the quick and poynant brevity of it (which is an high imitation of Nature in those sudden gusts of passion) to mingle with it; and this, joined with the cadency and sweetness of the rhyme, leaves nothing in the soul of the hearer to desire. 'Tis an art which appears; but it appears only like the shadowings of painture, which being to cause the rounding of it, cannot be absent; but while that is considered, they are lost: so while we attend to the other beauties of the matter, the care and labour of the rhyme is carried from us, or at least drowned in its own sweetness, as bees are sometimes buried in their honey. When a poet has found the repartee, the last perfection he can add to it, is to put it into verse. However good the thought may be, however apt the words in which 'tis couched, yet he finds himself at a little unrest, while rhyme is wanting: he cannot leave it till that comes naturally, and then is at ease, and sits down contented. (I. 103–4)

Though Neander does emphasize conspicuous artistry more than Crites, the two remain in substantial agreement, at least with regard to end or effect. Admittedly, the artist is conspicuously present in Neander's description, but precisely in the act of concealing his art. The effect of Neander's position, thus, is not an obtrusive mediation between the play and the audience, which he wishes as much as Crites to avoid, but rather the audience's intensified clarity of apprehension. Like 'the shadowings of painture', rhyme establishes a precision of line;

the sense of artistic control thereupon leads away from itself and back to the subject, 'the other beauties of the *matter*'. (I read this as: 'the other beauties, that is, those of the matter, the meaning'.)

Like Crites, thus, Neander aims at perspicuity, though he is inclined to see the goal's being reached through a greater sense of artistic control. Neander had implied this pleasurable sense of an artist in complete control of his materials earlier in his defense of English variety ('infinitely pleasing to be led in a labyrinth *of design*'), and Dryden himself was getting at the same thing in his first critical essay:

...to conduct his imaginary persons through so many various intrigues and chances, as the labouring audience shall think them lost under every billow; and then at length to work them so naturally out of their distresses, that...the spectators may rest satisfied. (I. 2)

Moreover, throughout his criticism, the figures Dryden uses to describe the kind of artist he admires all tend to emphasize this conspicuous control. The most frequent is the horseman – 'Let not them be accounted no poets, who choose to mount, and show their horsemanship'[20] (II. 101); the next most frequent, the performer on the ropes[21]; while the swordsman (I. 26), the 'skilful chess-player' (I. 88) and the 'skilful lapidary' (I. 146) have the same effect as well. For Dryden this effect has been achieved above all by Virgil, with his freedom 'to confess as well the labour as the force of his imagination', (I. 16) and a sustained figure describing Virgil in *A Parallel* is probably the clearest of all in defining it:

Virgil is so exact in every word, that none can be changed but for a worse; nor any one removed from its place, but the harmony will be altered. He pretends sometimes to trip; but it is only to make you think him in danger of a fall, when he is most secure: like a skilful dancer on the ropes...who slips willingly, and makes a seeming stumble, that you may think him in great hazard of breaking his neck, while at the same time he is only giving you a proof of his dexterity. (II. 148–9)

Here is the reality, the archetype which gives significance to the unconscious parody represented by Flecknoe in the *Essay*, as it will to the unconscious parody represented by Mac Flecknoe in Dryden's most famous poem thirteen years later.

I have, it seems, started talking about practical implications after all. They *are* there, in a way. In reading about bad playwrights in the *Essay*, the kind whose actions are 'laboured and driven on', the kind who 'embarrass, or cumber themselves with too much plot', it is difficult not to think – or think that Dryden is not thinking – of bad stylists, corrupt metaphysicals like Cleveland or Wild. And the *Essay* makes us think of good stylists as well, those who exhibit qualities that we enjoy in Dryden's or Pope's couplets, that sense of sure and brilliant control. Johnson's view of the couplet, in Paul Fussell's paraphrase, seems to be describing an effect similar in many ways to the one endorsed by Dryden's *Essay*: It

forces the ordering of the perceiver's mind so that it may be in a condition to receive the ordered moral matter of the poem...[It] serves an attention-calling function; it hammers into the consciousness of the perceiver the recognition that a formal process is at work, a process comprising elements of ceremony, self-awareness, artifice and control.[22]

And as for Virgil's performance on the tightrope, the effect has been put more prosaically by Donald Davie in his description of the diction of some mid- and late-eighteenth-century poets: 'One feels...that a selection has been made and is continually being made, that words are thrusting at the poem and being fended off from it'.[23]

But these are only general implications. When it comes to immediately practical issues, the *Essay* isn't much help. 'The discussions', Donald Davie has said elsewhere, are 'nebulous. Dryden could have asked, or implied, the questions: Am I, in my next play, to observe the Unities? Am I to take Corneille for my model or Shakespeare?'[24] Davie is quite right; such questions are not answered; conclusions are not reached. Or rather, too many conclusions are reached. The metaphors are an example of this. When Eugenius speaks about a broad imitation, what exactly is he asking for? What is the tenor – to say nothing of the vehicle? The metaphor, we feel, does serve to express a genuine theoretical difference between him and Crites, and a true substantive difference of opinion as well; yet it would nonetheless be quite conceivable to justify a given play – *Epicoene*, perhaps – with the theory of either one.

If my description of Dryden's *Essay* in this chapter is accurate, then it is a *deliberately* 'nebulous' work. As a conscious strategy it stresses particular opinions far less than the process of theoretical reasoning by which they are reached. In fact, one might say that the process is the conclusion. The ideal held up by the *Essay* is, I repeat, comprehensiveness, the location of different kinds of literary value and the insistence that legitimate theory (and practice) should be responsive to them all. For this reason, Davie's transforming his description into an objection seems to me silly – as if one complained, returning to my earlier example, that the *Four Quartets* lacked a good plot. There is no reason to take Dryden's deliberate inconclusiveness as a necessary fault, as an attempt, in Hume's words, 'to put something over on his audience by means of specious verbal resolutions of irreconcilable differences'.[25] Sometimes verbal resolutions are not specious, even if they cannot be transferred very easily to the real world of rocks and stones and trees and Corneille and Shakespeare. There are times when abstraction, when theory somewhat removed from practice, is distinctly useful, notably when one needs to define new forms. For Dryden at the beginning of his theatrical career, faced with many useful examples to imitate in the drama of his own and other ages and cultures, yet with no single example wholly satisfactory in itself, this may have been exactly such a time.

In this context, I'd like to return to the question I asked earlier: How, or to what extent, can Dryden's *Essay* illuminate the rest of his criticism? The answer to 'how' is – with great difficulty. The other essays are more immediately concerned with practical implications. To be sure, the extent to which they are governed by the works they introduce can be exaggerated. Typically, Dryden only starts with the occasion; before long he is discussing the issues suggested by the particular work at hand in a relatively general way. Nonetheless, the greater freedom from immediate practical concerns does make the *Essay* a special case. Inevitably, to some extent, Dryden has made certain decisions, has *acted* in writing the poem or play which he is introducing, and an act is never so 'pure' as a generalized program for action, which is what I think the *Essay* represents.

And yet perhaps the *Essay*'s nearly unique generality is an advantage in another sense. Dryden's development, a clear sense of the way his critical ideas progress over the years, has never been satisfactorily articulated.[26] Recent efforts by Aden and Hume are all to the good, but the job as a whole still needs doing.[27] What we require, first of all, is a framework sufficiently general to encompass the whole. Perhaps the *Essay* provides it. Perhaps the comprehensiveness that it espouses was a consistent value throughout the various changes of emphasis over the years. Can we say that general viewpoints often remain recognizable? that the *Defence of the Epilogue* or the *Preface to Troilus and Cressida*, in their tendency to stress justness of imitation, read as if written nearly wholly from Crites's point of view? that *An Essay of Heroic Plays* and *The Author's Apology*, in stressing elevation, give dominance to the kind of position expressed by Neander? Can we find general evidence that Dryden himself was consciously aware of limiting his perspective, as we can find particular evidence in the case of the *Defence of the Epilogue*, where he describes his attack on the stylistic incorrectness of the Jacobeans as 'so fruitful, in so small a compass'.[28] (I. 169) And if so, if Dryden's shifts of emphasis are so quick (*An Essay of Heroic Plays* and the *Defence* were written in the same year; the epilogue defended occurs at the end of the play introduced by *An Essay of Heroic Plays*), will we have to junk totally the idea of 'periods', so useful for describing courses of development? And what about Dryden's later essays which turn away from the drama, where the topics themselves, let alone emphases, change? Are the values described by the *Essay* sufficiently general and suggestive to be meaningfully applicable there?

I don't mean to minimize the difficulties in answering such questions as these. For one thing, although I have made special claims for the *Essay*'s generality, a good case could be made that *The Grounds of Criticism in Tragedy*, although attached to the *Preface to Troilus and Cressida*, is an independent piece of at least equal generality, and the systematic neoclassical theory of tragedy that is attempted in *The Grounds* goes, it must be admitted, against the emphasis I have been placing on Dryden's doubleness. Moreover, even if the *Essay*'s doubleness can be accepted as an embracing perspective, there would be enormous problems in applying it to Dryden's criticism as a whole; it would require at once enough overview to see similarities and a clear eye for the very real differences that exist, over the years and from piece to piece, without which Dryden's criticism would be dully monolithic. All this notwithstanding, the questions I ask above aren't neutral questions – if such things exist. The answers, I tend to feel, are generally yes, and I hope that I have gathered enough material in these two chapters to suggest that these may be reasonable hypotheses. But they are hypotheses only, and the work of establishing a truly convincing perspective that would allow us to see Dryden's criticism 'all, all of a piece throughout' has yet to be done.

3

CLASSICISM AND DRYDEN

I have been trying to describe what I take to be the characteristic structure of Dryden's critical thought. My aim now is to justify *classical* as an appropriate epithet to describe this structure. The special affinities between Dryden and classicism have been recognized from the very beginning, since Dryden himself frequently and self-consciously defined his literary endeavors in the context of Greek and Roman achievements. Modern scholars, perhaps drawing impetus from Mr Eliot, have examined Dryden's classicism in a variety of aspects – his knowledge or use or translation of ancient languages, poetry, critical principles, rhetorical theory, themes; and William Frost's recent article is a splendid synthesis of this work, as well as an addition to it.[1]

My aim here, though, is somewhat different. I am not trying to specify aspects of Dryden's thought or work for which there are ancient sources or precedents. Indeed, as the order of words in the title probably suggests, my attention is no longer centered on Dryden himself (though I trust that the preceding chapters suffice to guarantee him a kind of continuing presence in the discussion below, at least by implication, and I shall be returning to him from time to time and for a bit at the end of the chapter). My major focus is now broader, covering a variety of other figures who collectively illustrate a classical mode within which I feel Dryden is properly located. Like Ralph Cohen in his extremely important recent article on Augustan poetry, I am trying to describe 'what modern critics call "the mode of existence" of a work or works, rather than their...sources or ideas'.[2] This description is based on the assumption that

Josephine Miles has expressed in *Eras and Modes in English Poetry*: 'Certain modes...are discernible in the structures of language, and certain eras seem to have aptitudes for one or another of these modes.'[3] I believe that among writers like Aristotle, Plutarch, Horace, Longinus, Boileau, Bouhours, Dryden, Pope – that among these an 'aptitude' exists for the balanced mode, the classical poise of the golden mean, and this is the mode I try to describe in the first section below.

There are problems here which should be addressed at the outset. Obviously I cover an enormously varied range of work, ancient Greek and Roman, seventeenth- and eighteenth-century English and French, in the process riding roughshod over distinctions between 'classical' and 'neoclassical' or 'Augustan'. Quite a few recent studies have questioned the usefulness of over-ambitious synthesis: The generalizations to which they lead often don't do justice to individual cases, or if they do they're likely to be meaninglessly low common denominators.[4] I'm sympathetic to such objections. It seems to me true that the business of literary criticism is best conducted in the area of the concrete and the specific; it seems to me true also that the abstractions of literary history are inherently unsatisfactory, since any complex phenomenon is by definition more various than the schemes we derive from it. But these abstractions – metaphysical, Petrarchan, sublime, baroque, symbolist, imagist, romantic, post-modern and the others – serve a real function (why else do we persist in inventing, replacing and refining them?) as a natural, continuing endeavor of the mind to articulate a context within which a concrete awareness may be sharpened. In this chapter, such a context will be perforce untidy. I haven't forgotten that the authors I treat vary widely in subject matter, in sophistication, in quality and in importance. I don't mean to suggest that the mean radically structures every utterance of all of them, that they all wrote always like each other, or that the works of each one don't themselves vary widely; nor to suggest that the mean is exclusively classical, that we will find no examples of it in other periods among figures whom, on the face of it, we would balk at calling classical. But the 'aptitudes' that Josephine Miles mentions are realities (as her statistical appendices tend to demonstrate), and I hope that my rather long and many quotations immediately below serve not only to describe the mean as precisely as possible, but to suggest its frequency of occurrence among the authors and periods in question.

One final point, however, perhaps already implied: My aim is not to write or even to sketch a *history* of the classical mean. Conceivably enough material is gathered to represent the beginning of a history, but I make only occasional attempts to trace lines of development or describe any transmission of influence. Largely I ignore the question, from whom did Dryden learn the mean? All I wish to suggest is that he did learn it, that he knew it well, so well indeed that 'learning' and 'knowing' are probably misleading terms; and that this is true as well about the other writers that I have mentioned.

In the *Nichomachean Ethics*, Aristotle discusses the mean of virtue as 'something median between excess and deficiency'.[5] As an example, 'If ten is many and two is few, six is taken as the median'. (*ibid.*) The mean, though, is not a static or absolute concept; it varies from individual to individual. The median in relation to one person might be seven, to another five, depending upon the person's temperament and disposition. Nor is the mean a negative concept; that is, it is not predicated essentially upon the avoiding of extremes, but upon positive action.

To experience...[emotions] at the right time, toward the right objects, toward the right people, for the right reason, and in the right manner – that is the median and the best course, the course that is a mark of virtue. (1106[b])

Moreover, although 'in respect of its essence and the definition of its essential nature virtue is a mean,...in regard to goodness and excellence it is an extreme'. (1107[a]) That is, because virtue exists as one among many human possibilities, including excess and deficiency, it may be seen as the avoiding of extremes; but with relation to an absolute good, virtue is seen as a positive, as an action. 'There cannot be an excess and deficiency of self-control and courage – because the intermediate [such as self-control or courage] is, in a sense, an extreme'. (*ibid.*)

I have emphasized the dynamic and positive aspects of the mean for it is these that we are likely to lose sight of in our contemporary sense of the concept. H. D. F. Kitto warns that, although

the doctrine of the Mean is characteristically Greek, . . . it should not tempt us to think that the Greek was one who was hardly aware of the passions, a safe, anesthetic, middle-of-the-road man. On the contrary, . . . when he spoke of the Mean, the thought of the tuned string was never very far from his mind. The Mean did not imply the absence of tension and lack of passion, but the correct tension which gives out the true and clear note.[6]

In Aristotle's list of virtues, the mean is not primarily characterized by carefulness in avoiding the extremes, but by the more positive force of the Greek *aretē* (which, like the Latin *virtus*, is always the occasion for a translator's apology). In ethics, it is the proper action based upon the proper emotion, towards the right object in the right manner. The mean between rashness and cowardice is not, as we might tend to think, prudence – but courage. In giving and taking money, the excess is extravagance, the deficiency stinginess, and the mean, not as we might think, economy – but generosity.[7] What we think of as safeness or carefulness or prudence or economy – Polonius's wisdom – is more closely related to deficiency than to the mean. It is essentially a negative expression, *not too much*, rather than the positive, *enough*. An example of this quality of enough is the mean between intemperateness and insensibility, self-control, the Greek *sōphrosynē*, which

describes the full knowledge of one's limitations in a positive as well as negative sense: the *sophron*, who possesses this virtue, knows what he is capable of as well as what he is incapable of doing. 'Temperance', which is often used to translate this concept, is entirely negative, and is nowadays almost exclusively applied to abstention from alcoholic beverages, a connotation entirely uncharacteristic of the Greek word; 'moderation', too, has largely negative connotations and has, in addition, a flabbiness that is alien to the Greek term. Though SELF-CONTROL is also more negative than positive in modern usage, if the word is taken more literally than it usually is, i.e., if 'control' is not merely taken as 'restraint', but also as 'mastery', it comes closer to *sōphrosynē* than most alternative renderings.[8]

Though positive thus, the mean is perceived by contrast to the negative or negatives. Plutarch puts this very clearly in his well-known explanation in the *Life of Demetrius* for including bad figures among his good ones.

Medicine, to produce health, has to examine disease, and music, to create harmony, must investigate discord; and the supreme arts, of temperance, of justice, and of wisdom...are acts of judgment and selection, exercised not on good and just and expedient only, but also on wicked, unjust, and inexpedient objects.[9]

The mean participates positively in qualities that have always within them the potentiality to become extremes, particularly excesses; courage runs the risk of rashness, generosity the risk of extravagance. Demetrius and Antony are

two persons who have abundantly justified the words of Plato, that great natures produce great vices as well as virtues. Both alike were amorous and intemperate, warlike and munificent, sumptuous in their way of living and overbearing in their manners. (*ibid.*)

To be greatly courageous or generous – perhaps, simply, to be great – one is in danger of becoming at least a social nuisance, or even a violator of the most sacred taboos and a blasphemer against the gods. One thinks of Philoctetes or Oedipus; in fact the idea seems to be central to Sophocles's sense of tragedy.

The mean, of course, can define literary as well as moral virtues. Aristotle's discussions of stylistic propriety in the *Rhetoric*, for example, are frequently shaped by the concept of the mean.[10] Horace's *Ars Poetica* is full of passages that illustrate the positive values of the stylistic mean by warning against the inevitable dangers of stylistic excess and deficiency – passages such as the following:

I try to be terse, and end by being obscure; another strives after smoothness, to the sacrifice of vigour and spirit; a third aims at grandeur, and drops into bombast; a fourth, through excess of caution and a fear of squalls, goes creeping along the ground.[11]

Longinus in *On the Sublime* is perhaps even more explicit.

Turgidity seems to be one of the most difficult faults to avoid, for those who aim at greatness try to escape the charge of feeble aridity and are somehow led into turgidity, believing it 'a noble error to fail in great things'. As in the body, so in writing, hollow and artificial swellings are bad and somehow turn into their opposite, as, they say, nothing is drier than dropsy.

While turgidity attempts to reach beyond greatness, puerility is its direct opposite, altogether a lowly, petty, and ignoble fault... Beauties of style, great ability, and also the wish to please contribute to effective writing, yet these very things are the elements and sources of failure as well as of success.[12]

According to Grube, 'That particular vices of style are the close neighbors of particular virtues is a commonplace of ancient criticism'.[13] And of modern criticism as well, in the classical period. The mean informs the statement of Boileau's Horatian and Longinian *Art Poétique* (1674). For example:

> Qui ne sçait se borner ne sceut jamais écrire.
> Souvent la peur d'un mal nous conduit dans un pire.
> Un vers estoit trop foible, et vous le rendez dur.
> J'évite d'estre long, et je deviens obscur.
> L'un n'est point trop fardé, mais sa Muse est trop nuë.
> L'autre a peur de ramper, il se perd dans la nuë.
>   Voulez-vous du public meriter les amours?
> Sans cesse en écrivant variez vos discours.
> Un stile trop égal et toûjours uniforme,
> En vain brille à nos yeux, il faut qu'il nous endorme.
> On lit peu ces Auteurs nez pour nous ennuyer,
> Qui toûjours sur un ton semblent psalmodier.[14]

Again it must be emphasized that this is essentially positive in describing the mean of good quality. Boileau's warning about extremes establishes the limits (*se borner*), and the establishment of limits *defines* in the root sense the area within which good writing can take place. Boileau's couplet immediately following is an explicitly positive definition. The earlier feebleness and obscurity, extremes because they ignore the values suggested by the other, now combine to form the true mean, both smooth and strong:

> Heureux, qui dans ses vers sçait d'une voix legere,
> Passer du grave au doux, du plaisant au severe!

Dominique Bouhours's contemporary discussion of *le bel esprit*, a quality with at once literary and social applications, also exemplifies the informing concept of the mean in its positive sense.[15] At the basis of *le bel esprit*, according to Bouhours, is 'un discernement juste et délicat', and this combination of qualities Bouhours calls good sense:

Le vrai bel esprit… est inséparable du bon sens, et c'est se méprendre que de le confondre avec je ne sais qu'elle vivacité qui n'a rien de solide. Le jugement est comme le fond de la beauté de l'esprit, ou plûtot le bel esprit est de la nature de ces pierres précieuses qui n'ont pas moins de solidité que d'éclat. Il n'y a rien de plus beau qu'un diamant bien poli et bien net; il éclate de tous côtés et dans toutes ses parties… C'est un corps solide qui brille; c'est un brillant qui a de la consistance et du corps. L'union, le mélange, l'assortiment de ce qu'il a d'éclatant et de solide fait tout son agrément et tout son prix. Voilà le symbole du bel esprit, tel que je me l'imagine. Il a du solide et du brillant dans un égal degré; c'est, à le bien définir, le bon sens qui brille. Car il y a une espèce de bon sens sombre et morne qui n'est guère moins opposé à la beauté de l'esprit que le faux brillant. Le bon sens dont je parle est d'une espèce toute differente: il est gai, vif, plein de feu. (pp. 150–1)

Le bel esprit, thus, is the mean between somber good sense and false brilliance. 'Ce juste temperament', as Bouhours calls it just afterwards, (p. 152) exists in the balanced response to both judgment and brilliance. This is perhaps why

les véritables beaux esprits sont si rares: des qualités aussi opposées que la vivacité et le bon sens, la délicatesse et la force, sans parler des autres, ne se rencontrent pas toujours ensemble. (p. 165)

The Soame-Dryden translation of Boileau's *Art Poétique*, published 1683, was no doubt instrumental in popularizing the mean in England. Here is how they translate the couplet I quoted earlier:

> Happy, who in his verse can gently steer
> From grave to light, from pleasant to severe.[16]

But the idea goes back in England at least to Jonson (not a surprising figure to appear in this classical context), who remarks in *Timber, or Discoveries* (1620–35?) that,

Others that in composition are nothing but what is rough and broken: *Quae per salebras altaque saxa cadunt*…They would not have it run without rubs, as if that stile were more strong and manly, that stroke the eare with a kind of unevenesse…Others there are that have no composition at all, but a kind of tuneing and riming fall in what they write. It runs and slides, and onely makes a sound. Womens-*Poets* they are call'd, as you have womens *Taylors*.

> They write a verse as smooth, as soft as creame,
> In which there is no torrent, nor scarce streame.[17]

Between Jonson and Dryden, the idea appears in fragmentary forms in a variety of figures,[18] but it is Dryden's voice that one tends to hear in the familiar passages in Pope:

> And praise the *Easie Vigor* of a Line,
> Where *Denham's* Strength, and *Waller's* Sweetness join.

> Waller was smooth; but Dryden taught to join
> The varying verse, the full resounding line,
> The long majestic march, and energy divine.[19]

As for Dryden himself, the mean appears frequently in his criticism, as we have seen. Like others, he often expresses it in terms of negatives. The best known example of this, to us at least, is his description of the two 'extremities' of poetry, Wild and Flecknoe, at the beginning of the *Essay*, but this is only one among a great many such instances.[20] In Dryden too, the mean is essentially positive, 'partaking of...both', as he puts it describing Plutarch's belief in demons:

He thinks it absurd that there should be no mean between the two extremes of an immortal and a mortal being; that there cannot be in nature so vast a flaw, without some intermedial kind of life, partaking of them both.[21]

In this context, Dryden's comment in the *Preface to Troilus and Cressida* that Shakespeare sometimes 'distinguished not the blown puffy style from true sublimity' (I. 224) reflects more an interest in defining the boundaries of the true sublime than in simply debunking Shakespeare for exceeding them. In the same way, though he attacks the false brilliance of Chapman's conceits in the *Preface to the Spanish Friar*, 'those glaring colours ...a cold, dull mass, which glittered no longer than it was shooting', he is quick to remind his readers of the true brilliance of 'the lofty style in Tragedy, which is naturally pompous and magnificent' (I. 246) – the style, that is, generated not only by the fancy but by the judgment as well.

As so often, Dryden's norm for the proper style is exemplified by Virgil, and it is in his description of Virgil that the mean as an essentially positive criterion is expressed most clearly. From the *Preface to Sylvae* (1685): Virgil 'shines, but glares not'. (I. 256) From *A Parallel* (1695), after quoting a figure from the *Aeneid*: 'How warm, nay, how glowing a colouring is this!' (II.

150) Or, later in the same essay: Virgil 'knew the difference betwixt a glaring colour and a glowing'. (II. 152) Here is the true elevation, a glowing and a warmth, that was carried to excess by Chapman, with his glaring and coldness, or by Lucan and Statius, the defining extremes in *A Parallel*, who 'often ventured...too far; our Virgil never'. (II. 149) At the same time, Virgil goes far enough, unlike the deficient French in the *Dedication of the Aeneas* (1697), who 'are so fearful of a metaphor, that no example of Virgil can encourage them to be bold with safety'. (II. 229) Bold with safety – this balanced response to two different literary values is evident in that remarkably compressed formula, once again from *A Parallel*, that Virgil 'had judgment enough to know daring was necessary'. (II. 149) Virgil partakes of both; neither rash nor cowardly, he is, one might say, courageous in his style, and this is the proper style for a heroic poem.

The mean, then, describes a dynamic balance between different kinds of values. These values never lose their individual identities; they are comprehended by the mean but never synthesized into a transcendent unit. This is an unresolvable dualism, but what is striking about it is how comfortably unresolved it is. That is, the writers who tend to articulate their work by means of this very open organizing principle seem to feel no pressure to close it. This easy, un-anxious acceptance of dualism, or of multiplicity for that matter, is more than a characteristic of literary style. Or rather, as an aspect of style, it implies something broader. 'A different meter is a different mode of thought', T. S. Eliot once said[22]; or as Josephine Miles puts it, 'A pervasive sentence structure may well have both an effect and a purpose, a relation to larger cultural matters.'[23] This relation between style and sensibility occupies me now. If the mean, or an aptitude generally for loose structural unities, may characterize a classical mode, what assumptions does this mode imply concerning such matters as human nature, the moral judgments that are appropriate responses to human action, the nature of reality itself? Can one infer, from a classical mode, the outlines of what one might wish to call a classical sensibility?

I am trying to draw such inferences now, with the full knowledge that I can be at best suggestive and certainly not definitive. My focus is primarily on Plutarch's characteristic ways of organizing narrative materials in the *Lives*, but in order to establish a context for my claim that Plutarch exemplifies a classical response to experience, I indulge first of all in some generalities, ranging widely among some figures who seem to me similar to Plutarch and even more widely among other figures who seem to me different. In fact my emphasis is initially on the different figures, for like Erich Auerbach, who in the first chapter of *Mimesis* illustrates Homeric style by referring it to the very dissimilar style of the Old Testament, I am trying to describe by contrast, to clarify a classical attitude by setting it up against a different mode of literary representation and a different set of assumptions.

This constrating mode might be characterized variously as abstract rather than particular, closed rather than open, metaphysical rather than material, Platonic rather than Aristotelian, Christian rather than classical. Such distinctions no doubt perform the reverse of a clarifying function at this point, but the patient reader will, I hope, find them eventually meaningful. In the mean time let me suggest that the salient assumptions of this contrasting mode have been described by (among others) Joseph A. Mazzeo, D. W. Robertson, Jr, and Stanley Fish.[24] In particular Fish's recent contribution to both literary theory and seventeenth-century studies is valuable for its lucid exposition of this contrasting mode. 'The Aesthetic of the Good Physician', as Fish characterizes Augustinian dialectic, is at once a way of reading and of living that involves 'a continual exercise in translation, a seeing through the literal contexts of things (objects, events, and persons) to the significance they acquire in the light of a larger perspective', (p. 25) which turns out to be the transcendent unity of God's law. This seems to me in nearly every way contrary to the classical mode. In the classical mode the reader is invited precisely not to see through, but to see, to trust the untranscended particularity of phenomenal experience, to affirm the existence of all its rich variety and multiplicity of implication, perhaps even its contradictoriness, untranslated and unmerged into the 'larger perspective' of a supernatural resolution.

I begin with one of the many notorious acts recorded in Plutarch's *Life of Alcibiades*. Meeting secretly with Spartan ambassadors who had come to Athens with terms aimed at preventing a seemingly imminent war, Alcibiades convinces them to deny that they are plenipotentiaries (which, in fact, they are); and when they do so, he rises to denounce them at a popular assembly, they are discredited (as is, incidentally, Alcibiades's chief rival in Athens), and war follows. After narrating this event, which I have much abridged, Plutarch makes the following comment.

No man commended the method by which Alcibiades effected all this, yet it was a great political feat thus to divide and shake almost all Peloponnesus, and to combine so many men in arms against the Lacedaemonians in one day before Mantinea; and, moreover, to remove the war and the danger so far from the frontier of the Athenians, that even success would profit the enemy but little, should they be conquerors, whereas, if they were defeated, Sparta itself was hardly safe. (p. 242)

This comment is noteworthy in so casually balancing the method and the effect of Alcibiades's action. The former receives general moral censure; what Alcibiades did was wrong. The latter deserves commendation; on purely practical grounds, the consequences of Alcibiades's action were fortunate. Plutarch recognizes that this action may be viewed from two different perspectives, but he does not offer to decide which perspective is more important. Much more space is given to the action's good practical results than to its bad moral methods, but this is simply because practical results may be many in number and thus accumulated in a long list; the length of this list does not tip the balance in favor of the practical, against the moral perspective. Rather, these two perspectives, these two kinds of judgment, are allowed to coexist within a loose but single structure, component elements within the long sentence, separate but equal, held together by the quite deliberately indecisive *yet*.

In a nut shell then, what Plutarch says is this: *Alcibiades's act is morally bad; on the other hand*, to use one of Dryden's favorite transitions, *it is practically good*. Against this poised judgment we may contrast the following passage from Andreas Capellanus's *Art of Courtly Love*:

Now the clerk is considered to be of the most noble class by virtue of his sacred calling, a nobility which we agree comes from God's bosom...But so far as this nobility goes, a clerk cannot look for love, for on the strength of it he ought not devote himself to the works of love but is bound to renounce absolutely all the delights of the flesh...A clerk ought therefore to be a stranger to every act of love and put aside all uncleanness of body, or he will deserve to be deprived of this special nobility granted him by God. But since hardly anyone ever lives without carnal sin, and since the life of the clergy is, because of the continual idleness and the great abundance of food, naturally more liable to temptations of the body than that of any other man, if any clerk should wish to enter into the lists of Love let him speak and apply himself to Love's service in accordance with the rank or standing of his parents, as we have already fully explained in regard to the different ranks of men.[25]

As in Plutarch, we are confronted here with a balance, or an apparent balance, between moral and practical considerations, in this case between the injunction to priestly celibacy on the one hand and the weakness of the flesh and those qualities of priestly life, idleness and abundance of food, that encourage sensual indulgence on the other. But in Andreas's passage the balance cannot be truly realized, because of the informing hierarchical assumptions of the Christian context. The moral injunction to renounce is an absolute which renders the practical availability of means to indulge, a relative considera-tion, of no ultimate weight whatsoever. In loosely relating the two – and Andreas's style, like Dryden's or Plutarch's, is based upon loose relations – Andreas is not so much open-minded as either mindless or ironic (which of these two is still, I believe, a contentious issue among medieval scholars).

Radically different assumptions about experience underly the passages from Plutarch and Andreas. In the hierarchical framework that gives point (or perhaps lack of point) to Andreas's work, the purpose of human life is single and absolute – salvation. Subordinate goals are valued in propor-tion to their consistency with this primary one. Moreover, since salvation is achieved – to whatever extent human agency may be said to achieve it – by congruence with prescriptions whose source and significance derive from outside human nature (fulfilling God's law), and since relative goals tend to be defined by reference to strictly human institutions, there is a conflict likely, if not indeed necessary, between primary and subordinate goals. It may seem fine to be a good citizen, but not according to the rules of the City of Man; *or*, folly to the world may be true wisdom; *or*, it profits no man to store up earthly treasures at the expense of his soul (to paraphrase and conflate some familiar passages). Apparent relative goods, then, may be no good at all. In this context the *visibilia*, the public forms and social norms used to attribute value to human endeavors – to call a man a good citizen, or soldier, or politician, or merchant, or writer – are at best not very reliable. The goodness of an action is a much more private affair, inhering, as Aquinas puts it, rather in 'the interior act of the will' than in 'the external action'.[26] The action in fact may be totally irrelevant to a true determination of the interior measure.

Plutarch's thought is nowhere so rigorously hierarchical. Salvation is not an issue for Plutarch, and lacking such a clearly defined and absolute *telos*, he is in a position to be a great deal more flexible in his judgment of human action and human nature. The value of an action is not determined by reference to an absolute, immutable and otherworldly code. Rather, it is the product of a number of potentially conflicting variables in the social context, such as the practical concerns of the immediate situation and the particular laws of a given culture at a given time. As for Plutarch's flexible concept of human nature, the following comment about Alcibiades usefully specifies the relevant assumptions:

His conduct displayed many great inconsistencies and variations, not unnaturally, in accordance with the many and wonderful vicissitudes of his fortunes; but among the many strong passions of his real character, the one most prevailing of all was his ambition and desire of superiority, which appears in several anecdotes told of his sayings whilst he was a child. . . (p. 234)

Plutarch's distinction here between 'conduct' and 'real character' is a basic distinction throughout the *Lives* between a man's behavior (*ethos*) and his basic unchanging nature (*physis*). Plutarch recognizes the split between inner and outer man, but this is not the absolute split that Aquinas assumes. Though the 'variety' of a man's actions offers 'inconsistent' evidence, it is possible nonetheless to perceive the 'prevailing' figure in the carpet. Real character 'appears in' actions (or 'anecdotes' of actions), which are thus, after all, a reliable kind of evidence. Moreover, while real character may be derived by abstracting

74

from the variety of action, the reverse is also true. That is, action, as a response to a variety of public and social pressures (the 'many and wonderful vicissitudes of fortune'), itself (and 'not unnaturally') contributes to the definition of a man's character. As J. R. Hamilton puts it in his recent commentary on the *Life of Alexander*, Plutarch believes that a man's character 'is not only revealed by his actions but is formed by habitual or repeated action and by his reactions to events'.[27]

Hamilton goes on to point out that Plutarch's belief is probably derived from the Peripatetics, and it may be called a typical belief of the Greeks, perhaps even of the ancients generally, who tended to see reality and character in nature and in action, at least as much as in consciousness. Such a view helps to define some of the conspicuous differences in tone and texture between classical and Christian epic. An epic that begins, 'Arms and the man I sing', is more fundamentally committed to the arena of public, heroic actions than a poem that begins, 'A gentle knight was pricking on the plain.' Indeed, perhaps the fundamental problem of Christianizing classical epic resided in the different relative weights given to public and private, to 'external actions' and 'interior acts of the will'. Allegory, or a symbolic method in general, was a solution that frequently suggested itself (Boiardo, Ariosto, Spenser and in a different way Chapman) as a means to direct the reader's attention beyond accident to essence. If the use of a symbolic approach may be said to imply a critique of classical epic, such a critique is sometimes rendered explicit. In the Ulysses episode of the *Divine Comedy*, for instance (*Inferno*, XXVI), the truly stirring speech not to deny experience 'to this so brief vigil of the senses' manages to compress into a few lines what is felt to be the informing spirit of the adventurous, classically heroic stance. In the suddenness of Ulysses's fate ('as One willed the sea closed over us'), we are confronted with a literally shocking revelation of the inner emptiness of such an outwardly impressive stance. Other works treat the same discrepancy in a more comic way. I am thinking here of the witty, sustained juxtaposition of different hunts in *Sir Gawain and the Green Knight*, in which we are shunted back and forth between *boudoir* and forest, gradually led to the recognition of a concept of heroism which is equally appropriate to either milieu – or rather, so essentially an inner quality that it is independent of any milieu and any external posture. Or, a grimmer sort of comedy, the particularly Renaissance form of mock epic[28] in the Council Scene of Shakespeare's *Troilis and Cressida* (I. iii), or Milton's version of 'the great consult' in *Paradise Lost* or, in the same poem, the battle in heaven. In all of these the typical posture of the classical hero is declared to be only an absurd kind of posturing.

Tragedy offers another generic basis for comparison, if we may consider the following quotations as suggesting characteristic attitudes:

> It was long ago that someone first said:
> You cannot know a man's life before the man
> has died, then only can you call it good or bad.

> There's a special providence in the fall of a sparrow.
> If it be now, 'tis not to come; if it be not to come,
> it will be now; if it be not now, yet it will come;
> the readiness is all. Since no man, of aught he leaves,
> knows, what is't to leave betimes? Let be.

The first passage, the opening words in Sophocles's *Women of Trachis* (Jameson translation), has the quality of traditional wisdom, commonly accepted truth, which indeed it seems to have been among the Greeks. The 'someone' cannot really be identified. In the *Ethics* (1100[a]), Aristotle attributes the idea to Solon, and it may be found also in Herodotus and Euripides.[29] Its scepticism and doubt, its profound sense of the insecurity of the human condition in which happiness can suffer a sudden dramatic reversal due to causes (if there are causes) not necessarily subject to human understanding – all this makes the statement eminently appropriate to a tragic point of view; and not only to Greek tragedy, but to Shakespeare as well. Edgar's familiar words in *Lear* – 'And worse I may be yet; the worst is not/So long as we can say "This is the worst".' – also focus on the folly of assuming that the universe is shaped according to our desires or consistently with our understanding. In fact, Samuel Johnson interpreted Hamlet's speech above in much the same way:

Since *no man knows aught of* the state of life which *he leaves*, since he cannot judge what other years may produce, why should he be afraid of *leaving* life betimes? Why should he dread an early death, of which he cannot tell whether it is an exclusion of happiness or an interception of calamity.[30]

But Hamlet (and *Hamlet*) seem to me to be saying something far more deeply sceptical. Not merely do we lack the ability to predict the future; we cannot even understand past and present. The play's interrogative mood, established in apparently simple terms at the beginning ('Who's there?'), deepens in a series of increasingly difficult and, we come finally to realize, impossible questions to answer: is the ghost to be trusted? how can a man smile and be a villain? how can anyone with eyes leave a fair mountain to batten on a moor? what dreams await us after the sleep of death? what is the chief end of man's existence and what distinguishes him from angel and beast? These questions are impossible to answer because they inquire into a condition of abstract or spiritual reality for which all available sources of evidence, all the forms, moods and shows of behavior, are not reliable guides. The only thing certain in life, as the graveyard scene plangently expresses, is that it ends. But death itself offers no retrospective clarity and no revelation. As the priest tells us about Ophelia, 'Her death was doubtful.' The doubt (a word echoing throughout the play) surrounds of course not the fact but the meaning of her death. Did she commit suicide or not? The question is a hard one first of all because we don't see Ophelia drown; our information is second-hand, available in Gertrude's moving but not very definitive description. More than this, however, even if theatrical problems were solved and we were somehow allowed a direct view, even if we saw Ophelia falling like unripe fruit (a 'green girl', her father calls her) from a tree, we wouldn't be able to answer the question. For the question centers on the spirit, the purity or impurity of Ophelia's soul. The law and theology are available in the play to provide the necessary illusion of a coherent framework within which to act. They help the priest to decide whether Ophelia should be buried in hallowed ground, whether to accord her whole or 'maimèd rites'. But like all human institutions, the law and theology cannot pluck out the heart of the mystery. This remains an exclusively private matter between Ophelia and her God, beyond objectification.

The ghost had said it at the beginning: The secrets of his

prison-house have to remain secret; eternal blazons, if uttered to ears of flesh and blood, would literally rip the living human body apart. The condition of human life is, by definition, one of fundamental ignorance of the deepest meaning of human life. This radical doubt is sustained not only to but through the very end. Whether Hamlet enters into a state of grace, fulfills divine providence and justly purges Denmark, or whether he goes mad, abandons responsibility for his actions and contributes to a meaningless carnage – these are the poles within which the interpretative faculty struggles at the end of the play. We don't know, of course; the action on stage is amazingly swift; slowed down in the study, it is no less mystifying, for like all actions, it can reveal nothing more than tentative in this area. 'No man of aught he leaves knows' holds true about art as well as life. Eliot was right in a way in saying that the play lacks an objective correlative. What he didn't seem to realize is that the play assumes that life lacks an objective correlative. And this assumption, as I said at the beginning, is more radically sceptical than Sophocles's. Sophocles (in rather crude paraphrase) says that one can't reach a verdict until all the evidence is in. By the end of *Hamlet*, all the evidence *is* in, but no verdict can be reached.

The last few pages are no doubt too compressed and full of sweeping generalizations to be wholly convincing in themselves, but perhaps they furnish a context within which I can deliver on my promised intention to describe Plutarch. A good place to begin is the question of the overall purpose and unity of the *Lives*, if only because it is a much debated topic. The following suggestions have been offered: that Plutarch wished to demonstrate the superiority of Greek to Roman culture; that he wished to justify Roman culture to the Greeks; that he wished to explain to the Romans and the Greeks the virtues of the other's culture. All these suggestions are unconvincing and may be easily refuted by referring them to the details of the text,[31] but their distortion of detail is the function of a more general misrepresentation, namely the assumption that there *is* in Plutarch an overall structure, a governing significance to which all details are subordinated. One searches largely in vain in the *Lives* for the generalization to which all the concrete events lead, the abstract *significatio* to which, as in the medieval bestiaries, one is invited to relate the *natura*, or the twenty-four separate narrative units.

This is not to deny that there is a unifying structure in Plutarch's *Lives*, or better, a series of unifying structures of increasing magnitude – within each Life, within each set of Lives with its summary comparison, finally within the work as a whole. But it is the looseness of these structures that results in the particular easiness that the commentators on Plutarch, like the commentators on Dryden, have often noticed. To begin with the Life, the smallest unit: As I've mentioned, each Life is unified by the *physis*, the basic unchanging nature revealed in the conduct, or *ethos*, of its subject. Nonetheless, because a man's nature is revealed in his actions, with all their 'many and wonderful vicissitudes', the events in a man's life tend typically to be seen as discrete occurrences, important in themselves but not necessarily for their relevance to any subsuming abstract pattern. I cite an instance of this from the *Life of Demetrius*:

Let us here record an example in the early life of Demetrius, showing his natural humane and kindly disposition. It was an adventure which passed betwixt him and Mithridates, the son of Ariobarzanes, who was about the same age with Demetrius, and lived with him, in attendance on Antigonus [Demetrius's father]; and although nothing was said or could be said to his reproach, he fell under suspicion, in consequence of a dream which Antigonus had. Antigonus thought himself in a fair and spacious field, where he sowed golden seed, and saw presently a golden crop come up; of which, however, looking presently again, he saw nothing remain but the stubble, without the ears. And as he stood by in anger and vexation, he heard some voices saying Mithridates had cut the golden harvest and carried it off into Pontus. Antigonus, much discomposed with his dream, first bound his son, by an oath, not to speak, and then related it to him, adding that he had resolved, in consequence, to lose no time in ridding himself of Mithridates, and making away with him. Demetrius was extremely distressed; and when the young man came, as usual, to pass his time with him, to keep his oath he forbore from saying a word, but, drawing him aside little by little from the company, as soon as they were by themselves, without opening his lips, with the point of his javelin he traced before him the words 'Fly, Mithridates'. Mithridates took the hint, and fled by night into Cappodocia, where Antigonus's dream about him was quickly brought to its due fulfilment; for he got possession

of a large and fertile territory; and from him descended the line of
the kings of Pontus, which, in the eighth generation, was reduced
by the Romans. This may serve for a specimen of the early goodness
and love of justice that was part of Demetrius's natural character.
(p. 1075)

In this passage the action is sandwiched between two statements
naming the quality it is said to illustrate – Demetrius's 'natural
humane and kindly disposition', his 'goodness and love of
justice'. The action does indeed illustrate the quality, but in its
circumstantiality of description, it tells us more in a sense than
we need to know; the chaff (to use the familiar medieval terms,
still current in the Renaissance) has not been pared to expose
the kernel of significance. Why are we told that Mithridates is
about the same age as Demetrius? why is the dream given in
such detail? why is the city into which Mithridates flees
specified? why are we told that the dream came true, and
beyond, why that Mithridates's own descendants were ultimately 'in the eighth generation...reduced by the Romans'?

These details do not contradict the assertion of Demetrius's
goodness and love of justice, but they do not affirm it either, and
this is typical of Plutarch. For readers and writers educated in
a different tradition from Plutarch's, trained not to see but to
see through, such a tolerant attitude to the raw material of
history would not be natural, perhaps not even possible. I am
thinking of Shakespeare's Roman plays, where time after time
events that are only loosely related by Plutarch within the framework of a man's life are transformed into unifying *symbols* whose
meaning is related to an over-arching significance. Thus, to
take a small but typical example, Plutarch's 'three-and-twenty
wounds' in the *Life of Caesar* (North translation) becomes 'three
and thirty wounds' in *Julius Caesar* (v. i. 53), because of the
play's persistently ironic view of the relation between Caesar
and Christ, between Rome and Christian civilization. On a
larger scale, Shakespeare's transformation of Plutarch's Coriolanus has been brilliantly described by Willard Farnham:

The overlying haughtiness...becomes an underlying pride, a
spiritual flaw reaching to the depth of his being...Moreover, the
wrath of Shakespeare's Coriolanus is much more clearly subsidiary
to pride than the angry impatience of Plutarch's Coriolanus is

subsidiary to haughtiness. Shakespeare's Coriolanus is often a wrathful man, but always and before all else he is a proud man.[32]

This is exactly to the point. The loose structure of Plutarch's balance ('His good qualities and his bad', as Farnham notes, 'were quite separate') tolerates a wide variety of different, even inconsistent, character traits. Shakespeare's much more rigorously unified view, however ('the good and the bad... [become] seemingly inseparable and even seemingly interdependent'), is a hierarchy culminating in a single 'spiritual' quality which 'always and before all else' defines the character, and to which everything else is 'subsidiary'.

Before moving on to the next unit, the set of Lives, I would like to say a word about Plutarch's digressions which, like Dryden's, are often noted in conjunction with the easiness of his style; and rightly so, for they are an aspect of the same habit of mind. It is easy to list examples of Plutarch's digressions, not so easy to explain them, and yet an explanation is important, because digressions are an essential aspect of Plutarch's narrative method, not an occasional accident. That is, Plutarch is inherently digressive, even when he is not writing what we would tend to call a digression. The so-called digressions occur when the narrative stops and a semi-scientific inquiry begins into such subjects as whether human will is present in divinely inspired actions (pp. 284–5) or whether statues can talk. (pp. 288–9) But these are only the most conspicuous examples of the breaking of continuity, a phenomenon which occurs all the time in Plutarch. Consider the following:

But for all this, Cleopatra prevailed that a sea-fight should determine all, having already an eye to flight, and ordering all her affairs, not so as to assist in gaining a victory, but to escape with the greatest safety from the first commencement of a defeat.

There were two long walls, extending from the camp to the station of the ships, between which Antony used to pass to and fro without suspecting any danger. But Caesar, upon the suggestion of a servant that it would not be difficult to surprise him, laid an ambush, which, rising up somewhat too hastily, seized the man that came just before him, he himself escaping narrowly by flight.

When it was resolved to stand to a fight at sea, they set fire to all the Egyptian ships except sixty. (p. 1140)

I include the sentences preceding and following the ambush paragraph in order to suggest the context. In fact, the context has been developing for several pages, perhaps for the whole *Life of Antony*: This battle will be the crucial defeat, and Antony's accession to Cleopatra's desire that it be fought at sea is the culminating instance of his uxorious folly, for he was much better prepared to fight on land. Is the ambush a digression? In a way it is, no less so than the earlier examples concerning human will or statues talking, since the narrative may be said to be interrupted. In this case, however, the narrative is interrupted not by exposition but by another piece of narrative, one which, however, is not effectively related to the main narrative focus. That is, one does not see Antony's escape here as ironic in terms of his imminent defeat, or as a warning of his imminent defeat, or as building suspense towards his imminent defeat. Or perhaps one sees it as all these, but my point is the same. Plutarch does not specify the significance of the event in terms of an overall structure, the context of the whole. Quite simply this is, to use one of Dryden's favorite words, *another* event that happened to Antony about this time. Obviously, digressions are relative phenomena. A piece of writing seems to be digressive, to depart from an area, in proportion to one's sense of the narrowness of this area. And for Plutarch, the defining limits of an area, in this case the area of human character, are flexible indeed; they are simply the man's birth and death and all the events that happen to him in between. Within this loose unity, Plutarch shows us 'simply the quiet existence and operation of things in accordance with their natures'. The words are Schiller's to describe the effects of Homer's digressions, and they make us wonder whether these are digressions at all.[33]

To move now to the larger unit, Life-Parallel Life-*synkrisis*. This unit too is unified, but very loosely. About half the time the notion of analogy or parallelism is posited at the beginning, rather like the notion of Demetrius's goodness and love of justice; and once posited, forgotten. Or if Plutarch doesn't forget about it, he points transitionally to the notion of parallelism either at the end of the first or the beginning of the second Life in the pair. But such transitional pointers are brief and casual: 'Such was Solon. To him we compare Poplicola, who received this later title...' – and we are off into Poplicola's story. (p. 117) Only in the *synkrisis* is the parallelism sustained in any way, and these summary comparisons are indeed important in reinforcing the sense of a unity. But again, a loose unity. If Plutarch were a more tight unifier, these *synkrises* would be not merely important but all-important, the end towards which the whole process has been developing, a conclusion truly conclusive. They are not. That they are expendable is suggested by their absence in five cases, but even if it could be proved that these five were lost (and it is not assumed so), the *synkrises* could still not be called crucial. They are very brief, generally no more than about one-fifteenth as long as the two Lives that they sum up. More important is the fact that their function is, indeed, only to sum up.

For example, consider the following:

There was no law to prevent Demetrius from marrying several wives; from the time of Philip and Alexander it had become usual with Macedonian kings, and he did no more than was done by Lysimachus and Ptolemy. And those he married he treated honourably. But Antony, first of all, in marrying two wives at once, did a thing which no Roman had ever allowed himself; and then he drove away his lawful Roman wife to please the foreign and unlawful woman. And so Demetrius incurred no harm at all; Antony procured his ruin by his marriage. *On the other hand*, no licentious act of Antony's can be charged with that impiety which marks those of Demetrius. Historical writers tell us that the very dogs are excluded from the whole Acropolis because of their gross, uncleanly habits. The very Parthenon itself saw Demetrius consorting with harlots and debauching free women of Athens. The vice of cruelty, also, remote as it seems from the indulgence of voluptuous desires, must be attributed to him, who, in the pursuit of his pleasures, allowed or, to say more truly, compelled the death of the most beautiful and most chaste of the Athenians, who found no way but this to escape his violence. In one word, Antony himself suffered by his excesses, and other people by those of Demetrius. (p. 1154; my emphasis)

This paragraph is concerned with comparing the licentiousness of Demetrius and Antony and is divided roughly into two parts, on either side of that transition so familiar to readers of Dryden, *On the other hand*. In the first part their marital indulgences are compared, and Antony appears to be judged the less moral. In the second Plutarch judges Demetrius more harshly for his whoring in temples. But if one expects a hierarchical conclusion, the determination of a preference, the conclusion that Plutarch reaches, 'in one word', frustrates this expectation. In telling us that in their excesses Antony suffers and Demetrius caused others to suffer, Plutarch's focus is not on consciousness, not on motivation, not on the state of the doer's soul, but rather, again, on the consequences of action. Indeed, this was his perspective in the conclusion of the first part of the paragraph. Though the moral perspective is available in preferring Demetrius's polygamy to Antony's, this is not an absolute preference. Their actions are identical and it is only the cultural relativism that determines the conclusion. Antony was wrong not in relation to an immutable proscription handed down from a source outside nature, but in relation to the laws of his own particular environment. Though in Rome, he did as a Greek might. Again, Plutarch finds his norms in the arena of the visible, of public action.

As such the paragraph, like Plutarch's *synkrises* generally, is in a way inconclusive. He brings into closer proximity comparable actions that he has already narrated in the preceding *Lives*, but without relegating them to some higher judgment, without transforming the discourse to some higher mode. To speak symbolically, Action One in the *Life of Antony* and Action One in the *Life of Demetrius* are, in the *synkrisis*, expressed as One-and-One, not as Two. In the summing up, the components never lose their individual identities; nothing new is *revealed*. It is this sort of inconclusiveness that troubles Barrow, who feels that in his *synkrises* Plutarch 'sometimes seems to find it difficult to make out his case; to us it is obvious that the original choice was at fault [though]...perhaps from Plutarch's own rather circumscribed point of view there was a real link'.[34] The inconclusiveness of Plutarch's *synkrises*, however, is not due to the accidents of history by which resemblances clear in the author's day are no longer apparent. Rather, this inconclusiveness is a measure of Plutarch's respect for not-so-cold and not-so-dull facts, for the 'quiet existence and operation of things in accordance with their natures', a realm of being too compelling to be transformed into abstract values. To say that Plutarch does not 'make out his case' is to approach his Hellenistic sensibility with Hebraistic demands, to reveal oneself as a teleologue;

for Plutarch, narrating the events is in itself to make out his case.

In discussing Plutarch as an exemplar of classicism, I have mentioned Dryden only occasionally and parenthetically. Any systematic or sustained comparison between the two of them doesn't seem to me in order, since after all, Plutarch's *Lives* and Dryden's essays are different genres – moral biography and history on the one hand, literary criticism on the other. Nonetheless, I hope that even my perfunctory references to Dryden suggest how numerous and basic are the points of similarity between him and Plutarch; and it might not be inappropriate to specify some of them now as a kind of *synkrisis*.

In terms of a specific literary technique they are similar in their aptitude to use comparison, and to use it in a rather special way. In both comparison serves primarily to make the reader aware of different perspectives, not to determine a preference.[35] In terms of style and linguistic structure, both Plutarch and Dryden tend towards the flexibility articulated typically by the mean. Neither is given much to abstraction in the sense of a governing idea to which all particular phenomena must be referred. The phenomena are, to be sure, unified, contained within a single area, but a remarkably large area; they are interrelated within a single conceptual framework, but loosely, and by means of relatively unspecific transitions. The resulting mode in both Dryden and Plutarch is very respectful of the differences that exist in particular points of view, and of the values that exist in a variety of points of view. Both affirm the rich multiplicity of experience and the appropriateness of a comprehensive response to it. In these respects, both Dryden's criticism and Plutarch's *Lives*, for all their distinctness of identity from each other, may be understood as typical expressions of a classical sensibility.

Dryden read Plutarch, wrote about him and was connected (however casually) with the collective enterprise that has come down to us as the 'Dryden translation' of the *Lives*. I haven't appealed to this kind of evidence, not because it seems to me unimportant, but because the relation between Dryden and Plutarch (or perhaps between Dryden and classical writers generally) seems to me more profound than a matter of sources, influences and models. In concentrating on mode and on the relation between mode and sensibility, I have tried to suggest a shared way of seeing things that, while certainly conscious, is also deeper than consciousness.

This perhaps furnishes a way of distinguishing Dryden from earlier and later writers that we might also wish to characterize as classical. The classicism of the early Renaissance involved a marked interest in ancient models – social, philosophical and literary; as Bolgar points out, moreover, this interest was more solidly rooted in classical scholarship than was the same kind of interest in Dryden's period.[36] But even as they promoted classical studies, the Humanists felt stresses in assimilating them into a Christian point of view; and perhaps my references earlier to authors of a contrasting mode (Ariosto, Shakespeare, Chapman, Milton, *et al.*) suggest that Renaissance poets also tended to maintain an element of aloofness from, even to some extent disapproval of, the values and the forms of the classical models that they were imitating. In Dryden, however, this reserve of distance has been bridged, and the poise of a classical structure informs his own utterances. He himself seems to have felt no sense of radical inconsistency between classical antiquity and Christianity, and as James Johnson shows, his contemporaries generally shared this feeling, respecting equally and with no particular sense of stress the authorities of Christian and pre-Christian culture, both of which they regarded as 'classic' in a less circumscribed sense.[37]

In going to Schiller ('the quiet existence...') and to Arnold (Hebraism and Hellenism) for my terms, I have alluded obliquely to classicisms later than Dryden's, to Romantic and Victorian Hellenism. There is more than a declared interest in antiquity involved here; Josephine Miles demonstrates that in poets like Arnold and Swinburne, the 'smooth line and balanced structure' along with the vocabulary of Dryden's mode renews in strength.[38] But there is a certain polemical quality in these figures that distinguishes them from Dryden, a kind of special pleading and self-consciousness. It is obvious in Swinburne – 'Thou hast conquered, O pale Galilean; the world has grown grey from thy breath'; and even Arnold, who recognized the values of both Hebraism and Hellenism, who wanted above all a full human expression that would balance the two, writes persistently with an anxious sense of the difficulty of achieving such a balance, of worlds dying while others strive to be born. What is remarkable about Dryden is that the balance is not willed into existence, but effortlessly *there*, in his smooth transitions from French to English, from Horace to Juvenal, from Homer's Greece and Virgil's Rome to England in the Restoration; as fully realized in Dryden's criticism as it is in his poetry, as Josephine Miles has described it:

As God, king, and man are seen to feel much alike and to work much alike, in the same rich realms, as even the fields and skies are humanized, as Homer is seen in Virgil, and the Old Testament in the New, classicism establishes its time of balance, between the England of Jonson and the England of Blake, in Dryden's golden line and golden mean.[39]

PART TWO: CONTEXT

4

CORNEILLE AND THE QUESTION OF CULTURAL INFLUENCE

Having described Dryden's theory of literature and a tradition of classicism within which to locate it, I turn now to consider various questions of relationship, influence and response: In what way is Dryden enriched by his reading of contemporary French critics? How is Dryden affected by the pressures of an earlier, native critical tradition, and how in turn does he affect later English theory? What interactions exist between his criticism and his poetry? In some places I shall be urging a reconsideration of traditional conclusions, as in this chapter's suggestion that in many significant respects the familiar rôles of free-and-English Dryden and restrained-and-French Corneille should be reversed. In other places my aim is to reanimate traditional concepts, as in the fifth chapter where I try to find new usefulness for the venerable 'transitional figure' as a phrase to describe Dryden's historical position in English criticism. But my primary and unchanging purpose throughout the remainder of this book, though it is often only implied, is to suggest the relation between what I have called 'structure' and 'context'. In Dryden's organic assimilation of foreign critical theory into a native tradition, in his easy tolerance of old and new, in the remarkable diversity of his poetry – in all these instances I find illustrations of a flexibility which allows differences to coexist meaningfully in a broad but definite area, the poise which I have tried to suggest as the hallmark of Dryden's sensibility.

Writing about the *Essay* only three years after its composition, Dryden called it 'a little discourse in dialogue for the most part borrowed from the observations of others', (i. 112) and commented that

> those propositions [in the *Essay*]...are not mine (as I have said), nor were ever pretended so to be, but derived from the authority of Aristotle and Horace, and from the rules and examples of Ben Johnson and Corneille. (i. 125)

Not just in the *Essay* but throughout his criticism, Dryden 'borrows from the observations of others'. Such borrowing can vary in length from pages of direct quotation or paraphrase (generally, as we would expect, in the later essays) to short paragraphs. Most often the borrowings are in effect footnotes interpolated into the body of Dryden's text, passing acknowledgments to critics from whom he has taken, or to whom he can attribute, a particular observation, such as his expression of debt in the *Preface to Troilus and Cressida* to 'Bossu, the best of modern critics', for the point that the rules were formulated 'by men of transcendent genius'. (i. 211) In another interpolated footnote Dryden cites Aristotle along with Longinus and Horace in *The Author's Apology* as authorities who share his opinion that 'Heroic Poetry...has ever been esteemed, and ever will be, the greatest work of human nature', adding that, but for his recognition that 'quotations are superfluous in an established truth', he would 'reckon up, amongst the moderns, all the Italian commentators on Aristotle's book of poetry; and, amongst the French, the greatest of this age, Boileau and Rapin'. (i. 181)

Dryden reckons them up anyway. He is rarely above quoting an authority in support of an established truth, even without the playful *occupatio* of this last passage. 'I have endeavoured in this play', he says about *All for Love*, 'to follow the practice of the Ancients, who, as Mr. Rymer has judiciously observed, are and ought to be our masters.' (i. 200) This kind of strictly unnecessary massing of authority may be understood in part as a natural result of Dryden's rôle. Not simply a critic, he served his contemporaries also as scholar, literary historian, and teacher, and one of Dryden's pedagogical functions was to make the insular English aware of the existence on the continent of a venerable tradition of intelligent and careful literary criticism to which nothing at home could be compared. Like any pedagogical writer, he sometimes spares himself the cruel labor of going through his note cards to substantiate an assertion that seems to be self-evident. Sometimes, on the other hand, he interpolates such unnecessary notes into his text as the ones I have been quoting above.

Dryden tended to err more on the side of generosity than economy, and this tendency may help to explain the contemporary views of him as unoriginal, as a plagiarist.

> So does he shine, reflecting from afar
> The rays he borrowed from a better star;
> The rules which from Corneille and Rapin flow,
> Admired by all the scribbling herd below.[1]

But Dryden is scrupulous to distinguish his pedagogical from his theoretical rôle. Like a proper scholar, he directs his reader to previous scholarship without necessarily committing himself to accepting all of its ideas. Concerning his longest direct quotation, Dryden says, 'I will take my rise from Bellori, before I proceed'. (ii. 125) That is, he uses Bellori as the starting point for the discussion. Indeed in this particular instance Dryden cannot fully accept Bellori's idealistic theory of art, and he quickly adds a corrective passage quoted from Philostratus, expounding a more naturalistic kind of theory. But Philostratus, Dryden adds, does not fully represent his position either.

Thus, as convoy-ships either accompany or should accompany their merchants, till they may prosecute the rest of their voyage without danger; so Philostratus has brought me thus far on my way, and I can now sail on without him. (ii. 124)

When Dryden finally sails into port, he is in possession of his own theory, not Bellori's or Philostratus's, though one which these earlier critics helped him to understand and articulate again – in the sense that one can relearn what one already knows. 'Both these arts...are not only true imitations of Nature, but of the best Nature, of that which is wrought up to a nobler pitch'. (ii. 137) Dryden, typically, *uses* earlier critics. They are available to be learned from, but not to obviate additional thought on his own.

I am now almost gotten into my depth; at least, by the help of Dacier, I am swimming towards it. Not that I will promise always to follow him, any more than he follows Casaubon; but to keep him in my eye, as my best and truest guide; and where I think he may possibly mislead me, there to have recourse to my own lights, as I expect that others should do by me. (II. 53)

The writing of criticism was an adventure for Dryden, an exploration, part of whose excitement was the discovery of realms of thought already explored by earlier adventurers. But at every point, and especially in the last leg of the voyage, Dryden recognizes the need 'to have recourse to my own lights'.

What was exciting for Dryden probably seems the reverse of exciting for us. Tracing Dryden's path like a hummingbird's from one to another of the grey eminences in the continental neoclassical establishment – this is the stuff that source studies are made of, and source studies are legendarily dull. In part the problem is the nature of the particular material: The dramatic issues debated under the aegis of the rules no longer engage our interest. But the problem is also partly the kind of study itself, which still typically follows the pattern described regretfully by Louis Bredvold in an important article published in 1950: An intensive examination of 'the sources' is followed by a rapid reading of a mass of the literature supposed to be influenced, and 'the accumulating of similarities is then presented as a demonstration of influence'. But this need not as well as should not be the case, and Bredvold offers the following alternative:

The emphasis might better be reversed. It is the literature that is influenced that must be studied profoundly, for the influence is significant only as a phase of its history. It is the organism that assimilates the influence which must be understood in all its individuality, its native tendencies, its past history as well as its present condition. Only the influence which is thus assimilated is really worth studying.[2]

I am not sure that I accept wholly this reversal of emphasis. Better, certainly, to emphasize the influenced rather than the influencing literature, but why emphasize either at the expense of the other? Shouldn't we try to understand *both* bodies of literature in all of their individuality, native tendencies, history and present condition?

Still, what is so good about Bredvold's essay is that he speaks about 'organisms' and 'assimilation' – that he recognizes the responsibility of 'source study' or 'comparativist study' to respond to a vital and dynamic reality. These are not old books influencing old books, but living minds learning from living minds. Very good minds, generally, too – and if we keep this in front of us, perhaps we can find more interest in the particular issues debated, not in themselves necessarily (in themselves they are, most of them, pallid), but in their ability to engage the active and lively intelligence of very bright men, some of whom wrote poetry that we still read with immense enjoyment. I am concerned with two such men here, Dryden and Corneille. Corneille was, in the words of the anonymous contemporary slur I quoted earlier, one of the men from whom 'the rules flowed' to Dryden. I like the metaphor, even if its context is misleading. Rivers flow, and the flowing of rivers is in some ways like 'the growth of a poet's mind'; rivers have sources too, and in tracing the active course from Corneille to Dryden, perhaps we can chart the growth of a critic's mind.

But Corneille is not truly the source, the origin. Beyond him stretches a vast tradition of French and Italian theory, and his *Discours* were written in large part as a response to this tradition. This tradition – in all its individuality, native tendencies, history as well as present condition – helps us to recognize the organic vitality of Corneille's own critical achievement. Thus the story is more complicated and more interesting; there are more than two characters. But there remain two major characters, and I hope that both of them, Dryden and Corneille, emerge as kinds of heroes in the pages that follow.

In 1657, François Hédelin, the Abbé d'Aubignac, published *La Pratique du Théâtre*,[3] a book that alternately censured and praised Corneille's plays, in general according to their departure from or proximity to the traditional canons of dramatic propriety as established by French and Italian theoreticians of the sixteenth and seventeenth centuries. *La Pratique* served as the immediate occasion for Corneille's three *Discours*, which were included in the 1660 edition of his *Oeuvres*. However, it was not only to *La Pratique* that Corneille was responding, for d'Aubignac's work had awakened those issues, supposedly dormant for twenty years, that were involved in *La Querelle du*

Cid, the literary battle that followed upon the appearance in 1636 of Corneille's most famous play.[4] Corneille had not been silent during *la Querelle*, but the moratorium imposed on further discussion by Richelieu had prevented him from replying in a formal way to the most extensive criticism directed against him, *Les Sentiments de l'Académie sur le Cid*. Doubtless the material of the *Discours* had been on Corneille's mind for some time, waiting for such an opportunity as d'Aubignac's treatise presented him to break silence gracefully. Certainly, too, Corneille felt a greater self-confidence by 1660, with a long and successful dramatic career behind him, and with the ample opportunity to fill in the gaps in his knowledge of the commentators on Aristotle of whom, he says in the *Examen* of *Mélite*, he had been completely ignorant when he began writing for the theater.[5] In any case, Corneille's *Discours* are essentially apologetic in the old sense, according to the ancient principle of warfare that attack is the best defense. If he had been criticized by theoreticians who held his plays up to the rules, now he would criticize the theoreticians, by holding their rules up to the standard of his plays and the undeniable popular acclaim that had been accorded these plays.

To begin with, then, the unities themselves as regarded generally in neoclassical theory prior to Corneille: It has often been pointed out that the three unities are not to be found as such in Aristotle's *Poetics*, but rather are the products of Italian theory in the sixteenth century.[6] Their theoretical basis is generally the same as we remember from Dryden's *Essay*. Since the play lasts but a few hours in presentation, its subject should be similarly limited. Playing time should be in close proportion; thus the unity of time. Unity of place is a corollary of this idea which, as René Bray describes it, 'se dégage lentement de l'unité de temps'.[7] Since the dramatic time lasts only a few hours, one must not suppose the dramatic geography to extend to any great distance. It is not until 1570, in Castelvetro's commentary upon the *Poetics*, that the unity of action is brought together with time and place. Castelvetro rejects the Aristotelian grounds for unity of action, basing the rule rather upon the need to obey the other unities. In Bray's paraphrase, dramas 'ne peuvent mettre en scène qu'un seul héros et une seule action: deux actions ou deux héros séparés forceraient le poète à sortir du temps et du lieu qui lui sont assignés'.[8] In the excessively assertive nature of his thought, Castelvetro is, as often, somewhat eccentric. But the assertion itself, the subordination of action to time and place, is in the mainstream of the tradition.

It is in the *Troisième Discours, des Trois Unités*, the piece which had the most powerful influence on Dryden, that Corneille confronts neoclassical theory on this point. The first thing to notice is the order in which Corneille considers the unities: 'D'action, de jour, et de lieu'. It is usual among Italian and French neoclassical critics to begin with time and place and defer action till last. Corneille is not unique (Chapelain had adopted the same order earlier), but Corneille's order does mark a break from the norm; and in a critical tradition in which – its tendency towards polemics notwithstanding – strong disagreement is often rendered in terms of subtle shades of nuance, such an abnormality is significant. Since action is the only unity that is mentioned in the *Poetics*, Corneille's order may be taken as an attempt to return to Aristotelian purity. But Corneille has no vested interest in explicating Aristotle accurately. When he points out deviations from the *Poetics* on the part of earlier commentators, it is either to establish a precedent for his own wish to interpret Aristotle according to his own lights, as the others had, or to cast doubt on the trustworthiness of these later commentators as possessors of revealed literary truth. His reversal of the traditional order of the unities is simply the first indication (first for our purposes) of his unwillingness to accept the traditional theory underlying the unities, and his objection to their status as prescriptive law.

Corneille spends over half of the *Troisième Discours* in discussing the unity of action, before finally arriving at a discussion of the unities of time and place. At this point his tone indicates an evident impatience with theoretical niceties. He begins with the unity of time – however, not by stating the principle behind the rule, but by referring to the 'dispute fameuse' between the proponents of the natural and the artificial day (p. 137; it is a question of whether Aristotle intended a day of twenty-four or twelve hours). After dwelling – not lovingly, to be sure – on the details of this 'famous controversy', Corneille immediately turns to state his own position.

Et pour moi, je trouve qu'il y a des sujets malaisés à renfermer en si peu de temps, que non-seulement je leur accorderais les vingt-quatre heures entières, mais je me servirais même de la licence que donne ce philosophe de les excéder un peu, et les pousserais sans scrupule jusqu'à trente. (pp. 137–8)

By going directly to the trivial details of critical exegesis, Corneille by anticipation trivializes the principle itself. And by implying the triviality of the principle, Corneille allows himself the dignity of appearing to be – as, to be sure, he really is – a man of common sense, a pragmatist opposed to the excesses of the pedants and theoreticians. To cast further doubt on the usefulness of the principle, Corneille hereupon includes a paragraph of details of those classical playwrights who were forced into absurdities by the demands of unity of time; Euripides, for example, in whose *Supplices* only a brief chorus fills in the time between Theseus's departure from Athens to Thebes and the return of a messenger from Thebes to Athens with the news of Theseus's victory. 'Ethra et le choeur', Corneille says with what one imagines is a triumphant smile, 'n'ont que trente-six vers à dire.'[9] (p. 138)

It is only now that Corneille introduces the theoretical principle itself. The passage is worth quoting in full, if only because it establishes the precedent he will follow in his discussion of unity of place.

Beaucoup déclament contre cette règle, qu'ils nomment tyrannique, et auraient raison, si elle n'était fondée que sur l'autorité d'Aristote; mais ce qui la doit faire accepter, c'est la raison naturelle qui lui sert d'appui. Le poème dramatique est une imitation, ou pour en mieux parler, un portrait des actions des hommes; et il est hors de doute que les portraits sont d'autant plus excellents qu'ils ressemblent mieux à l'original. La représentation dure deux heures, et ressemblerait parfaitement, si l'action qu'elle représente n'en demandait pas davantage pour sa réalité. Ainsi ne nous arrêtons point ni aux douze, ni aux vingt-quatre heures; mais resserrons l'action du poème dans la moindre durée qu'il nous sera possible, afin que sa représentation ressemble mieux et soit plus parfaite. Ne donnons, s'il se peut, à l'une que les deux heures que l'autre remplit ...Si nous ne pouvons la renfermer dans ces deux heures, prenons-en quatre, six, dix, mais ne passons pas de beaucoup les vingt-quatre de peur de tomber dans le dérèglement, et de reduire tellement le portrait en petit, qu'il n'aye plus ses dimensions proportionées, et ne soit qu'imperfection.

Surtout je voudrais laisser cette durée à l'imagination des auditeurs, et ne déterminer jamais le temps qu'elle emporte, si le sujet n'en avait besoin. (p. 139)

Corneille is somewhat disingenuous at the beginning of this passage. Who indeed has been inveighing against this rule, though subtly, if not himself in the previous pages? The invocation of Aristotle's authority can scarcely be completely serious, since Corneille himself has pointed out that there is no unity of time as such in the *Poetics*. The theoretical statement that follows, however, is in itself forceful and unqualified. As Homer and Nature, Virgil found, were the same, so, Corneille tells us, both Aristotle and natural reason argue for the unity of time. In fact, Corneille states the principle in its most rigorous form, as many of the theoreticians had previously, most recently d'Aubignac: 'Il seroit même à souhaitter que l'action du Poëme ne demandast pas plus de temps dans la verité que celuy se consume dans la représentation.'[10] But the context he has created makes it unnecessary for Corneille to worry too much about the theory. He will simply excise all references in his plays to the passage of time and 'would leave this duration up to the audience's imagination'. This, I believe, is what is called cutting the Gordian knot.

This is also exactly his strategy in discussing the unity of place. Again he begins with certain objections and qualifications, and only then does he state the theoretical principle in its most rigorous form.

Je souhaiterais, pour ne point gêner du tout le spectateur, que ce qu'on fait représenter devant lui en deux heures se pût passer en effet en deux heures, et que ce qu'on lui fait voir sur un théâtre qui ne change point, pût s'arrêter dans une chambre ou dans une salle suivant le choix qu'on en aurait fait.[11] (pp. 143–4)

Corneille quickly adds that, 'Souvent cela est si malaisé...qu'il faut de nécessité trouver quelque élargissement pour le lieu, comme pour le temps.' (p. 144) Again, after stating the rule, Corneille subordinates it to 'nécessité', the obviously more pressing demands of practical dramaturgy. As Barnwell says, 'Clearly, Corneille is unwilling to sacrifice *un beau sujet*...in order to comply with a rigorous interpretation of the rules.'[12]

91274

Corneille invents what Schérer calls 'le lieu composite',[13] which refers simply to any and all unspecified places within a single city. His strategy, as with the unity of time, is simply to exclude any specific references to place from his plays. 'Qu'aucun des deux lieux ne fut jamais nommé, mais seulement le lieu général.' (p. 146) And once again, it is implied, Corneille will trust the audience's imagination.

Corneille's diminution of the authority of the unities is part of his rejection – or, at least, his rigorous qualification – of the major theoretical principle upon which the unities are based, *la vraisemblance*. *La vraisemblance* means, literally, the semblance of truth, and this semblance was preferred to the truth itself when the latter might interfere with either of the ends of poetry, pleasing or instructing. For example, in the case of a historical subject that strained credibility – that is, where truth was stranger than fiction – a fidelity to the recorded story would result in an unconvincing drama. And if an audience could not believe in the play, it would never be pleased. But the other poetic end, instruction, 'leading men to virtue', was involved even more significantly, as Chapelain tells us:

Les...anciens...tous d'un accord ont banni la vérité de leur Parnasse...nul ne faisant état de l'y rappeler que lorsqu'elle s'accommoderait à...la justice et à la raison, et qu'elle vêtirait la vraisemblance, laquelle en ce cas et non la vérité sert d'instrument au poète pour acheminer l'homme à la vertu.[14]

This position, established as early as Maggi or Scaliger,[15] was based upon the same need for establishing the subject's credibility, for if the audience could not believe in the subject, not only would pleasure be denied, but instruction would be made impossible. Moreover, *la vraisemblance* satisfied the moral end by ordering disordered history, by universalizing history's particularity, and by rendering poetic justice where history sometimes left its heroes unrewarded and its villains unpunished. The failure to observe *la vraisemblance* and the failure to instruct were the two most insistent objections made to *Le Cid* during the *Querelle*.

With varying degrees of impatience, Corneille refuses to accept the arguments of the traditional theory that endowed *la vraisemblance* with such importance. Years of success on the stage inclined him to treat the problem of belief as a red herring. He has full confidence in the ability of the audience to enjoy the play, without his having to make pointed reference to the unities in order to establish credibility. 'I would leave it up to the imagination of the spectator.' For a similar reason, he is much more willing to bring back historical subjects unchanged, to recall the truth which, according to Chapelain, the ancients had unanimously banished from their Parnassus. Because of his trust in the audience's imagination, he is less worried than are the traditional theoreticians about the demands such subjects might make upon credibility. Moreover, once a subject becomes valid because it is based on historical actuality – and this is what Corneille argues for – then the poet's liberty is enlarged to choose among a vast body of material – myth and legend as well as history in the modern signification. Such an enlargement of valid material liberated Corneille to find the kind of subject, 'le beau sujet', particularly adapted to his dramatic talents.[16] Corneille rejected the idea that historical subjects were invalid on moral grounds by denying that literature had any explicit and requisite end to instruct its audience (a position nearly unique in France with slightly greater precedent among the Italian critics). He rejected *la vraisemblance* as the over-arching criterion for creating or judging poetry, 'systematically [reducing]...verisimilitude to an attribute of the *acheminements* of the plot...plausible motives and incidents leading up to an event'.[17] This systematic reduction is undertaken in the *Deuxième Discours*, subtitled 'De la tragédie et des moyens de la traiter selon le vraisemblable ou le nécessaire', in which Corneille subordinates *le vraisemblable* to *le nécessaire*.[18] In fact, necessity is the highest principle in Corneille's theory. It alone 'nous peut autoriser à changer l'histoire et à nous écarter de la vraisemblance'. (p. 118) But in a sense, necessity is not what we think of as a theoretical principle at all. Necessity, he tells us, 'n'est autre chose que *le besoin du poète pour arriver à son but ou pour y arriver ses acteurs*'. (p. 118) That is, any obstacle to the working out of plot may be removed by appeal to *le nécessaire*, so long as the effect is consistent with the end of the poet to please his audience – 'de plaire selon les règles de son art'. (p. 118)

'According to the rules of his art' – this qualification introduces one of the most interesting questions about Corneille's criticism. After such a radical rejection of the theoretical bases for the rules, why does he feel it necessary to make public displays of genuflection before them? It would have been open to him to dispose of them with a casual 'n'importe!' like Samuel Johnson in the *Preface to Shakespeare*. (Johnson's disposition of the probable-marvelous issue in connection with *Paradise Lost* also comes to mind.) But Corneille eschewed this alternative of summary dismissal and, indeed, entered with apparent gusto into what might seem to be the jejune labor of spinning webs of theory around self-conscious misinterpretations of Aristotle. The question remains, why?

In part the answer may lie in the fact that the rules to some significant extent were of genuine practical use to him. If he is himself stricter than most contemporaries in endorsing some of d'Aubignac's prescriptions – for instance, on the *liaison des scènes*, the introduction of all important characters in Act I, and the avoidance of soliloquies – it may be because such rules tended to produce the compression and intensity which, as Will Moore and others point out, contribute essentially to his plays' dramatic vitality.[19] Then, too, there is something in Barnwell's suggestion that Corneille adopted the meticulousness of the earlier theoreticians because 'he had to please his audience... and the tastes of his audience were in some measure influenced by men like d'Aubignac'.[20]

But this is not the whole truth, for the pressure on Corneille is internal as well; as Bray points out concerning the rules, Corneille was 'forcé par son siècle *et par lui-même* de les admettre'.[21] Even granting his basic pragmatism, we should recognize a strong element in Corneille's sensibility that respects the rules *as rules*. The old wheeze about Norman legalism perhaps shouldn't be discounted altogether; and Corneille, a lawyer's son, received both Jesuit and legal training. More serious evidence is provided by the plays themselves, which consistently dramatize conflicts between instinct and prescription, the basic drive towards freedom and the restraining influences of tradition. The old cant phrase was 'love vs. honor', and the old cant view that the plays support the claims of the latter. But recent work (by Borgerhoff, Moore, Schérer, *et al.*) has removed Corneille from this procrustean 'classical' bed, suggesting that his characters do not so much submit their private beings to the supposedly higher claim of the public order as achieve – or try to achieve – an accommodation for self-expression within the framework of the social structure. In this view instinct has its own legitimate claim, and the spokesmen for public morality are seen to have a certain element of paternal posturing about them. It might even be argued that the torn, Cid-like heroes smack in their self-dramatizations just a bit of *miles gloriosus*, a residue of Matamore never wholly forgotten from *L'Illusion Comique*. Such a view of Cornélien drama perhaps clarifies his criticism by analogy, rendering the apparent contradiction between medium and message in the *Discours* less perplexing. With its primary emphasis on freedom, but its respect nonetheless for the pressures of tradition, a respect woven into the meticulous texture of the discussion, Corneille's criticism may embody in its own (and admittedly less dramatically engaging) way, the same kind of conflict as one finds at the center of his plays.

As we can see from all this, Corneille was indeed tremendously important for Dryden. In fact, John Aden suggests that Dryden may have written the *Essay* with the *Troisième Discours* open at his side, pointing out that he 'cites Corneille by name or virtually so eight times in the *Essay*'.[22] There are, in addition, plenty of other instances where Dryden has quoted or paraphrased Corneille without bothering to acknowledge him, as my notes earlier should have shown. Direct quotation or paraphrase aside, the *Discours* provided Dryden with a wealth of material, discussions of dramatic propriety concerning a variety of different issues – the unities, 'relations' (narrated material), *liaison des scènes*, for examples; and this at a time when Dryden, at the beginning of his criticism and with no wholly relevant native tradition to draw upon, must have been especially eager to find ways of talking intelligently about the drama. Probably more important than any of this is the general similarity in temperament between the two critics, which has been pointed out before. Ker comments about Corneille that, 'Like Dryden, . . . his business as a critic [was] to find some compromise between freedom and authority.' (I. xix) A. F. B. Clark has said, after noting Corneille's influence on the *Essay*: 'Though there is no explicit borrowing from Corneille in Dryden's other essays on dramatic subjects, they are nearly all characterized by that judicial balancing between the rules and the artistic need of individual liberty which the author no doubt learned from Corneille's *Discours*.'[23] I cannot muster the certainty of Clark's 'no doubt', but this seems generally true. Corneille, with his rejection of what Dryden called 'a servile observation of the unities', with his insistence upon the importance of pleasure, must have seemed a kindred spirit. Dryden must have gained enormously in self-confidence (not, of course, that he was constitutionally deficient in this quality) to find how closely the views of the most successful dramatist in France (and France, since the Restoration at least, was acknowledged in England as the literary capital of Europe) corresponded to his own.

Yet when all this is said, if we look more closely into the correspondence between Corneille and Dryden, salient differences become immediately apparent. For instance, only in the most general way can we legitimately identify their two positions towards the unities as, say, qualified acceptance, for there are two very different kinds of acceptance involved. For Corneille, as always, pragmatism *omnia vincit*, and his commitment to the rules is a function of the dramatic advantages derived from observing them. In fact these advantages are never really gone into in the *Discours*, but they may be inferred from his plays' dependence upon concentration. For Dryden, on the other hand, the unities serve to introduce the crucial theoretical question of the proper mimetic relation of art. They embody the concept of a just imitation of nature which is essential to his theory, not only in the *Essay* but in other pieces as well. For this reason, it is important to note that Dryden's discussion of the unities follows the normal traditional order (time, place, and then action) from which Corneille had deviated, and that Dryden's frequent borrowings from Corneille of examples of absurdity into which 'a servile observation' of the unities may lead are offered only *after* the principle itself is stated, by Crites, in what we may call its pure form.

Just as there is a profound difference between Corneille's and Dryden's acceptance of the unities, so there is a profound difference in the way that they qualify their acceptances. Both, certainly, appeal to the kinds of pleasure which too strict an observance of the unities prevents, but the basis of the appeal once again emphasizes the differences between Corneille's pragmatic and Dryden's theoretical nature.

For Corneille, pleasure is what is pleasing – what had pleased the audiences at his plays for a quarter of a century. He rarely goes beyond the experiential question – does it work? Thus in the *Troisième Discours*, discussing whether or not to present actions which are subordinate to the main design, Corneille tells us that the dramatist need choose only 'celles qui lui sont les plus avantageuses à faire voir, soit par l'éclat et la véhémence des passions qu'elles produisent, soit par quelque autre agrément, qui leur soit attaché'. (p. 126) This does not wholly ignore the question why an action might please or displease, be advantageous or disadvantageous, but it relegates it to a subordinate clause where it is given rather perfunctory and inconclusive treatment ('soit par l'éclat..., soit par quelque autre...'). A few pages later, discussing narrations in which the events occurred earlier than the action of the play, he tells us:

Ces narrations importunent d'ordinaire, parce qu'elles ne sont pas attendues et qu'elles gênent l'esprit de l'auditeur...[Mais celles] qui se font des choses qui arrivent, depuis l'actoin commencée, font toujours un meilleur effet, parce qu'elles sont attendues avec quelque curiosité. (pp. 130–1)

In this passage, pragmatism again; the dynamics of pleasure, the reason *why* an action might be 'avantageuse à faire voir', is rooted in the most basic verifiable phenomena of audience response – boredom, expectation, curiosity.

As one final example, here is Corneille rejecting cruel actions in the *Deuxième Discours*:

Il faut examiner...[si l'action] n'est point si cruelle, ou si difficile à représenter, qu'elle puisse diminuer quelque chose de la croyance que l'auditeur doit à l'histoire...Lorsque cet inconvénient est à craindre, il est bon de cacher l'évènement à la vue, et de le faire savoir par un récit...C'est par cette raison qu'Horace ne veut pas que Médée tue ses enfants, ni qu'Atrée fasse rôtir ceux de Thyeste devant le peuple. L'horreur de ces actions engendre une répugnance à les croire, aussi bien que la métamorphose de Progne en oiseau et de Cadmus en serpent, dont la représentation presque impossible excite la même incrédulité quand on la hasarde aux yeux du spectateur. (p. 102)

Most of this is devoted to the immediate practicalities of *mise-en-*

scène, rejecting actions that present insuperable production problems; again, the author writes as a man of the theater, a practicing playwright. In mentioning the relation between cruelty and belief, Corneille introduces a question that bristles with theoretical implications; but he is obviously not interested in them. What is it about the audience's powers of belief, or its psychology, that is reluctant to accept cruelty? Corneille does not really answer this question; the fact of such disbelief is all he needs to know. In this sense, the horror and cruelty are problematical in exactly the same way as the metamorphoses. They both present insuperable obstacles to the practical attainment of dramatic success. Actually Corneille is subscribing here to an aspect of the traditional theory, *les bienséances externes*, which emphasized the necessity for rendering the action conformable to the particular taste of the audience. ('Si le Sujet n'est conforme aux sentimens des Spectateurs', d'Aubignac tells us, 'il ne réussira jamais.'[24]) But Corneille's attachment to the concept is only a commitment to an isolated aspect of the theory which in general, focusing on the problem of belief as it does and offering *la vraisemblance* as a solution to this problem, Corneille tends to disregard.

Dryden clearly owes something to these passages of Corneille. In fact, as Lisideius he translates the first passage quoted, urging the representation of only those actions which are 'advantageous to have performed', commending Corneille for what he 'says judiciously'. (I. 64) And, moreover, as Neander he makes uses of the doctrine of *bienséances externes*:

Whether custom has so insinuated itself into our countrymen, or nature has so formed them to fierceness, I know not; but they will scarcely suffer combats and other objects of horror to be taken from them. (I. 74)

But Lisideius's translation occurs a page after an extremely complex theoretical discussion of narrations in which it was decided that only those 'actions which can be imitated to a just height' ought to be presented on stage, and Neander's remark is only a small part of an intricately involved argument in response to Lisideius's. In both these cases and indeed throughout the *Essay*, Dryden is much more interested than Corneille in speculating on the reasons for pleasure. Corneille's 'does it work?' becomes in Dryden, 'why does it work?' In attempting to answer this question, Dryden leaves the nearly exclusively pragmatic grounds on which Corneille's discussion is based in order to explore the mimetic question, examining the conditions in the relation between the play and nature which will tend to produce, or to prevent, the audience's pleasure.

To conclude then: Dryden learned much from Corneille, but he remained his own man. There are marked differences as well. as a general similarity in the critical temperaments of the two. While Corneille respects theoretical speculation, he is mainly concerned to defend his freedom as a practicing playwright. While Dryden has an obvious interest in practical matters, he is much more profoundly concerned with the theoretical issues. These differences in strategy, really in sensibility, are understandable in part as the results of differences in the situations in which each one found himself. Corneille wrote his criticism at a time when a great French drama was a *fait accompli* – indeed, a reality in the establishment of which he himself had played a major rôle; and when theory was serving not so much to nourish practice (at least not his practice) as to inhibit it. How much d'Aubignac's book galled him one can hardly guess – a pedantic theoretician presuming to advise the world about 'the *practice* of the drama', and daring to damn Corneille himself with faint praise. Corneille is in no measure an antinomian, about to reject theory *per se*, but a sustained irony, intentional or not, runs through the *Discours*, as he beats the pedants at their own game, splitting the hairs that they had split already until there is nothing left for the naked eye to see – and then deciding in favor of the poet's freedom. Nothing is quite so grimly funny, in its own (and, one feels, not altogether disingenuous) way, as the conclusion to the *Deuxième Discours*, in which Corneille supplants *la vraisemblance*, the chief theoretical principle of a century-old tradition, with the new principle of *le nécessaire*, which turns out – despite all the impressive machinery of periphrasis, pseudo-Aristotelian authority and definitive italics – to mean: 'making things easier for the poet'.

Dryden's situation when he was writing the *Essay* was quite different. Where Corneille looked back over an established dramatic career, Dryden looks ahead to establishing one. Where in France criticism was a tradition so venerable as to approach, perhaps, ossification, so respected as, perhaps, to inhibit art, in

England there was nearly no critical tradition, the great dramatic art of the 'last age' was no longer a wholly useful model, and Dryden was forced to wander in strange seas of thought, relatively alone. Nearly thirty years later, Dryden described the circumstances under which the *Essay* was composed –

When I was myself in the rudiments of my poetry, without name or reputation in the world, having rather the ambition of a writer, than the skill; when I was drawing the outlines of an art, without any living master to instruct me in it; an art which had been better praised than studied here in England, wherein Shakespeare, who created the stage among us, had rather written happily, than knowingly and justly, and Johnson, who, by studying Horace, had been acquainted with the rules, yet seemed to envy to posterity that knowledge, and, like an inventor of some useful art, to make a monopoly of his learning; when thus, as I may say, before the use of the loadstone, or knowledge of the compass, I was sailing in a vast ocean, without other help than the pole-star of the Ancients, and the rules of the French stage amongst the Moderns. (II. 16–17)

Granted the tone of self-congratulation in this passage, and granted the fact that it was written so long after the *Essay*, I believe nonetheless that it more accurately describes Dryden's situation in 1665 than does the remark in the *Defence*, more polemical than factual, that 'those propositions. . . are not mine'. The felt need expressed retrospectively here was surely genuine; it was for theoretical at least as much as practical guidance, for a conceptual framework within which to discuss and understand dramatic poetry. In this felt need Dryden's criticism is very different from Corneille's; at the same time this is the felt need that in large measure is satisfied by Corneille's criticism.

And it is appropriate to be reminded in conclusion, as this passage does, how Dryden conceived of criticism as an exploration of the world of ideas, rich with the exciting possibility of discovery. This excitement included the reading of earlier criticism and the help derived from it. Dryden's famous description of Jonson in the *Essay* is applicable to himself: 'He invades authors like a monarch; and what would be theft in other[s]. . .is only victory in him.' (I. 82) I conclude with Dryden's justification for using Shakespearean and Homeric parallels in a scene from his *Troilus and Cressida.*

We ought not to regard a good imitation as a theft, but as a beautiful idea of him who undertakes to imitate, by forming himself on the invention and the work of another man; for he enters into the lists like a new wrestler, to dispute the prize with the former champion. This sort of emulation, says Hesiod, is honourable... – when we combat for a victory with a hero, and are not without glory even in our overthrow. Those great men, whom we propose to ourselves as patterns of our imitation, serve us as a torch, which is lifted up before us, as high as the conception we have of our author's genius. (I. 206)

I have been trying to describe an example of literary influence. My first purpose is to move people, in the light of my conclusions, to re-assess the nature of Dryden's relation to Corneille. The usual view of this relation, that Dryden was freely English and Corneille rigidly French, seems to me the reverse of accurate in many important respects. Inaccurate, at least, in terms of what freedom and rigidity are usually taken to mean – the one a disregard for theoretical rules, the other a felt need to establish them. In other respects, of course, Dryden *is* a free spirit, freer than Corneille. A page of each convinces absolutely of this. Perhaps, then, we should rethink our terms. Freedom and rigidity are terms to describe a sensibility, not necessarily a particular substance of belief. Corneille might emphasize 'enlarging' the rules so that the poet is liberated to fulfill his primary end, pleasing the audience; but he expresses this emphasis in terms of a doctrinaire principle: *le nécessaire*. Dryden might emphasize the need for establishing rules, but this emphasis is expressed with Dryden's characteristic flexibility and open-mindedness, a casual *sprezzatura* (even in the relatively formal *Essay*) which is vastly freer in tone than Corneille. At the root of the difficulty, I believe, is the conception that the rules, as a belief, and freedom, as a quality of mind, are, first, subject to direct comparison and, second, that this comparison is a contrast, that the two are absolutely contrary to each other. The nineteenth-century ghost, again; it would be nice to remove that cold hand once and for all.

This brings me to my darker purpose. In rethinking Dryden and Corneille, perhaps we should rethink English and French generally, or more generally still, the way we tend to regard the transmission of cultural influence. The relation between Corneille and Dryden is a rather special one, and I don't wish to generalize too quickly on the basis of this one example. Still, if we take a figure like Rapin who is more representative, arguably, of 'pure' French neoclassicism, we find that even he, as received by the English, fails to fit the rôle to which Atkins assigns him – a pernicious incarnation of orthodoxy against which English critics strive valiantly (and finally successfully) to assert their independence. Nor, on the other side, is Boileau a conquering hero, not at least in the way Clark describes him, overwhelming the helpless English, for a time anyway, with a *Blitzkrieg* of doctrinaire theory. The erroneousness of these views has been amply demonstrated,[25] but what disturbs me about them is not so much their substance as the dominant metaphor by which they conceive of these international literary relations: namely, warfare, covert or declared.

This concept is still in the air, even in recent critics who are far more responsive to the reality of French-and-English during the Restoration. Consider the following from Sutherland's volume in the Oxford History of English Literature:

In the late 1670s and the early 1680s, when the work of Rapin, Boileau, and Le Bossu became better known, and when Rymer set himself up as their English salesman, Dryden came over – for some time at least – to the neo-classical point of view...[Rapin, Boileau and Le Bossu] could not possibly be ignored, and for some time *diverted* English criticism from its *normal* easy-going course.[26]

This may be factually quite accurate but still, I'd argue, misleading. True, Dryden tended more towards the regularity of the French in the years specified, but the emphasized words suggest that the French influence was a perversion; in this context, to declare that Dryden 'comes over' to the French view is nearly to characterize his movement as a departure from the underground into the collaborationists camp.

I don't mean to put words into anyone's mouth, nor even to suggest that submerged warfare metaphors are totally out of place in describing Anglo-French critical relations during the period. For an age that, presumably 'wearied into peace', kept asserting its standards of civility, the later seventeenth century certainly expended a great deal of powder and shot on literary matters. From Sprat's quarrel with Sorbière in the sixties to the battle of the books in the nineties, the tone is frequently bellicose, both generally and especially with reference to the French influence. The literary issues were never wholly removed from politics, not even in Dryden himself. Sutherland again (p. 401):

As late as 1697 he breaks out characteristically: 'Let the French and Italians value themselves on their Regularity; Strength and Elevation are our Standard.' Some twenty years earlier he had objected to 'our *Chedreux* critics' who formed their judgements on the practice of the French dramatists, and he had asserted his own independence: 'But for my part, I desire to be try'd by the Laws of my own Country; for it seems unjust to me, that the French should prescribe here, till they have conquer'd.'

But there is much less of this kind of outburst than one tends to remember. Hume surely exaggerates in his recent comment that 'cosmopolitanism' as a tag for Dryden 'fits only to the extent that Dryden could and did read French. He was consistently... patriotic and is always concerned about coming out ahead of the French, even though he freely drew on them.'[27] Dryden is not always concerned about beating the French; he's not even usually concerned with this. Indeed, this is not even his primary concern in the first passage that Sutherland quotes ('Let the French...'). Seen in context – and I discussed the passage at length in considering Dryden's style (pp. 30–35) – Dryden's concern may be secondarily to claim greater virtues for the English, but it is primarily to recognize the different virtues on both sides.

Dryden (to paraphrase André Gide) should not be understood too quickly. Because of his habits of style, his tendency to isolate particular aspects without insistently relating them to the over-riding point, Dryden is especially apt to be quoted out of context. And for the same reason, quoting Dryden out of context is especially apt to misrepresent him – not to communicate false information but to fail to communicate the whole truth. (Perhaps this is why Aden's *Dictionary*, so useful to consult, is not so satisfactory to browse through as J. E. Brown's comparable work on Johnson.) In focusing on the relation between Corneille and Dryden in this chapter, I've tried to do justice to the full context as I understand it. Believing with Josephine Miles that 'foreign need not necessarily mean hostile or opposed, but rather, simply different, irrelevant until made relevant by context', I'd suggest that 'English *and* French' would have better fit Dryden's characteristic endeavor in this area than the heading Aden chose, 'English *vs.* French'. And I'd suggest that we might consider as a general proposition that the assimilation of French influence into English criticism, even in the form of a temporary action to which a reaction set in after the early eighties, is not so much a diversion from the norm as a totally healthy development by means of which the norm is enriched.

The idea of warfare needn't – and probably shouldn't – be totally junked, but we should understand it in the spirit of Dryden's description of Jonson, invading other authors like a monarch. There is a good deal of cooperation implied here, an international community of authors. Within this community, of course, there are differences, separate identities, private and distinctly national purposes to be served. And in this sense Dryden takes only what he needs or can use from Corneille, only what he can assimilate into a native tradition, the primacy of whose interests he never tires of asserting. But he *does* take, copiously and with grateful acknowledgments, not just from Corneille but from Le Bossu, Horače, Longinus, Heinsius, Dacier, Bellori, Philostratus, Rigaltius, Casaubon – from all 'those great men, whom', in criticism as well as poetry, 'we propose to ourselves as patterns of our imitation'. The outbursts of literary patriotism would have no meaning without deference to these authorities; the deference is only genuine because it is in turn deferred to the self and indigenous demands. These are the constituent elements of an outlook that has rightly been called cosmopolitan; these are the components of a truly civilizing and civilized sensibility.

5

DRYDEN, OLD AND NEW

In the *Essay* Dryden called himself, or an important aspect of himself, Neander, the new man. The innovative rôle that he is usually assigned in the history of English criticism is one that he was aware of himself. A conscious self-projection as a modernist occurs not just in the *Essay*, but, in one form or another, in practically every piece of criticism that he wrote. Another kind of evidence for Dryden's novelty, and again one present throughout the body of his criticism, is his ambivalent attitude towards the literary tradition of the Renaissance. The 'last age' figures prominently in Dryden's imagination, and though he sometimes looks upon it as a happy age before the flood whose literary masterpieces are transcendent achievements beyond the reach of himself and his contemporaries, he also writes often about it as a less civilized period whose poetry, for all its greatness of soul, could not hope to compete with the refined artistry of 'this age'. Such an ambivalence is in no way unique to Dryden; every writer, one supposes, looks upon the past 'with parted eye', finding at once models to emulate and to reject; many writers, besides, look upon themselves as attempting something new. Dryden's attitude towards the past, however, is characterized by a particular intensity of self-consciousness, especially revealed in those frequently recurring terms – this age, the last age – and one feels that his critical endeavor is genuinely new in a qualitative way: an expression of taste that is not merely the inevitable evolutionary development of a tradition, but an abrupt break from it as well.

My first concern in this chapter is to describe Dryden's departure from the Renaissance tradition, a departure which I locate in terms of a single issue of literary theory, figurative language. Metaphor is much discussed by Dryden and by Renaissance critics, among whom there is sufficient agreement to justify speaking of a tradition; so there is material here for a legitimate comparison. I wish, then, to adopt a different historical perspective, relating Dryden not to the past but to the future, to the profoundly new developments of the late seventeenth and early eighteenth centuries. One such set of developments may be located in Locke and Addison – Locke because he systematized new assumptions about the nature of reality, our perception of reality, and the rôle language plays in this perception; Addison because he self-consciously transferred these assumptions into literary theory. Addison is a particularly significant figure for my purposes here as a kind of *terminus ad quem*, for in his systematic explicitness, he defines clearly a position towards which Dryden's innovations were tending.

Many people have written about a 'shift' or 'shifts of sensibility' in the late Renaissance, focusing on significant changes in style, or critical theory, or conceptions of literature, or in the religious and social structure, or in attitude towards experience in general.[1] I am in substantial agreement with what I understand to be the drift of modern scholarship in this area. I've perhaps helped to clarify a few points and outline a few new connections, but my main interest here is not so much in these late Renaissance changes *per se* as in the pressure which such changes might have exerted on Dryden, whose criticism was composed in their midst. As another way of putting this, I am not writing history in this chapter, or I am writing history of a deliberately biased kind. My treatment of Addison is a case in point. I shamelessly approach Addison in terms of the old metaphysical concerns of Renaissance theory, the relations of poetry to reason and truth, not for what this perspective can tell us about Addison (indeed, one of Addison's achievements was to render it definitively obsolete),[2] but for the way it can clarify Dryden's peculiar historical situation. For Dryden, even as he moves towards a position like Addison's, maintains his bases firmly in a Renaissance context. Such an ambivalent relation to change is inherently problematic, for the demands of old and new, metaphysical and empirical, are vastly different. The problem for Dryden was to articulate a structure sufficiently flexible to accommodate the demands of both – a theory in which literature must fulfill the residual requirements of tradition within a radically innovative set of assumptions. Dryden's way of handling (I do not say solving) this problem is another illustration of the vitality of his intelligence.

When Dryden discusses the use of figures, he insists almost invariably upon the criterion of decorum, and in this respect he is completely consistent with both Renaissance and ancient traditions.[3] However, his frequent and intense objections to excessive boldness or 'hardness' of figure suggest strongly that he defines the limits of propriety with a special and a new strictness. Even the figures that he chooses to commend, moreover, imply the same new rigor. For example, he praises a figure from the *Aeneid* in the following way:

Speaking of Misenus, the trumpeter, [Virgil] says:

> . . .quo non praestantior alter
> Aere ciere viros, . . .

and broke off in the hemistic, or midst of the verse; but in the very reading, seized as it were with a divine fury, he made up the latter part of the hemistic with these following words:

> . . .Martemque accendere cantu. [*Aeneid*, VI. 165]

How warm, nay, how glowing a colouring is this! In the beginning of his verse, the word *aes*, or brass, was taken for a trumpet, because the instrument was made of that metal, which of itself was fine; but in the latter end, which was made *ex tempore*, you see three metaphors, *Martemque, – accendere, – cantu*. Good Heavens! how the plain sense is raised by the beauty of the words! (II. 150–1)

I quote the passage in full because the tone is significant. Dryden nowhere else becomes so excited in praising figurative boldness, but one may wonder where this extraordinary boldness resides. *Martemque accendere cantu*, 'kindling Mars with his song'; where are the three metaphors? *Mars* is metonymy; for the warlike spirit, which the plain sense demands, is substituted the god of war, with which it is closely associated. Like the metonymy in the previous hemistich, brass for trumpet, like most metonymies, this is a relatively inconspicuous, a soft figure, for the reason recognized by the author of the *Rhetorica ad Herennium*: The transference is made between terms which are already close together and is thus 'abundant not only amongst the poets and orators but also in everyday speech'.[4] The metaphor in *kindling* is the same as in a *heated* argument, once again so close to the ordinary patterns of the language that one tends not to notice it as a trope. In Dryden's time, when the humors psychology was still current if no longer necessarily generally accepted, the notion that Mars could be kindled must have seemed even less of a deviation from the norm than it does today. *With his song* is the most hidden of all the metaphors. It is based upon the fact that song is music of the human voice, not music of an instrument like the trumpet, but every Latin dictionary I have checked not only gives the metaphorical sense (so common a metaphor it was), but does so without even noting it as in any way a departure from the norm.

Admittedly, the cumulative effect of the three figures is substantial, but with allowances made for this, the intensity of Dryden's reaction is still significant of his relatively narrow sense of metaphoric propriety. If this Virgilian hemistich represents the outer limits of boldness, it is understandable that Dryden feels it continually necessary to censure particular figures as excessively bold, rash and hard – as figures which go beyond the legitimate limits. In *The Author's Apology* where the subject receives its closest theoretical examination, Dryden tells us that 'Poetic Licence' involves 'speaking things in verse, which are beyond the severity of prose', and in both its larger and its more strictly defined stylistic aspects – the latter being either tropes 'if this licence be included in a single word', or figures 'if in a sentence or proposition' – this Poetic Licence 'consists in fiction'. (I. 188–9) This fictional quality, this sense of departure from the norm of literal description, is what seems particularly to trouble Dryden, and to judge from the following comment in the same essay, it is this which he wishes to keep under control: 'You are not obliged, as in History, to a literal belief of what the poet says; but you are pleased with the image, without being cozened by the fiction.' (I. 185)

Not surprisingly, then, Dryden's praise for metaphors that conform to his sense of propriety is often predicated explicitly on a kind of softening effect which ensures that we are not 'cozened by the fiction'. He praises a couplet from Cowley's *Davideis* (iii. 385–6) –

The valley, now, this monster seem'd to fill;
And we, methought, look'd up to him from our hill

– with the comment that 'the two words, *seemed* and *methought*, have mollified the figures'. (1. 185) A figure from Virgil (*Aeneid*, VIII. 691–2) receives the same kind of commendation:

> ...credas innare revulsas
> Cyclades, aut montes concurrere montibus altos.

Virgil, Dryden comments,

knew the comparison was forced beyond nature, and raised too high; he therefore softens the metaphor with a *credas*: you would almost believe that mountains or islands rushed against each other.
(II. 153)

Here, finally, is Dryden's approval of Ovid's 'modesty' in a figure from the *Metamorphoses* (1. 175–6):

'Tis true, no poet but may sometimes use a catachresis:...And
Ovid once so modestly, that he asks leave to do it:
...quem, si verbo audacia detur,
Haud metuam summi dixisse Palatia caeli. (1. 52)

In all these cases Dryden's praise is for a verbal sign post that informs the reader of the presence of a deviation from normal language. *Seemed, methought, you might believe, if I dare say so* – all these expressions serve notice that the poet is speaking what is not literally true.

Moreover, even where there is no explicit warning, the kind of figure which Dryden most often commends acts upon the reader in such a way as to imply such a warning. Here are examples from Cleveland (*Rupertissimus*, 39–40) and Virgil (*Aeneid*, VIII. 91–3):

> For beauty, like white powder, makes no noise,
> And yet the silent hypocrite destroys.

> ...mirantur et undae,
> Miratur nemus insuetum fulgentia longe
> Scuta virum fluvio pictasque innare carinas.

> In wonder the waves, in wonder the unwonted woods
> view the far gleaming shields of warriors and the
> painted hulls floating on the stream.[5]

These passages make use of personification and a kind of grammatical transference in which significances usually conveyed adverbially are rendered by means of adjectives. It would be more usual to say that white powder destroys silently; more strictly speaking, it is the *intrusion* into the woods of the shields and hulls that is 'unwonted'. Well over half the figures chosen by Dryden to illustrate proper boldness are characterized either by personification or this kind of grammatical transference or both together.[6]

The effects of this kind of figure have been brilliantly described by Donald Davie, who finds it a common device in the later eighteenth-century poets, Langhorne, Goldsmith, Gray, Johnson and, in the following passage, Shenstone:

> So first when Phoebus met the Cyprian queen,
> And favour'd Rhodes beheld their passion crown'd,
> Unusual flowers enrich'd the painted green,
> And swift spontaneous roses blush'd around.

The image comes out of common poetic stock...Shenstone refreshes it. It is just as logical to describe the flowers as unusual, swift and spontaneous as it is to describe their flowering in those terms. But because we had thought of these as features of the event, not of its effects, Shenstone presses upon our notice the logic of his transference of these terms to the roses. The logic of the usage being thus impressed upon us, these words strike us as dry and prosaic; and they have the effect of a taunting gravity and sobriety, which chastens the reader as it pleases him.

Moreover, by taking adverbs and turning them into other parts of speech, the poet leaves the verb singularly naked and powerful. Probably there was something in the metrical exigencies of the couplet which demanded that the verb should beat so sharply into the line, pinning it and making it quiver...This habit of throwing metaphorical force from noun to verb produces personification.[7]

For my particular purposes here, I would like to emphasize, among the many points that Davie makes, the way this kind of figure 'presses upon our notice the logic of...[the] transference'. This kind of metaphor makes us aware that it is a metaphor. Though it does not contain an explicit sign post extrinsic to itself, a *credas* or a *methought*, its own process serves as a kind of sign post. Of course, to some extent every metaphor calls attention to itself, but this sort acts to inform the reader not merely that a metaphorical process is at work, but that the poet himself is aware of it and that the reader needn't worry about it. Its effect is to invite the reader on a temporary holiday with the author, during which responsibilities for reporting or perceiving with literal accuracy are abandoned. The plain sense is left behind so obviously that the figure is a particularly conspicuous one, but in such a way as to become inconspicuous. No reader is likely to be fooled by this trope and thus, being spared the task of having to solve a linguistic puzzle, of having to examine the significance of its departure from the literal norm, is left free simply to appreciate the expressive elegance. He is 'pleased with the image, without being cozened by the fiction'.

I turn now to the first part of this formula, a pleasing image. Still in *The Author's Apology*, Dryden borrows Longinus's definition of 'imaging' (*On the Sublime*, chapter xv) as

a discourse, which, by a kind of enthusiasm, or extraordinary emotion of the soul, makes it seem to us that we behold those things which the poet paints, so as to be pleased with them, and to admire them. (I. 186)

The passage characterizes imaging in terms of two separate aspects, the subject of the discourse ('those things which the poet paints') and its effect upon the reader ('so as to be pleased with them, and to admire them').[8] About the first aspect I am not sure what Dryden intends. There are times when 'those things which the poet paints' seems to refer primarily to the phenomena of the external world, as in Dryden's complicated definition of 'the proper wit of an Heroic or Historical Poem' in the *Preface to Annus Mirabilis*: 'It is some lively and apt description, dressed in such colours of speech, that it sets before your eyes *the absent object*, as perfectly, and more delightfully than nature.' (I. 14, 15; my emphasis) On the other hand, Dryden's example of 'excellent imaging' in *The Author's Apology* itself suggests otherwise. The example is taken from Cowley (*Davideis*, I. 79): 'Where their vast courts the mother waters keep'. The metaphors here, Dryden admits, are subject to ridicule if taken literally, as some would insist. The streams would be daughters ('*mother* waters'), 'bound, in all good manners, to make courtesy' to their sovereigns ('vast *courts*'). In this case, the subject of the image must refer to some poetic significance rather than to an event or phenomenon such as we might perceive in the external, real world. (Indeed, one feels that a 'methought' or some other interpolated 'as it were' would have diminished the vulnerability of Cowley that Dryden recognizes to a strict literalist's ridicule.)

In the *Preface to Troilus and Cressida*, when Dryden discusses Shakespeare's figures, he seems to wish it both ways. This discussion too begins with ridicule, though Dryden's own in this case, of literal absurdities in the player's speech in *Hamlet* (II. 88; see I. 225–6). It moves, then, to praise for a different Shakespearean passage, 'one of his passionate descriptions' in *Richard II* (v. ii. 23–36) of the deposed king, riding into London, contemptuously ignored by his former subjects. Here is Dryden's comment:

The painting of it is so lively, and the words so moving, that I have scarce read anything comparable to it in any other language. Suppose you have seen already the fortunate usurper passing through the crowd, and followed by the shouts and acclamations of the people; and now behold King Richard entering upon the scene: consider the wretchedness of his condition, and his carriage in it; and refrain from pity, if you can. (I. 226)

What exactly does this word-painting, or this combination of painting and of words, show us? Is there a distinction between the entrance of the king upon the scene that we are asked to 'behold', and the wretchedness of his condition that we are asked to 'consider'? Or is the wretchedness of his condition a matter of pale complexion, dirty and tattered clothes – physical appearances, the same order of being as 'his carriage in it'; in which case are 'behold' and 'consider' interchangeable terms? Again, is this a real occurrence, a natural event, or a distinct poetic subject, the state of a human mind and soul, that we are invited to perceive?

Here the two are distinguishable but not really distinct, and perhaps the question cannot be answered. On the other hand, the second aspect of good imaging, its operation on the reader, is less ambiguous. It pleases us by its appeal to our sight; we are moved because we are made to see. In this respect the different passages are all consistent: 'suppose you have already seen', 'it sets before your eyes', 'makes it seem to us that we behold'. As Dryden says after reporting the kind of ridicule to which

Cowley's line is open, 'But an image, which is strongly and beautifully set before the eyes of the reader, will still be poetry when the merry fit is over, and last when the other is forgotten.' (I. 188) Thus, whatever the subject of the image, we can be fairly certain about its effect and its quality: It pleases us as a forceful and clear pictorial presentation that appeals to our eyes.

'You are pleased with the image, without being cozened by the fiction.' This formula may be said to epitomize Dryden's attitude towards figure, and I wish now to describe its departure from traditional norms. There is nothing new, certainly, in Dryden's recognition that metaphor involves fiction; this was commonly assumed from the earliest times in ancient rhetorical theory,[9] and, in the Renaissance, the fictional process of metaphor receives a special emphasis. Puttenham, for example, calls metaphors

trespasses in speach, ...occupied of purpose to deceive the eare and also the minde, drawing it from plainnesse and simplicitie to a certain doublenesse, whereby our talke is the more guilefull & abusing. (p. 154)

What is new in Dryden is the felt need to 'soften' this fictional process, to render tropes either inconspicuous or conspicuous in ways that free the reader from the burden of rational analysis. Traditionally this kind of analysis was valued, was, indeed, conceived to be pleasurable rather than burdensome. Cicero supposes that 'to jump over things that are obvious and choose other things that are far-fetched' (*longe*) is precisely what causes the delight of metaphor: 'The hearer's thoughts are led to something else and yet without going astray, which is a very great pleasure.'[10] Cicero may speak here for the tradition generally, not only of ancient but of Renaissance theory: Aristotle, Quintilian, 'Cornificius' and the others; Sherry, Wilson, Peacham and the others. The collective effort of these critics, in classifying the schemes and tropes, in distinguishing among and naming the various specific ways 'to jump over' the obvious and choose the distant – this effort assumes that pleasure inheres in a conscious analytical awareness of the fictional process of verbal interchange.

This sort of purposeful deception is assumed to be instructive as well as pleasurable. Metaphor can sometimes get at the truth which plain statement cannot reach. Cicero and Quintilian both value its ability to suggest significance beyond those available to literal language,[11] and Renaissance writers again emphasize this value in a particularly insistent way. Puttenham remarks about synecdoche that its effect is 'to drive the hearer to conceive more or lesse or beyond or otherwise then the letter expresseth', and later concerning the same trope, 'It encombers the minde with a certain imagination, what it may be that is meant, and not expressed.' (p. 185, p. 195) John Hoskins in his *Directions for Speech and Style* (*c.* 1599) says of hyperbole: 'Sometimes it expresseth a thing...in flat impossibility, that rather you may conceive the unspeakableness than the untruth of the relation.'[12] The reason for this particular insistence in the Renaissance is not difficult to guess, for it is perhaps the most fundamentally sustaining belief, common to all Renaissance critics, that the poet's task is to go beyond the literal, the mere appearances of nature. So Sidney, in disparaging the 'brazen' nature of sense impressions which 'the poet, disdaining to be tied to any such subjection', rejects for the golden new nature, found 'freely ranging only within the zodiac of his own wit'.[13] So Puttenham, in his equally famous defense of poetic imagination, *euphantasiote* rather than *phantastici*, as 'a representer of the best, most comely and bewtifull images or appearances of things to the soule and according to their very truth'. (p. 19) So Spenser too, in a less famous but no less compelling passage, the Proem to Book II of *The Faerie Queene*, in which an unnamed critic who rejects 'Faerie lond' as 'painted forgery' is urged to 'advise' himself 'with better sence': There is more to reality than 'that which he hath seene', and it is to this expanded concept of reality that the poet's imagination is responsive.

There are distinctions to be made among these writers. Only Sidney would have poetic imagination reject material reality totally. Puttenham's 'very truth' and Spenser's 'better sence' suggest that intelligible order may be perceived or inferred within or beyond – but not wholly independent of – the phenomena of nature, and their position seems to be more in the mainstream of Renaissance thought.[14] But however they may differ in detail, it is the general framework shared by these writers and by all Renaissance critics which is important for our purposes. If the poet's task is to express the natural order and not the mere appearances in nature, metaphor is a particularly useful – indeed, a necessary – tool. Its effect is to force upon the reader an awareness of analogies among creatures and created things and thus a meaningful relation between what might merely appear to be a flux of objects or events. This effect is evident in the extraordinary figure of '*Parabola*, or Resemblance misticall', as Puttenham calls it, which, by 'applying one naturall thing to another, or one case to another, infer[s]...by them a like consequence in other cases' (p. 245); or, more commonly, in synecdoche, the effect of which is that

by part we are enforced to understand the whole, by the whole part, by many things one thing, by one, many, by a thing precedent, a thing consequent, and generally one thing out of another by maner of contrariety to the word which is spoken. (p. 185)

In fact, not just parabola or synecdoche, but metaphor in general 'enforces' us to a recognition of an underlying order and unity in created nature. Hoskins says that,

though all metaphors go beyond the signification of things, yet are they requisite to match the compassing sweetness of men's minds, that are not content to fix themselves upon one thing but they must wander into the confines; like the eye, that cannot choose but view the whole knot when it beholds but one flower in a garden of purpose; or like an archer that, knowing his bow will overcast or carry too short, takes an aim on this side or beyond his mark. (p. 8)

In this particularly suggestive passage, Hoskins in effect defines metaphorical language as the mediator between the natural order ('a garden of purpose') and the ordering capacity of consciousness ('the compassing sweetness of men's minds').

I turn now to Dryden's concept of a pleasing image which is also a significant departure from Renaissance tradition. Renaissance writers make probably as much use as Dryden of figures taken from painting in order to discuss poetry, but they consistently reject the representational implications that such figures might suggest.[15] They tend, moreover, not to emphasize a clear pictorial presentation, a picture powerfully appealing to the reader's eyes. Peacham, for instance, writes that

Allegorie serveth most aptly to ingrave the lively images of things, to present them under deepe shadowes to the contemplation of the mind, wherein wit and judgement take pleasure, and the remembrance receiveth a long lasting impression.[16]

There is no appeal here to the eye; indeed, the 'deepe shadowes' of metaphor serve purposefully to frustrate such a direct mode of apprehension in favor of the more complicated sorts involving the mind, wit, judgment and memory. Sidney makes the same point more explicitly in his remark that the epic poet 'sets her [virtue] out to make her more lovely in her holiday apparel, to the eye of any that will deign not to disdain until they understand'. (p. 119) The eye by itself does not find the image lovely, indeed would reject it; it is to the understanding, the mind's eye, that the appeal is made.

It is specifically and only for its appeal to the mind's eye, 'the sight of the *soul*', that Renaissance critics value poetry's pictorial power. Poetry can furnish not so much sights of things as insights into moral concepts – such, Sidney tells us, as would 'lie dark before the imaginative and judging power, if they be not illuminated or figured forth by the speaking picture of poesy'. (p. 107) This ability to figure forth is the special advantage of the poet, the source of his superiority to the philosopher:

for whatsoever the philosopher saith should be done, he giveth a perfect picture of it..., for he yieldeth to the powers of the mind an image of that whereof the philosopher bestoweth but a wordish description, which doth neither strike, pierce, nor possess the sight of the soul so much as that other doth. (p. 107)

Sidney's argument here is a common one, built upon traditional assumptions. The superiority of the sight to the other senses, a time-honored Platonic idea (*Phaedrus*, 250^d), in conjunction with the sometimes sadly uttered commonplace of Renaissance psychology, that the mind can be reached only through the senses, leads to Sidney's statement that 'even those hard-hearted evil men who think virtue a school name... [would nonetheless] steal to see the form of goodness (which seen they cannot but love) ere themselves be aware'. (p. 114) Bacon, who of course felt profoundly ambivalent towards poetry and rhetoric, offers nonetheless the same kind of argument:

For Plato said elegantly (though it has now grown into a common place) 'that virtue, if she could be seen, would move great love and affection'; and it is the business of rhetoric to make pictures of virtue and goodness, so that they may be seen. For since they cannot be showed to the sense in corporeal shape, the next degree is to show them to the imagination in as lively representation as possible, by ornament of words.[17]

In relation to this context we should not misinterpret Sidney's praise for the poetic qualities of the prodigal-son parable in the Bible: 'Truly, for myself, me seems I see before my eyes the lost child's disdainful prodigality, turned to envy a swine's dinner.' Sidney's praise is not for the pictorial quality as such, but for the way in which a moral quality, prodigality, or the consequences of this quality, is rendered through the senses so that it might 'more constantly (as it were) inhabit both the memory and judgment'. (p. 109) In the same way, David's 'notable *prosopopeias*' in the Psalms, 'when he maketh you, as it were, see God's coming in His majesty', Sidney declares to be 'a heavenly poesy, wherein almost he showeth himself a passionate lover of that unspeakable and everlasting beauty to be seen by the eyes of the mind, only cleared by faith'. (p. 99; Sidney's *as it were* and *almost* in the last two quotations are highly significant) When Puttenham tells us that 'the matter and occasion leadeth us many times to describe and set foorth many things, in such sort as it should appeare they were truly before our eyes', he too is emphasizing the 'notability' of such *prosopopeias* as occur at the beginning of the *Romance of the Rose*, 'describing the persons of avarice, envie, old age, and many others, whereby much moralitie is taught'. (p. 238, p. 329) To the extent that the sense of sight is appealed to in these passages, it is only through necessity, as a temporary measure, and finally as a means effectively to convey a kind of awareness beyond that available to the eyes.

Dryden's attitude towards metaphor is radically innovative, and it is more than a matter of a new idea about a particular literary device. Whether consciously or not, Dryden departs from the broad, basic assumptions about literature and reality that had underlain traditional rhetorical theory. Another passage from Hoskins can serve to make these assumptions explicit.

The conceits of the mind are the pictures of things and the tongue is interpreter of those pictures. The order of God's creatures in themselves is not only admirable and glorious, but eloquent; then he that could apprehend the consequence of things, in their truth, and utter his apprehensions as truly were a right orator. Therefore Cicero said much when he said, *dicere recto nemo potest nisi qui prudenter intelligit.*

The shame of speaking unskilfully were small if the tongue were only disgraced by it. But as the image of the king in a seal of wax, ill represented, is not so much a blemish to the wax or the signet that sealeth it as to the king whom it resembleth, so disordered speech is not so much injury to the lips which give it forth or the thoughts which put it forth as to the right proportion and coherence of things in themselves, so wrongfully expressed. (p. 2)

Hoskins makes three assumptions: 1. External reality is the ordered creation of God. 2. This ordered creation may be apprehended by the human mind. 3. This apprehension may be expressed in language. These assumptions are sufficiently flexible to allow for a number of different styles, or stylistic tendencies, that we know to have existed during the Renaissance. The passage seems primarily the basis for a logical and direct style, the simple uttering of the apprehended eloquence of God's order. On the other hand, it by no means precludes stylistic ornament; as a means of not 'speaking unskilfully', a kind of rhetorical elaborateness might indeed be justified as appropriate to suggesting the consummate artifice of God as revealed in His creation. While the passage, then, seems to be the product of Ramist influences, it is neither surprising nor inconsistent for Hoskins to quote Cicero and, a page later, to list a very heterogeneous group of sources for his *Directions* – 'taken out of Aristotle, Hermogenes, Quintilian, Demosthenes, Cicero, and some latter, as Sturmius and Tallaeus'. Moreover, while Hoskins's passage does not readily fit into the Attic mold (the mind's apprehension of reality seems too direct for this), its assumptions in no way preclude an 'anti-Ciceronian' position. There are, of course, real differences between these three kinds of Renaissance style; but the boundary lines between them cannot be drawn too firmly. They are not mutually exclusive, either in strict logic or in historical fact.[18] They may diverge in the specific ways that they conceive the mind's apprehension of reality and the utterance of this apprehension to be best accomplished, but they nonetheless share in a general way an acceptance of Hoskins's three assumptions.

Not so Dryden's concept of figurative language, or Restoration style and theoretical norms for style generally. The new emphasis on perspicuity and conversational directness in verse and prose, the swelling critical chorus of trope-damning – these later seventeenth-century developments seem to be built, con-sciously or not, upon assumptions contradictory at least to the second of those above – namely, that the mind is unequal to the object, that the mind's apprehension of reality and external reality itself are two different orders of being.[19] This split between mental and physical reality I take to be one crucial determinant of the new literary sensibility, because of its im-plications for language. Words, because they can name only our impressions of things and not the things themselves, are in-herently limited in trustworthiness. One consequence of this is the establishment of a new hierarchy of verbal usages, cor-responding (not coincidentally, I would argue) to the values revealed in Dryden's discussion of metaphor: Tropes, blatantly fictional, removed in their very essence from objective pheno-mena, are the least trustworthy; images appealing forcefully to the eyes, on the other hand, are the most trustworthy, for it is through the sense of sight that we obtain our most reliable knowledge of external reality. But another consequence is even further-reaching, based on the inherent general untrustworthi-ness of all kinds of verbal usages; the extreme implication of this position calls for language to wither away and die. What results from this specifically is, in effect, a theory of stylelessness (itself, of course, a theory of style), which indeed comes close to explicit articulation in Locke and Addison, the two figures I am pri-marily concerned with here. As for the general results, they involve a fundamental reconstitution of esthetic theory, with new and vastly different demands made upon literature – but this reconstitution and Dryden's relation to it will not be my concern until the last section of this chapter.

Let me begin with a word about Hobbes. In the first chapter of *Leviathan* (1651) Hobbes tells us that 'there is no conception in a man's mind, which hath not at first, totally, or by parts, been begotten upon the organs of sense'.[20] This begetting, according to Hobbes, is provoked by a pressure from external objects upon the sense organs which transmit it through the nervous system to the brain and heart. The reception of this pressure causes 'a resistance, or counter-pressure, or endeavour of the heart to deliver itself, which endeavour, because *outward*, seemeth to be some matter without'. (I. i. p. 2) 'Seemeth to be', but isn't, and this is the crucial point. Hobbes is very insistent upon keeping separate the internal impression and the external object. Although the sense impression is *caused* by the object, it cannot be said to *inhere* in it: 'All...qualities, called *sensible*, are, in the object that causeth them, but so many several motions of the matter, by which it presseth our organs diversely.'[21] (*ibid.*) Hobbes concludes his chapter by attacking scholastic epistemology, with its assumption of a natural affinity between consciousness and objective reality:

But the philosophy-schools, through all the universities of Christendom, grounded upon certain texts of Aristotle, teach another doctrine, and say, for the cause of *vision*, that the thing seen, sendeth forth on every side a *visible species*, in English, a *visible show, apparition*, or *aspect*, or *a being seen*; the receiving whereof into the eye is *seeing*. And for the cause of *hearing*, that the thing heard, sendeth forth an *audible species*, that is an *audible aspect*, or *audible being seen*; which entering at the ear, maketh *hearing*. Nay, for the cause of *understanding* also, they say the thing understood, sendeth forth an *intelligible species*, that is, an *intelligible being seen*; which, coming into the understanding, makes us understand. I say not this, as disproving the use of universities; but because I am to speak hereafter of their office in a commonwealth, I must let you see on all occasions by the way, what things would be amended in them; amongst which the frequency of insignificant speech is one. (I. i. p. 3)

In tone as well as subject, this passage recalls Bacon with his angry but amused irony directed against the schoolmen, spinning verbal webs out of their minds instead of directing their attention outwards to things; and like Bacon, Hobbes has little use for the language of received wisdom – 'absurd speeches, taken upon credit, without any signification at all, from deceived philosophers, and deceived, or deceiving schoolmen'. (I. iii. p. 17) In particular Hobbes's objections are directed against language that is abstracted from sensory experience. He lists offending kinds of words and expressions at the end of his chapter, 'Of Speech': new words; contradictions and inconsistencies; value terms, especially moral qualities; and finally 'metaphors and tropes', because they 'can never be the true grounds of ratiocination'. (I. iv. pp. 27–9)

However Locke may have diverged from *Leviathan*'s conclusions (especially in political theory), these assumptions of
Hobbes form the basis for *An Essay Concerning Human Understanding* (first published 1690). Like Hobbes, Locke makes a
rigorous distinction between external reality and the impression that it provokes internally on the mind. Like Hobbes, Locke
believes that words name only these impressions, not the objects
that provoked them; 'they are the signs of our *ideas* only and
not...things themselves'.[22] As a consequence of this, the order
that the mind may perceive is the mind's only, and our description of it only a nominal reality. And finally, like Hobbes, Locke
is suspicious of language in proportion as it is abstracted from
'the real existence of things': '*General* and *universal* belong not to
the real existence of things, but *are the inventions* and *creatures of
the understanding*, made by it for its own use, *and concern only signs*,
whether words or *ideas*'. (III. iii. 11) Since concepts of value,
'mixed modes' as he calls them, are assembled by the mind not
in order 'to copy anything really existing, but to denominate
and rank things as they come to agree with those archetypes or
forms it has made', they therefore 'must needs be of doubtful
signification'. (III. ix. 7) And, of course, Locke sees metaphor as
a particularly nasty form of verbal abuse. In focusing the
reader's attention upon verbal shifts, it pretends to create an
artificial verbal reality, and thus may be said to exemplify the
'*Fourth*...great *abuse of words*..., *the taking them for things*'. (III.
x. 14) In deliberately equivocating, metaphor willfully violates
the fifth of Locke's rules by which words are to make known the
ideas they stand for: '*constancy in their signification*'. (III. xi. 26) As
Locke remarks ironically, a less patient and incisive version of
the Baconian-Hobbesian tone, if all authors 'should *use the
same word constantly in the same sense*...many of the philosophers'
...as well as poets' works might be contained in a nutshell'.
(*ibid.*) Or, more straightforwardly:

All the artificial and figurative application of words eloquence hath
invented, are for nothing else but to insinuate wrong *ideas*, move the
passions, and thereby mislead the judgment, and so indeed are
perfect cheat. (III. x. 34)

I have emphasized the distrust in both Hobbes and Locke of
non-literal language, especially their distrust of metaphor. It

should be insisted that, although each attacks abuses of language, they both recognize that language, when properly used, is valuable and indeed necessary in order to record and order our impressions and communicate them to others. Nonetheless, given their basic epistemological assumptions, it must be recognized that there is a problem inherent in language itself. *Some* language is particularly distorting, and Hobbes and Locke direct their major attack against this kind – tropes, value concepts and the like. Still, *all* language is to some extent distorting. Even the most trustworthy words cannot serve to name objects themselves, only 'the consequences of things imagined in the mind'. Thus, while Hobbes and Locke concentrate on linguistic abuses, the implication is present in both that language itself, in its removal from the reality of material things, constitutes an abuse.

Locke is much more aware of this problem than Hobbes, or perhaps, simply, more troubled by it. Strictly speaking, it is a problem that admits of no satisfactory solution. Language is inherently abusive or potentially distorting because perception is inherently abusive or potentially distorting. There is simply no way by which the impression of an object can be guaranteed to conform precisely to the real qualities of the object itself. And here I must say a few words about Locke's distinction between primary and secondary qualities.[23] The former (a thing's shape, size, spatial location, velocity and degree of hardness) are alone truly qualities, characteristics of external being 'such as are utterly inseparable from the body, in what state soever it be'. (II. viii. 9) The latter (a thing's color, temperature, smell, taste and sound) are not truly qualities in the object but are mental impressions, the results of the object's ability to affect us, 'such *qualities* which in truth are nothing in the objects themselves but powers to produce various sensations in us by their *primary qualities*'. (II. viii. 10) Primary qualities alone are real, then, but it should not be inferred from this (as it sometimes is) that we may know them. Locke nowhere says that they are directly perceptible. Between the primary qualities of the object and our perception of them falls the same shadow as had fallen in Hobbes – that of the nervous system. (see II. viii. 11–12) Locke does believe, however, that there is a *similarity* between our ideas of primary qualities and these qualities, as distinct from

our ideas of secondary qualities which have no relevance outside consciousness, 'no resemblance...at all' to external reality.
(II. viii. 15) In this sense, our perception of primary qualities is
more likely to be true, that is, has *some* likelihood of accurately
reporting the truth, and this provides the best (really the only)
basis for knowledge. To the extent that we remove our ideas of
secondary qualities from serious study and limit ourselves to
ideas of primary qualities, we attain, not to certainty, but to the
greatest likelihood of true knowledge.

The crucial point for our purposes here is that *words do not aid
such a delimitation*. We may illustrate this point by means of two
words that are names for complex substances, *liquor* and *gold*
(Locke's examples, III. ix. 15–17). A word like *gold* can mean
one thing to one person and another to another, depending
upon the particular qualities attached to it. Though the qualities of gold are always united in nature, the qualities suggested
by *gold*, the nominal essence, are variable. This is because the
word, like all words, is a creature of the mind, and likely in
human practice to refer to secondary as well as to primary
qualities. Indeed, through long periods of usage, these words
have accrued significances, some of which do truly (or with
more likelihood of truth) resemble reality than others; yet these
significances have been accrued *indiscriminately* to the point that
it is impossible, or at least extremely difficult, to determine

which are those that are to make up the precise collection that is to
be signified by the specific name;...which obvious or common
qualities are to be left out; or which more secret or more particular
are to be put into the signification of the name of any substance. (III.
ix. 14)

Note that this is a difficulty inherent not just in a mixed
mode or a trope but in a specific name for a thing. (For a complex thing, to be sure, and names for simpler things are more
trustworthy, but even they are not wholly so.) Language, all
language, even the kind that we tend to call literal, is too firmly
allied to a distorting perceptive apparatus to be the most reliable
guide to reality. And indeed, in one of the most poignant passages in the *Essay*, language is itself *identified* as the distorting
aspect of our perceptive apparatus:

The great disorder that happens in our names of substances proceeding, for the most part, from our want of knowledge and inability to penetrate into their real constitutions, it may probably be wondered *why I charge this as an imperfection* rather *upon our words* than understandings. This exception has so much appearance of justice that I think myself obliged to give a reason why I have followed this method. I must confess, then, that, when I first began this discourse of the understanding, and a good while after, I had not the least thought that any consideration of words was at all necessary to it. But when, having passed over the original and composition of our *ideas*, I began to examine the extent and certainty of our knowledge, I found it had so near a connexion with words that, unless their force and manner of signification were first well observed, there could be very little said clearly and pertinently concerning knowledge, which, being conversant about truth, had constantly to do with propositions. And though it terminated in things, yet it was, for the most part, so much by the intervention of words, that they seemed scarce separable from our general knowledge. At least they interpose themselves so much between our understandings and the truth which it would contemplate and apprehend that, like the *medium* through which visible objects pass, their obscurity and disorder does not seldom cast a mist before our eyes and impose upon our understandings. (III. ix. 21)

Extraordinarily poignant as this passage is in its confessional quality, the ideas out of which it is constructed are altogether typical of Locke. The independence of knowledge from language is something that he assumes throughout the *Essay*, and even in admitting here 'so near a connexion' between knowledge and words, Locke does not concede that this is a necessary, still less a desirable connection. The more closely connected knowledge is to words, the less certain it will be as an accurate picture of reality.

To the extent that language can be made to coincide with our ideas of things, it will be a transparent medium, which does not 'cast a mist...upon our understandings'. To this end Locke tells us over and again to know what our words mean and to use language unequivocally. To this end also, Locke, in anticipation of two great intellectual achievements performed in England and France in the following century, proposes the undertaking of what appears to be a combination dictionary-encyclopedia, in order at once to create stability in the language and establish an accurate record of scientific knowledge attained to so far.

Yet Locke recognizes the difficulty if not impossibility of this task, and in another particularly significant passage, he offers an alternative proposal:

But though such a dictionary as I have above mentioned will require too much time, cost, and pains to be hoped for in this age, yet methinks it is not unreasonable to propose that words standing for things which are known and distinguished by their outward shapes should be expressed by little draughts and prints made of them. A vocabulary made after this fashion would perhaps, with more ease and in less time, teach the true signification of many terms...Such things as these, which the eye distinguishes by their shapes, would be best let into the mind by draughts made of them, and more determine the signification of such words than any other words set for them or made use of to define them. (III. xi. 25)

This will cut the Gordian knot. Instead of purifying the linguistic medium, such a dictionary will, as much as possible, eliminate it. It is not accidental that Locke speaks here about 'things ...which the eye distinguishes by their shapes'. We remember the sight figure quoted earlier (words, 'like the *medium* through which visible objects pass,...not seldom cast a mist before our eyes'), and indeed it is one of Locke's favorite figures.[24] The reasons for this are not hard to find. Sight is 'the most comprehensive of all our senses, conveying to our minds the *ideas* of light and colours, which are peculiar only to that sense; and also the far different *ideas* of space, figure, and motion'. (II. ix. 9) Not only are some major secondary qualities conveyed exclusively through the eyes; more important, it is in the main through the sense of sight that we receive most of our ideas of primary qualities and thus obtain the least distorted, most trustworthy perception of reality. This explains why a substance's

leading qualities are best made known by showing...For the shape of a *horse* or *cassowary* will be but rudely and imperfectly imprinted on the mind by words, the sight of the animals doth it a thousand times better. (III. xi. 21)

From this position it is not a long voyage to reach the Grand Academy of Lagado –

An expedient was therefore offered, that since words are only names for *things*, it would be more convenient for all men to carry about them such *things* as were necessary to express the particular business they are to discourse on.

– though Locke, man of common sense, recognizing that language is adequate for ordinary human communication, would never himself go so far.

The implications of this for literary theory are readily evident in Addison's *Spectator* papers on 'The Pleasures of the Imagination',[25] in which Locke's influence is clear and self-conscious from the very beginning:

Our Sight is the most perfect and most delightful of all our Senses. It fills the Mind with the largest Variety of Ideas, converses with its Objects at the greatest Distance, and continues the longest in Action without being tired or satiated with its proper Enjoyments... It is this Sense which furnishes the Imagination with its Ideas; so that by the Pleasures of the Imagination...I mean here such as arise from visible Objects, either when we have them actually in our view, or when we call up their Ideas into our Minds by Paintings, Statues, Descriptions, or any the like Occasion. (No. 411, pp. 535–6)

This last contrast is the basis for a distinction that runs throughout Addison's series, between what he calls the primary and the secondary pleasures of the imagination. The adjectives, of course, are taken from Locke, and although Addison does not use them with Locke's kind of complexity or technical precision, the basic framework is genuinely Lockean. The primary pleasures are derived from the actual experience of external reality. The secondary pleasures which are derived from art, however, more internal than external,

proceed...from that Action of the Mind, which compares the Ideas arising from the Original Objects, with the Ideas we receive from the Statue, Picture, Description or [musical] sound that represents them. (No. 416, pp. 559–60)

Addison attributes a great deal of significance to these secondary pleasures of the imagination. Indeed, in the crucial paper No. 418, he tells us that they 'are of a wider and more universal Nature than those it has, when joined with Sight'. (p. 566) Whereas the primary pleasures of the imagination are contingent upon the quality of the image beheld (only if the image is 'Great, Strange or Beautiful' will we be pleased), the secondary pleasures suffer no such limitations. Since the pleasure is derived not from the quality of the image, but from 'the Action of the Mind, which *compares* the Ideas that arise from Words, with the Ideas that arise from the Objects themselves', (pp. 566–7) then even 'the Description of a Dung-hill is pleasing to the Imagination, if the Image be represented to our Minds by suitable Expressions'. (p. 567)

There is a problem, though, in such a position, arising from the definitions that Addison has established for his major terms. The pleasures of the imagination, as distinguished in their original definition from those of the understanding,

have this Advantage, . . . that they are more obvious, and more easie to be acquired. It is but opening the Eye, and the Scene enters. The Colours paint themselves on the Fancy, with very little Attention of Thought or Application of Mind in the Beholder. (No. 411, pp. 537–8)

Strictly speaking, then, the 'wider and more universal' pleasure that Addison talks about in No. 418, should, as he himself admits, 'be more properly called the Pleasure of the Understanding than of the Fancy', and in this sense all esthetic pleasures involve pleasures of the understanding as well. Not only is the imagination delighted with a great, strange or beautiful image; there is also the mind's delight in the perception of analogy, the 'affinity' apprehended between the image as experienced from the artifact and the image as experienced from reality.

For it is this that not only gives us a relish of Statuary, Painting and Description, but makes us delight in all the Actions and Arts of Mimickry. It is this that makes the several kinds of Wit pleasant, which consists, as I have formerly shown, in the Affinity of Ideas: And we may add, it is this also that raises the little Satisfaction we sometimes find in the different sorts of false Wit. (No. 416, p. 560)

Addison frankly admits ignorance as to the cause of this delight in perceiving analogies. (We might note in passing that it is the kind of pleasure described over and again in traditional rhetorical theory as the mind's delight in metaphor – see Cicero and Hoskins, quoted p. 121 and p. 123 above.) Moreover, as the last sentence of Addison's statement just above implies, there is something troublesome about it. Given his Lockean assumptions, this is understandable, for inevitably the perception of these analogies involves a certain awareness of the artist's use of his materials. In the case of literary art, in order to compare the image experienced from the poem with the image experienced from reality, one must have a prior sense of both components of the comparison. This involves some understanding of the constituent elements not only of the real or objective image, but of the artificial or poetic image as well. These latter constituents are, of course, words, and it is this focus on words that primarily accounts for Addison's difficulty with the concept of the pleasures of the understanding. The *Spectator* papers on true and false wit (Nos. 58–62) to which he refers in the passage quoted above ('as I have formerly shown') describe the nature of Addison's difficulty quite clearly.[26] The major purpose of these papers is to define and distinguish between true and false wit. '*True Wit* consists in the Resemblance of Ideas, and *false Wit* in the Resemblance of Words.' (No. 62, I. p. 265) Resemblances between 'Ideas' (in Locke's sense, of course: 'sense impressions') are 'true' because firmly rooted in material experience. Resemblances between words, however, verbal play – puns, tropes, etc. – are removed from material experience: false. False wit, word dependent, may be detected by the test of translation. If it 'vanishes in the Experiment you may conclude it to have been a Punn'. (No. 61, I. p. 263) True wit, though, independent of words, is like the beautiful woman in an aphorism attributed to Aristinetus: 'When she is *dress'd* she is Beautiful, when she is *undress'd* she is Beautiful'. (*ibid.*)

Put simply, the trouble with the pleasures of the understanding is that they do not necessarily discriminate between true and false wit. The understanding, delighting in its ability to perceive analogy as a process, makes no prior demands upon the validity of the material analogized – that it be true and not false, that it consist of ideas close to reality and not merely words removed from reality. As Addison says, it 'makes *the several kinds* of wit pleasant', accounting not only for our appreciation of true wit, but also for 'the little Satisfaction we sometimes find in the different sorts of false Wit'. Addison's sneering 'little' and 'sometimes' should not be misinterpreted. In the *Essay* Locke had articulated the sad truth that he might have inherited from any one of a long line of dualists dating back to Plato – that no quantity of reasoned criticism is sufficient to weaken the nearly carnal appeal of verbal wit.

Eloquence, like the fair sex, has too prevailing beauties in it, to suffer itself ever to be spoken against. And it is vain to find fault with those arts of deceiving, wherein men find pleasure to be deceived. (III. x. 34)

And Addison, of course, knows this too. Punning, he tells us, has been 'recommended by the Practice of all Ages...It is indeed impossible to kill a Weed, which the Soil has a natural Disposition to produce'. (No. 61, I. p. 259) The satisfaction that the understanding takes in false wit is perhaps in terms of its value a *little* one; but its force is all too large, and in practical frequency, despite the wishful nature of Addison's *sometimes*, the experience occurs all too often.[27]

Addison cannot ignore or deny the operation of the understanding in esthetic experience. In view of the context suggested above, however, it is not surprising to find that he consistently attempts to minimize its importance and, on the other side, attempts to emphasize the primary pleasures of the imagination. Thus, after conceding that a good description even of a dunghill, 'of what is Little, Common or Deformed', is pleasant, Addison urges upon us that

the Description of what is Great, Surprising or Beautiful, is much more so; because here we are not only delighted with *comparing* the Representation with the Original, but are highly pleased with the Original it self. Most readers, I believe, are more charmed with *Milton*'s Description of Paradise, than of Hell; they are both, perhaps, equally perfect in their Kind, but in the one the Brimstone and Sulphur are not so refreshing to the Imagination, as the Beds of Flowers, and the Wilderness of Sweets in the other. (No. 418, p. 567)

The focus here shifts from the way the object is rendered by the artifact to the quality of the object itself. In the hierarchy of art forms that Addison establishes in No. 416, we recognize a similar desire to de-emphasize the importance of any esthetic rendering. 'Among the different kinds of Representation, *Statuary* is the most natural, and shows us something *likest* the object that is represented.' (p. 559) Painting, because the representation is only two-dimensional, comes second to sculpture, but ahead of verbal '*Description* [which] runs yet further from the things it represents than Painting; for a Picture bears a real Resemblance to its Original, which Letters and Syllables are wholly void of'. (*ibid.*) Last, for obvious reasons, is music.

For the same reason Addison tends to de-emphasize the rendering function of the artist. When Addison talks about the imagination of the poet, he is primarily inclined to focus on his receptivity to objects in nature, his experience of sense impressions.

His head must be full of the Humming of Bees, the Bleating of flocks and the melody of Birds. The Verdure of the Grass, the Embroidery of the Flowrs, and the Glistring of the Dew must be painted strong on his Imagination.[28]

And once the poet is thus 'stored with Country Images, if he would go beyond Pastoral, and the lower kinds of Poetry, he ought to acquaint himself with the Pomp and Magnificence of Courts'. (No. 417, p. 564) Amidst all this Addison does not totally neglect the poet's verbal ability or the expressive power of words, but he locates this last, as we would expect from a follower of Locke, nearly wholly in their ability to represent pictures of things. Though in passages I have quoted (and in passages I shall quote), Addison uses such terms as 'colours' and 'figures', it is clear from the context that he does not intend these terms to be understood in their traditional rhetorical senses – that is, as descriptions of certain kinds of verbal formulas, of relations of words *inter se*[29]:

Words, when well chosen, have so great a Force in them, that a Description often gives us more lively Ideas than the Sight of Things themselves. The Reader finds a Scene drawn in stronger Colours, and painted more to the Life in his Imagination, by the help of Words, than by an actual Survey of the Scene which they describe. In this Case the Poet seems to get the better of Nature; he takes, indeed, the Landskip after her, but gives it more vigorous Touches, heightens its Beauty, and so enlivens the whole Piece, that the Images, which flow from the Objects themselves, appear weak and faint in Comparison of those that come from the Expressions. The Reason, probably, may be, because in the Survey of any Object we have only so much of it painted on the Imagination, as comes in at the Eye; but in its Description, the Poet gives us as free a View of it as he pleases, and discovers to us several Parts, that either we did not attend to, or that lay out of our Sight when we first beheld it. As we look on any Object, our Idea of it is, perhaps, made up of two or three simple Ideas; but when the Poet represents it, he may either give us a more complex Idea of it, or only raise in us such Ideas as are most apt to affect the Imagination. (No. 416, pp. 560–1)

The power of words here is almost exclusively dependent on their ability to suggest images to the sight. It is nearly a paradox, then, that verbal images are stronger than actual images, and Addison's stammer when trying to find the explanation for this ('The Reason, probably, may be...') reflects a certain understandable uneasiness on his part. Those reasons that he does finally offer in no way contradict his exclusion of any but a pictorial power to language. The superiority of the poetic description to the actual sight is a function simply of the poet's ability to select and choose the objects he would put on display, to broaden or sharpen the focus of our view.

It follows from this that a painter who selected and focused his images in these ways would produce a work of art even more satisfactory to the imagination, because the experience of the images would approximate more closely the actual experience of such images. *A fortiori* a sculptor, and we needn't stop here. The logic of Addison's theory allows us to go beyond his hierarchy of art forms into nature itself. A natural sight that happens to have its component objects organized in a meaningful way would be, first of all, more pleasurable to the imagination than one not so organized; and this is what Addison tells us in his comment that 'we find the Works of Nature still more pleasant, the more they resemble those of Art'. (No. 414, p. 549) It also follows that an 'artistically' organized natural landscape, because its medium does not merely approximate but is identical to 'the Object that is represented', is more satisfactory *esthetically* than any artifact can ever hope to be. And indeed, in Addison's famous description of the *camera obscura* experiment, this is all but explicit:

The prettiest Landskip[30] I ever saw, was one drawn on the Walls of a dark Room, which stood opposite on one side to a navigable River, and on the other to a Park. The Experiment is very common in Opticks. Here you might discover the Waves and Fluctuations of the Water in strong and proper Colours, with the Picture of a Ship entering at one end, and sailing by Degrees through the whole

Piece. On another there appeared the Green Shadows of Trees, Waving to and fro with the Wind, and Herds of Deer among them in Miniature, leaping about upon the Wall. I must confess, the Novelty of such a sight may be one occasion of its Pleasantness to the Imagination, but certainly the chief Reason is its near Resemblance to Nature, as it does not only, like other Pictures, give the Colour and Figure, but the Motion of the Things it represents.[31] (No. 414, pp. 550–1)

This is the equivalent in esthetic theory for Locke's statement that *'Ideas of the leading qualities of substances are best got by showing'*.

Locke published his *Essay* towards the end of Dryden's life, and Addison's *Spectator* papers appeared a dozen years after Dryden's death; but empirical ideas were in the air during the early Restoration, in figures known to Dryden like Hobbes or Bishop Sprat, whose *History of the Royal Society* (1667) is a notable testament to the new way of looking at things: *'Experimental Philosophy*... opens our eyes to perceive all the realities of things: and clears the brain, not only from darkness, but false, or useless light.'[32] This is pure Locke, and so is Sprat's famous description (pp. 111–15) of the Royal Society's 'manner of discourse', with its strict banishment of metaphor (in urging which Sprat makes use again of the same sight metaphor as Locke will: 'how many mists and uncertainties, these specious *Tropes* and *Figures* have brought on our knowledg') and its insistence upon the closest possible proximity to 'Mathematic plainness' ('so many *things*, almost in an equal number of *words*'). Even more interesting and relevant, because concerned with literary rather than scientific discourse, is the Appendix on Wit (pp. 412–19), in which Sprat judges among various sources according to their ability to furnish 'images which are generally known, and are able to bring a strong, and a sensible impression on the *mind*'. In his reasons for rejecting the abstract sciences – 'they are... conversant about things remov'd from the Senses, and so cannot surprise the *fancy* with very obvious, or quick, or sensible delights' – Sprat's language directly anticipates Addison's. And in his emphasis upon clear and forceful imagery –

[wit founded] on the *Arts* of men's hands is masculine and durable: It consists of *Images* that are generally observ'd, and such visible

things which are familiar to men's minds...[The] *Works of Nature*
...will make the most vigorous Impressions of mens *Fancies*, becaus
they do even touch their *Eyes*, and are neerest to *Nature*.

– Sprat brings to mind his contemporary, Dryden, as well as
both Addison and Locke.

I am trying to suggest that the empirical assumptions underlying Locke's and Addison's systems were operative in the mid-
seventeenth century, in Dryden's time, even if they had not yet
become systematized. In terms of poetic theory, the most
significant of these assumptions was the rigorous separation of
function conceived to exist between imaginative and rational
faculties. It is Hobbes in *Human Nature* (x. 4) who seems to be
the first to contrast fancy and judgment in the special way of
later seventeenth-century critics. A good fancy, Hobbes tells us,
discovers

unexpected *similitude* of things, otherwise much unlike,...from
whence proceed those grateful similies, metaphors, and other tropes,
by which both *poets* and *orators* have it in their power to make things
please or displease, and shew well or ill to others, as they like themselves...[The judgment, on the other hand, discovers] *dissimilitude*
in things that otherwise appear the same. And this virtue of the
mind is that by which men attain to exact and perfect *knowledge*; and
the pleasure thereof consisteth in continual instruction, and in
distinction of places, persons, and seasons...(Vol. IV. pp. 55–6)

In this distinction, Hobbes was followed by More, Boyle,
Bishop Parker, Temple, Locke, Addison, Pope – in short, it was
a sustaining belief of the period.[33] The distinction between these
faculties corresponds to the split between mental constructs and
phenomena, words and things. Locke would insist upon this
distinction with much more rigor, and his suspicion of imaginative verbal usage is in proportion to this rigor. Nonetheless, a
distrust or trivialized view of poetry as a discourse removed from
the reasonable and the real is already quite common in the
1650s. Indeed, in Henry More's *Enthusiasmus Triumphatus* (1656)
poetry is not only essentially defined by, but valued for, its
purposeful distance from the real experience of life; the argument being that, in proclaiming its own irrelevance and
triviality, it renders itself harmless – an amusing, if trivial
game. More, having noted similarities between the complexions

of the poet and the enthusiast, notes also the following 'great difference':

A *Poet* is an *Enthusiast in jest*, and an *Enthusiast* is a *Poet in good earnest*; Melancholy prevailing so much with him, that he takes his no better then Poetical fits, and figments for divine inspiration and reall truth.[34]

Hobbes in *Leviathan* makes a point quite similar to More's. One legitimate purpose of language, he tells us, is 'to please and delight ourselves and others, by playing with our words, for pleasure or ornament, innocently', and the innocent nature of this verbal play is specified shortly thereafter in his comment that, compared to moral abstractions, 'metaphors, and tropes of speech...are less dangerous, because they profess their inconstancy; which the other do not'. (I. iv. p. 20 and p. 29) Hobbes is not talking specifically about poetry here, and in fact he may have been a declared friend to poetry – another salient distinction between him and Locke. But there remain implications here for poetic theory that cannot be ignored. They are, to adopt Dryden's formula, that poetry is a pleasing but non-cozening fiction.

This is the context within which Dryden wrote his criticism. As a poet, of course, he writes out of a different experience and with a different purpose than, say, Hobbes – let alone Sprat or More or Locke. Crane and Youngren are right to insist on such differences,[35] but the production of literature and criticism in the Restoration (as in any period) was not an endeavor carried out in isolation from scientific and philosophic thought. The empirical assumptions I have been describing are, demonstrably, part of the given premises in Dryden's essays. For him as for Hobbes, fancy and judgment are felt to serve markedly contrasting functions. The judgment is the distinguishing faculty, responsible for the accurate observation of nature and clarity of expression in the writing. The fancy, on the other hand, is endowed with the ability to heighten or enlarge nature from a strict representation of the way things are, and is the basis for the tropes and schemes in the expression, the 'Poetic License'. This distinction Dryden sometimes expresses with regard to the ends of poetry – fanciful discourse affects, rational discourse instructs – as he does in the *Preface* to *Religio Laici*:

The Expressions of a Poem, design'd purely for Instruction, ought to be Plain and Natural, and yet Majestick: for here the Poet is presum'd to be a kind of Lawgiver, and those three qualities which I have nam'd are proper to the Legislative style. The Florid, Elevated and Figurative way is for the Passions; for Love and Hatred, Fear and Anger, are begotten in the Soul by shewing their Objects out of their true proportion; either greater than the Life, or less; but Instruction is to be given by shewing them what they naturally are. A Man is to be cheated into Passion, but to be reason'd into Truth.[36]

This, however, is a very problematical position, for to make poetry wholly reasonable in the sense intended in this passage – that is, to limit the statement of poetry to an accurate description of objective reality – is to eliminate the element of fancy altogether, the pre-eminently poetic faculty, and thus to deny poetry its very being. As Dryden puts it in *An Essay of Heroic Plays*, 'Serious plays ought not to imitate conversation too nearly. If nothing were to be raised above that level, the foundation of Poetry would be destroyed.' (I. 148)

One obvious alternative is to go to the other extreme, to give fancy free rein, which is the basic position adopted by Dryden later in the same essay.

I am of opinion, that neither Homer, Virgil, Statius, Ariosto, Tasso, nor our English Spencer, could have formed their poems half so beautiful, without those gods and spirits, and those enthusiastic parts of poetry, which compose the most noble parts of all their writings. And I will ask any man who loves poetry...if the ghost of *Polydorus* in Virgil, the *Enchanted Wood* in Tasso, the *Bower of Bliss* in Spencer...could have been omitted, without taking from their works some of the greatest beauties in them. And if any man object the improbabilities of a spirit appearing, or of a palace raised by magic; I boldly answer that an heroic poet is not tied to a bare representation of what is true, or exceeding probable; but that he may let himself loose to visionary objects, and to the representation of such things as depending not on sense, and therefore not to be comprehended by knowledge, may give him a freer scope for imagination. 'Tis enough that, in all ages and religions, the greatest part of mankind have believed the power of magic, and that there are spirits or spectres which have appeared. This, I say, is foundation enough for poetry; and I dare further affirm, that the whole doctrine of separated beings, whether those spirits are incorporeal substances (which Mr Hobbs, with some reason, thinks to imply a contradiction), or that they are a thinner or more aerial sort of bodies (as some of the Fathers have conjectured), may better be explicated by poets than by philosophers or divines. For their speculations on this subject are wholly poetical; they have only their fancy for their guide; and that, being sharper in an excellent poet, than it is like it should be in a phlegmatic, heavy gownman, will see further in its own empire, and produce more satisfactory notions on those dark and doubtful problems. (I. 152–3)

Dryden never more than here sounds like a Renaissance theorist, and yet nowhere else are Dryden's differences from the Renaissance more clear, and more clearly a function of his empirical assumptions. For Dryden, meaningful knowledge seems to be limited to *scire*; for the Renaissance, meaningful knowledge may include the kind derived from empirical science, but always within the more comprehensive framework of understanding, *intelligere*, or some such unifying concept. Sidney tells us that

learning, under what name soever it come forth, or to what immediate end soever it be directed, the final end is to lead and draw us to as high a perfection as our degenerate souls, made worse by their clayey lodgings, can be capable of. (p. 104)

This perspective, which is conspicuous also in such works as Spenser's Letter to Raleigh or Milton's 'Of Education', allows Sidney to evaluate comparatively all of man's pursuits, all of his arts (or arts and sciences, in their modern significations), and to conclude that the art of the poet, ranging only within the zodiac of his own wit, is superior. Dryden, however, is denied this unifying perspective; for him, the knowledge that may be derived from empirical science is rigorously dissociated from all other kinds of knowledge. Such 'wholly poetical' discourse as he describes above may be, by identity, most purely itself, but it is also most irreparably disjoined from all other aspects of human experience. It is only 'in its own empire' – that is, concerning 'such things as depend...not on sense, and [are] therefore not to be comprehended by knowledge' – that poetry can 'see further'. Concerning the true knowledge derived from sense experience, poetry can see nothing and say nothing to us. Dryden cannot therefore legitimately compare poetry and science (or any other art), and indeed, he doesn't. He tells us only that the discourse of the liberated imagination is better poetry than it is science. Milton in the *Areopagitica* dares to affirm the superiority of poet Spenser as a teacher to theologians Scotus and Aquinas. While for Dryden, too, the poet is superior to the 'heavy gownman' in the capacity of his imagination to produce 'satisfactory notions' on metaphysical problems, the primary informing distinction in the passage is not between two kinds of metaphysical understanding, but between all kinds of metaphysical understanding on the one hand and any kind of physical understanding on the other. The latter remains the only area of which knowledge may be genuinely acquired, and neither poet nor gownman seems to help in furnishing instruction of this kind of knowledge. The differences between Dryden and Spenser are even more pointed than they are between Dryden and Milton. The unnamed critic in the Proem to Book II of *The Faerie Queene* who made reality coterminous with sense objects was treated as a straw man to be torn down in the process of erecting a defense of poetry. In Dryden's passage, however, his empirical assumptions are accepted as valid, and his charge that poetry is merely 'painted forgery' is not readily answerable.

Neither the position adopted in the *Preface to Religio Laici* nor the one in *An Essay of Heroic Plays* is very satisfactory. The latter is vastly better known and appreciated among commentators, presumably because of its greater friendliness to imaginative discourse, but this friendliness, I think, is only superficial. And in fact neither position can be called typical of Dryden's endeavor which is, rather, to strike a balance between these views, to tell us (and he is not unique in this respect[37]) that both fancy and judgment must combine in the production of poetry, despite – or perhaps because of – the sharp contrast in their functions. This position is stated most clearly in the *Defence of An Essay*, where Dryden rejects both kinds of extreme positions described above (see I. 113–14 and I. 121) in favor of the following:

Imagination in a man, or reasonable creature, is supposed to participate of Reason, and when that governs, as it does in the belief of fiction, Reason is not destroyed, but misled, or blinded; that can prescribe to the Reason, during the time of the representation, somewhat like a weak belief of what it sees and hears; and Reason

145

suffers itself to be so hoodwinked, that it may better enjoy the pleasures of the fiction: but it is never so wholly made a captive, as to be drawn headlong into a persuasion of those things which are most remote from probability: 'tis in that case a free-born subject, not a slave; it will contribute willingly its assent, as far as it sees convenient, but will not be forced. Now, there is a greater vicinity in nature betwixt two rooms than betwixt two houses; betwixt two houses, than betwixt two cities; and so of the rest: Reason, therefore, can sooner be led by imagination to step from one room into another, than to walk to two distant houses, and yet rather to go thither, than to fly like a witch through the air, and be hurried from one region to another. Fancy and Reason go hand in hand; the first cannot leave the last behind: and though Fancy, when it sees the wide gulf, would venture over, as the nimbler, yet it is withheld by Reason, which will refuse to take the leap, when the distance over it appears too large. (I. 127–8)

In general, at least, this would appear to be a more satisfactory position. By insisting that reason plays a part in poetry, Dryden can bring poetry closer to real knowledge, to provoking a kind of belief that is not wholly disjoined from real significance. Moreover, Dryden manages to accomplish this without denying poetry its essential nature; he denies the exclusive domination of imagination, but not its pre-eminence ('Imagination... governs...in the belief of fiction'). The resulting product has the advantages of any hybrid, strengthened through cross-breeding because it shares the values of the two different original strains.

Yet even here the problem cannot be called completely solved, even if we approach the argument theoretically, with a charitable disregard of practical implications.[38] Poetry remains primarily, if not wholly, unreasonable – reason is 'misled' or 'blinded' rather than 'destroyed'. On the other hand, what advantages might be said to inhere in the total liberation of the imagination are diminished. Its 'nimbleness' is 'withheld', and the 'pleasures of the fiction' are presumably reduced; the essential nature of poetry is adulterated if not denied. The hybrid may possess two different kinds of value, but it possesses neither kind fully. Perhaps the problem is incapable of solution, given empirical assumptions. Puttenham in an earlier age could distinguish between *phantastici* and *euphantasiote* (pp. 18–20) and Sidney between the 'delivering forth' that should be scorned as 'wholly imaginative' and the legitimately valued imaginative invention of the poet, 'freely ranging only within the zodiac of his own wit'. (pp. 100–1) But these distinctions are based upon a concept of reality, and of the rational faculty that deals with the real, much broader and more flexible than Dryden's. An ordered imagination, an intuitive reason[39] – these informing Renaissance concepts were unavailable to Dryden because – the point bears repetition – he lacked the Renaissance's unifying perspective.

If the new empiricism may be said to have created this problem for literary theory, it also solved it. Solved it in the sense that it brought with it a new set of terms within which literary theory was destined to operate. Renaissance theory tends to emphasize the metaphysical, the ability of poetic imagination to express 'the very truth'. With the distancing of truth, very or otherwise, with the new split between human consciousness and reality, it could no longer have made as much sense to focus on the relation between poetry and truth as on the relation between poetry and mind; the emphasis for literary theory tends to shift from metaphysical to psychological. The development of psychological criticism, with its beginnings in Locke and Addison, the first 'pre-Romantics', through Akenside and Burke, culminating perhaps in Coleridge – this is a familiar story and I am not concerned with it here except to say that Dryden has his place in it as well. Along with Hobbes[40] he helps to define a new psychological approach by tending to emphasize how poetry properly 'may descend to the sight' of its audience, to recall Neander's image. Dryden's departures from Renaissance views of figurative language may also be understood within this context. It was more meaningful, given his context and assumptions, to discuss what 'makes it seem to us that we behold those things which the poet paints, so as to be pleased with them, and to admire them', than to engage in the strictly verbal analysis of cataloging the various kinds of tropes. Such analysis belonged to an earlier period when the divine order was assumed to inhere in nature, and could be described by the ordering of words, which ordering was itself a function of imagination, *euphantasiote*, the divine inhering in human nature, the *logos*.

Yet Dryden is not altogether new, not a full-fledged psychological critic. Though he emphasizes the way poetry works on its readers, he consistently refers this pragmatic question to the mimetic, to the relation of poetry to reality or truth; he tends still to view poetry from a Renaissance perspective and by means of a Renaissance vocabulary. Again, his attitude towards metaphor is a kind of indicator. Dryden may be more strict than the Renaissance in his exemplary definitions of metaphorical propriety, but he is arguably less strict than such later critics as Goldsmith or Johnson.[41] It may be true that, in some fundamental way, metaphor in Dryden's theory is stripped of its traditional occupation. Nonetheless, Dryden insists upon metaphor as absolutely essential to poetry's being, and, the last among English critics to do so, he expresses this insistence in terms of the traditional vocabulary: figures, colors, tropes, ornament. There remains a strong commitment in Dryden to a declining idea, that some meaningful kind of reality may be apprehended through imaginative structures, abstract symbols, creatures of the mind – through words, in short.

In this respect he ought to be distinguished from even so historically close a follower as Addison, who operates much more fully within the context of the new sensibility. Here is Addison's well-known description of 'Mixt Wit':

a Composition of Punn and true Wit, . . . more or less perfect as the Resemblance lies in the Ideas or in the Words: Its Foundations are laid partly in Falsehood and partly in Truth: Reason puts in her Claim for one Half of it, and Extravagance for the other. (No. 62, I. p. 267)

This passage adopts Dryden's position in the *Defence of An Essay* with no significant changes, but with one crucially significant difference: For Addison, this mixed state is undesirable, preferable perhaps to false wit but inferior to true wit; for Dryden, on the other hand, it is desirable, a description of valid poetic experience in general. For Dryden as for Addison the lines are drawn between words and things, imagination (in the old sense) and reason; yet some residual instinct prevents him from Addison's assertion of the former's absolute irrelevance to reality. Addison's notion that wit is totally independent of language, equally beautiful whether dressed or naked, unchanged in translation – this is something Dryden cannot accept without major qualification:

for thought, if it be translated truly, cannot be lost in another language; but the words that convey it to our apprehension (which are the image and ornament of that thought,) may be so ill chosen, as to make it appear in an unhandsome dress, and rob it of its native lustre. (I. 242)

These differences between Dryden and Addison should not surprise us, and they are more than a function of Dryden's greater practical experience writing poetry and translating. For Addison, after all, close as he was historically to Dryden, did write a full generation later, and historically speaking this generation was a crucial period of time. Addison was much further removed from the 'last age' (indeed, for Addison it was not the last age) than was Dryden, for whom the old rhetorical tradition was still vital, available in the works of Hoskins, Peacham, Smith, Blount, *et al.*, published and republished through to the end of the seventeenth century.[42] And Donald Davie says well about Dryden that he was conservative as well as innovative, 'that he spent more time and energy trying to keep in touch with older native traditions than in breaking free of them'.[43] Not that Dryden isn't Neander, the new man, as I suggested at the beginning of this chapter, but he is Neander in the process of becoming, not yet fully defined. He accepts the implications of the new empiricism for poetic theory with many more residual commitments to the old ways than does Addison; or than does Edward Bysshe, Addison's contemporary. Bysshe's *Art of English Poetry* was *the* poetic handbook of the new age, reprinted nine times between its first appearance in 1702 and 1762, serving the eighteenth century as Sherry, Wilson, Puttenham, Hoskins and the others did the sixteenth and early seventeenth. Instead of analyzing and exemplifying tropes, however, Bysshe's major effort is to list in alphabetical order the 'Most Natural, Agreeable, and Noble *Thoughts*'. From how-it-is-written to what-is-written, from style to subject, and the revolution in taste is complete. It is a revolution that one feels would have been impossible but for Dryden, yet one which Dryden himself, because he was still too intimately allied to the traditions of the last age, could not or would not complete.

Nothing would be easier than to see Dryden's situation here as an anxious one – saddled with no-longer-workable traditions and seeking out not-yet-fully-realized ideas. In a certain sense this is an accurate view. Renaissance attitudes do lead a kind of twilight existence in Dryden, and the full implications of the new poetic do remain to be defined by later figures. Yet it would be terribly misleading to view Dryden as struggling between two worlds, one dying, the other striving to be born. There is little or no sense of struggle in Dryden. He seems perfectly content to live amidst these changes, to allow old and new enough room for themselves; again, what is so impressive about Dryden is his easy tolerance of difference. This tolerance may have been dictated in part by the circumstances in which he found himself, circumstances of rapid and radical change. Whether this is so or not, it was a tolerance well adapted to effecting change meaningfully, to bridging old and new. I am simply reviving here the hoary cliché of Dryden as a 'transitional figure'. As long as we recognize this description for what it is, a kind of critical tag which, like all short-hand denotations of complex phenomena, must be subject to constant revaluation and refinement, a guide by means of which to approach Dryden and not a blanket to cover him, then it seems to me still a useful one.

6

THEORY AND PRACTICE

Dryden's criticism is always intimately close to his poetic ambitions, constantly referred and often referring to his practice, alternately nourishing and nourished by his practice. It tells us what kind of poetry Dryden wants to write and what kind he feels he has written; the two are not usually the same. It is a rich and various body of material, expressing the interests of a very large-minded individual over a long period of time. Diversity is the central fact of its existence. For this reason it is difficult to generalize about. Such diversity must be honored, for it is a major factor in the attractiveness of his criticism, as it is of his poetry whose diversity it reflects. Dryden is *not* 'all, all of a piece throughout', and we shouldn't expect him or want him to be. Still it is possible to recognize certain similarities and congruities among his different poetic interests, a pattern around which other patterns tend to develop, enough to suggest a constancy of design.

Chronology, of course, helps in managing this intractable material; Dryden's criticism may be divided into two fairly distinguishable periods. The earlier, roughly the first fifteen years (1664–80), corresponds to the time when Dryden was most actively engaged in dramatic writing. He produced eighteen plays during this period, for fourteen of which he wrote critical essays. These prefaces and dedications provide a running commentary on what he has done and offer, however informally, a program for what he wishes to do. The vast majority of their critical energy is spent in trying to analyze dramatic propriety, especially often to determine the form of the heroic play. This constitutes a sustained critical endeavor, unified in an almost Aristotelian sense, with a beginning in the earliest prefaces, tentative and probative in tone, a middle in *An Essay of Heroic Plays* (1672) when the form seems to have crystallized, at least momentarily, in Dryden's mind, and an end in a series of essays in the late seventies which record the disappointment of failure, after which Dryden's interest in the theater, as either poet or critic, pretty much ends.

Dryden's first essay, the *Epistle Dedicatory of The Rival Ladies* (1664), begins with Dryden's remembering his play

when it was only a confused mass of thoughts, tumbling over one another in the dark; when the fancy was yet in its first work, moving the sleeping images of things towards the light, there to be distinguished, and then either chosen or rejected by the judgment. (I. 1)

He had hoped 'in that first tumult of thoughts' to have produced 'something worthy my Lord of Orrery' to whom the play is dedicated, but he was 'then in that eagerness of imagination, which, by overpleasing fanciful men, flatters them into the danger of writing'. Now that the play is finished Dryden is dissatisfied with it. Not only is this particular play imperfect; Dryden wonders how *any* play can help but be imperfect, 'for the stage being the representation of the world, and the actions in it, how can it be imagined, that the picture of human life can be more exact than the life itself is?' Dryden does not answer this question, but the difficulty of the poetic problem suggests to him the need for a charitable attitude towards the playwright:

He may be allowed sometimes to err, who undertakes to move so many characters and humours, as are requisite in a play, in those narrow channels which are proper to each of them; to conduct his imaginary persons through so many various intrigues and chances, as the labouring audience shall think them lost under every billow; and then at length to work them so naturally out of their distresses, that when the whole plot is laid open, the spectators may rest satisfied that every cause was powerful enough to produce the effect it had; and that the whole chain of them was with such due order linked together, that the first accident would naturally beget the second, till they all rendered the conclusion necessary. (I. 2)

Thus in a somewhat fragmented and inchoate manner, the ideas that appear in the first paragraph of Dryden's criticism are the major ones to which he will return repeatedly in the essays to follow – the places of fancy and judgment, imitation, variety of action, the sources of pleasure. The tone is dominated by the unanswered question, and by Dryden's dissatisfaction with what he has so far created.

In *An Essay of Dramatic Poesy* (1665) these fragmented ideas are brought together; the simile of a statue – a play, to be like nature, must be set above it – may be construed as an answer to the question left unanswered in the *Dedicatory Epistle*. A play *cannot* be more 'exact' (perfect, just) than life, but in being heightened it will 'descend in its just proportion'. It may be that the clarity of the *Essay* is a function of its remoteness from any particular poetic occasion (it introduces no play) and from the London theatrical scene generally (it was written in Wiltshire). Nonetheless, the *Essay* is directed towards the same end as all the critical prefaces written during this period, part of the same endeavor, an attempt to establish a form and style for dramatic propriety. It may have suggested an answer to the question – or questions, actually – raised by the *Dedicatory Epistle*, but these questions were of a kind that demanded repeated answers, none of which could be fully satisfactory without being embodied in the dramatic work itself.

Not surprisingly, then, the prefaces that follow *An Essay* return to a tentative and exploratory tone. The *Preface to Annus Mirabilis* (1666) is best known for its definition of true wit ('some lively and apt description...'). As he had in the *Dedicatory Epistle*, Dryden distinguishes between the functions of fancy and judgment, but characterizes them again as part of a single process. These earliest essays are marked by Dryden's strong sense at once of delight and of danger in the power of his imagination. In the *Dedicatory Epistle*, 'Imagination in a poet is a faculty so wild and lawless, that like an high-ranging spaniel, it must have clogs tied to it, lest it outrun the judgment'. (I. 8) In the *Preface to Annus Mirabilis*, Dryden uses the same figure, but he seems to be less worried about the lawlessness. Imagination is 'like a nimble spaniel, [which] beats over and ranges through the field of memory, till it springs the quarry it hunted after'. (I. 14) This ambivalence towards imagination, never fully resolved in Dryden's criticism, is particularly intense at this time. It is reflected in Dryden's attitude towards rhyme.

In the *Dedicatory Epistle* rhyme is viewed as properly circumscribing the fancy; in the *Preface*, however, where Dryden is much more at ease with the ranging spaniel of his imagination, rhyme is viewed as slavery.

The form with which the *Preface* is concerned is the heroic poem, not the heroic play. Yet the heroic poem is a major influence on the kind of drama Dryden wishes to write. The same tentativeness and uncertainty appears in Dryden's discussion of the heroic poem. *Annus Mirabilis* is, Dryden must admit, too short to be called true epic. Besides, its action is 'tied too severely to the laws of history'. (I. 11) Dryden was to become much more insistent later that a true epic poem had to be liberated from the demands of historical accuracy and literal truth. In 1672 he remarks that none of the epic poets 'could have formed their poems half so beautiful, without those·gods and spirits, and those enthusiastic parts of poetry, which compose the most noble parts of all their writings'. (I. 152–3) In 1697 he says that he 'could easily demonstrate, if there were need to prove it, or I had the leisure', that 'no heroic poem can be writ on the Epicurean principles'. (II. 210. 'Epicurean principles' in the cosmological rather than moral sense, Epicurus as a follower of Democritus's atomism. The context makes Dryden's meaning clear: No heroic poem can be written without a sense of the participation by the gods in the affairs of men.) At this early date, however, Dryden is relatively content to view his poem as a kind of sub-species of the true heroic poem. If not the thing itself, his poem is still close to it. Still, he is no more wholly satisfied with *Annus Mirabilis* than he had been with *The Rival Ladies*. Though he can tell what true wit ought |to be for the heroic poem, whether it is actually present in *Annus Mirabilis* he is not sure. 'Such descriptions or images, well-wrought, *which I promise not for mine*, are ...the adequate delight of Heroic Poesy.' (I. 18; my emphais) The *Preface to An Evening's Love* (1671) reveals a similar uncertainty, for although the essay states a preference for a higher kind of drama, *An Evening's Love* was itself a prose comedy with a 'little' action and characters of low quality.

An Essay of Heroic Plays (1672) is the clearest statement of Dryden's intentions in this first period of his criticism. Many if not most of his essays had implied cumulativeness as a desideratum – fancy *and* judgment, French *and* English, height *and* exactitude of description. *An Essay of Heroic Plays* makes this desideratum explicit. In the *Preface to Annus Mirabilis*, Dryden had distinguished between Ovid and Virgil, dramatic propriety and epic propriety. *Of Heroic Plays* predicates the form of its title on the combination of both the virtues of the drama and of the epic – the unified action and availability to the common apprehension of the one, the gravity and majesty of the other. For the first time Dryden writes as if he is presenting truth, not seeking it out. He seems, moreover, to be certain about the success of *The Conquest of Granada* (the heroic play to which this essay is prefixed); not that it is without errors, but Dryden is 'content to sit quietly; to hear my fortune cursed by some, and my faults arraigned by others, and to suffer both without reply'. (I. 159)

If it was a genuine tranquility, it proved short-lived. Beginning as early as the middle-seventies and continuing into the next decade, Dryden's criticism reflects a new uncertainty and a new exploratory mood. In such pieces particularly as the *Heads of An Answer to Rymer*, the *Preface to All for Love* and the *Preface to Troilus and Cressida* (1677, 1678 and 1679), Dryden is much more interested in formal neoclassical principles and much more insistent (along with Rymer, Rapin and Le Bossu) on the moral function of poetry. In the same period, Dryden's criticism betrays a growing sense of dissatisfaction with the drama. Much of this is a reaction to the contemporary theatrical situation, the audience's taste for elaborate and silly spectacle[1]; but much of it, too, reflects the sense of his own inability to realize a successful dramatic form. Thus, as early as 1676 in the *Dedication of Aureng-Zebe*, another heroic play, Dryden writes of his distaste for comedy, but more than this, his dissatisfaction with himself and with the theater in general. 'I desire to be no longer the Sisyphus of the stage.' In the drama, 'My predecessors have excelled me in all kinds.' He would 'make the world some part of amends for many ill plays by an heroic poem'. (Watson, I. 190–1) By the time of the *Dedication of the Spanish Friar* (1681) Dryden's dissatisfaction has become a general disgust. He condemns the theater for cheap illusionism, the audience for judging by appearances and himself for not having in his writing 'reached to those ideas that I had within me'. (I. 244) After *The Spanish Friar* Dryden disengages himself from the theater. With the exception of *The Duke of Guise* (1682), a rewriting in collaboration with Nathaniel Lee of his first play (it had never been performed, and Dryden's interest in it may have been more political than dramatic), Dryden writes nothing for the theater until *Don Sebastian* (1689), and *Don Sebastian*, as Dryden frankly admits in its *Preface*, was written because of financial hardship. He tells us there that he had left the stage with a 'loathing of it', convinced that the possibilities for 'humours comedy' had been exhausted, and that love and honor, which he had specified as the proper subjects for heroic plays, were 'the mistaken topics of tragedy'. (Watson, II. 45)

In this transitional period, Dryden's increased interest in the neoclassical critics and his gradual retreat from the drama are perhaps related phenomena. If French neoclassicism tended to emphasize the heroic mode and its attendant moral function, it may be precisely in terms of the epic element, the elevation central to its definition, that the heroic play was a failure. There is real evidence to support the recent view that Dryden was flirting with irony in the heroic plays.[2] Indeed, in the *Preface to Troilus and Cressida*, he laughs at one of Montezuma's similes from *The Indian Emperor* in much the same spirit as had provoked Buckingham to parody Dryden's 'new way of writing' in *The Rehearsal*.[3] But there is too much evidence against accepting King's view of a sustained and basic ironic intention in the heroic plays – evidence in Dryden's criticism, where the elevated mode is so often commended with great seriousness, and evidence in the heroic plays themselves, where comic effects seem unaccidentally part of a successful overall plan only from time to time. Perhaps too many different kinds of impulse are striving for expression in the heroic plays. One can admire the variety endorsed by Dryden's criticism, but the heroic plays seem to me not so much richly various in design as simply confused. And perhaps Dryden's disillusionment in this period reflects an awareness of such a confusion.

Even rhyme falls under the same encompassing shadow at this time. Though conceived of originally as a necessary aspect of the heroic play, essentially contributing towards the proper elevation, Dryden falls out of love with it during this period.

The metaphor is his own; as he writes in the Prologue to *Aureng-Zebe* (1675), 'Our author...to confess a truth, (though out of time)/Grows weary of his long-lov'd Mistris, Rhyme.[4] Dryden turns to blank verse for *Aureng-Zebe* and *All for Love*. He never rejects the theory justifying rhyme, nature wrought up to a higher pitch, but as he tells us in the *Preface to All for Love* (1678), it no longer seemed practically useful: 'Not that I condemn my former way, but that this is more proper to my present purpose'. (1. 200.)

However one explains it – the influence of neoclassical critics, a growing dissatisfaction with his own practice – Dryden's criticism changes markedly in tone after about 1680. There is little of the eager anticipation that had characterized the earlier criticism; Dryden no longer writes as if expecting revelation. The later essays are not unified by a central concern, as the earlier ones had been with their focus on the heroic play. Since less immediately concerned with the problem of defining a particular form, they are open to a wider range of interests, including some of a not strictly critical kind – biography (*Life of Plutarch*, 1683; *Life of Lucian*, c. 1696) and literary history (*A Discourse Concerning the Original and Progress of Satire*, 1692). The later essays are still occasional in nature, but the occasions tend to be different. Instead of exploring the literary problems he has met in writing a work of his own, Dryden in this period finds himself introducing either miscellanies and compilations for which he was not entirely responsible, or introducing his translations of other poets. Not that Dryden is more distant from the occasions later; he takes his editorial and translating tasks quite seriously. But with the different kind of occasion, Dryden finds himself placed in a different perspective, looking back upon the achievements of others rather than ahead to his own hoped-for goals. Such a perspective results in the inclusion of historical material and the estimates of earlier critics, and these inclusions tend to make the later essays longer and more formal than the earlier, less eagerly anticipatory, quieter.

If the later essays may be said to be unified by any single concern, it is translation. The overwhelming majority of the later criticism is occasioned by translation, and the principles of literary translation occupy the discussion in a number of these essays.[5] Dryden's theory of translation is stated first in a formal way in the *Preface to Ovid's Epistles* (1680); proper translation is called paraphrase, a mean between metaphrase and imitation. Metaphrase, literal accuracy, pays the proper respect to the sense and words of the original, but fails to realize that 'since every language is so full of its own properties,...what is beautiful in one, is often barbarous, nay sometimes nonsense, in another'. (I. 241) Imitation, as Dryden intended the term, has the same sense in Robert Lowell's usage today; the foreign poem becomes the occasion for a new poem in English. Imitation thus respects the native proprieties of English, but leaves the sense and words of the original too far behind, according to Dryden, to be the correct basis for translation. Paraphrase responds to the demands of both literal fidelity to the external source and internal beauty, verbal propriety. Dryden's concept of translation bears a striking resemblance to his theory of art as expressed in terms of original creation.

It is probably not accidental that translation began to occupy a place of prime importance in Dryden's criticism in 1680, at a time when the radical failure of the heroic play had been brought home to him. In effect Dryden seems to have devoted his energies to translation as a result of his failure to create a satisfactory mode. 'In effect', because no such causality is ever made explicit, but both the heroic play and translation may be seen as accommodating Dryden's overriding ambition, to write a heroic poem. It is virtually impossible to exaggerate the power of this ambition. H. T. Swedenberg has characterized it as 'obsessive',[6] noting how consistently Dryden tended to view the variety of poetic forms he employed as related in some way or other to the epic form. Along with historical poetry like *Annus Mirabilis*, political, panegyrical and satirical poetry all find a home in Dryden's mind under this broad roof, sub-species of epic if not fully epic themselves. Certainly the heroic play can be viewed in this light. Ker comments about *An Essay Of Heroic Plays* that Dryden 'is not really much interested in dramatic form, and though his present theme is Almanzor, it may be suspected that his heart is with the unwritten epic for which the right time never came.' (I. lvi) This is an overstatement; Dryden really was quite interested in the dramatic form, and many literary traditions besides that of heroic poetry seem to combine in the genesis of the heroic play (which and how many traditions is an old debate still unsettled). Nonetheless, Ker's suggestion is a valuable one, made by many other commentators as well.[7] As for translation, Dryden's main concern in the later criticism, its relation to Dryden's ambitions as a heroic poet is much less clear. After all Dryden translated a wide variety of material among many authors very different in style and sensibility, and with obvious dedication to them all. Still, Dryden's *Aeneid* is in many senses the culmination of the whole endeavor, the last major work he produced as a translator, the one he was proudest of, certainly the original poem that he most admired, the best of the best kind of poetry, 'undoubtedly the greatest work which the soul of man is capable to perform'. (II. 154) It is an interesting coincidence that Dryden's *Aeneid* was dedicated to the Earl of Mulgrave, for twenty-one years earlier, at a time when Dryden was first recognizing the failure of his drama to realize the ideas he had within, it was to the same Mulgrave that he had promised 'amends for many ill plays by an heroic poem'.

I don't wish to make too much of this coincidence or of any simple unity to Dryden's poetic career. As I said earlier (echoing virtually everyone who has written on the subject) diversity is the central fact of Dryden's poetry. Even limited to his two most sustained kinds of endeavor, drama and translation, his output is remarkably various – humours comedy, wit comedy, heroic tragedy; Ovid's *Amores, Art of Love, Metamorphoses,* Lucretius's *De Rerum Natura,* Horace's odes, Juvenal's and Persius's satires, all of Virgil, some of Chaucer and Homer and Boccaccio and Boileau. All this is to say nothing of Dryden's original non-dramatic poetry, which is again striking in its variety, particularly in poems of the middle and high-middle styles: satire, verse epistle, historical poem, panegyric, political poem. But the ambition to write an epic is a constant presence among these changes, a recurring theme, even a fundamental framework if we adopt Swedenberg's perspective.

Such a perspective leads to the conclusion that Dryden's criticism as a whole must be said to describe a failure; 'the right time never came' for the heroic poem. The heroic plays, as a deflection and accommodation of his impulse to write heroic poetry, are hardly memorable; and however well

Dryden's version of the *Aeneid* 'made amends' for them, it is not the original epic whose idea was within. This conclusion is a bizarre one, for we don't consider Dryden a failure. The hierarchy of genres no longer influences our judgments. We can value Dryden for his poetic achievements even if they are not epic, sensibly recognizing that his talent was a great one whether or not it was realistically suited to the stern demands of his elevated muse. Dryden, though, never could see things quite this way, even in the *Preface to the Fables*. This last piece is a real happy ending. The delight Dryden takes in his undiminished creative powers is infectious, wholly free from the self-serving quality that occasionally appears elsewhere, perhaps because he is so willing to admit and forgive, rather than defend, his own errors. But even here, in the context of a critical response to Blackmore's *minimum opus* ('The Guardian Angels of kingdoms were machines too ponderous for him to manage; and therefore he rejected them...'), he is led to a nostalgic reminiscence of his own heroic plans. 'I will only say, that it was not for this noble knight that I drew the plan of an epic poem on King Arthur, in my preface to the translation of Juvenal.' (II. 272) That epic ambition was there right to the end, and we, in looking into the relation between Dryden's theory and his practice, should take it centrally into account.

I turn now to *Mac Flecknoe*, a poem with many advantages as an illustration of Dryden's practice in relation to his theory. The poem, to begin with, is very well known, very much admired, and short enough to be given the detailed consideration it deserves. It was written in 1678, a time during which Dryden's criticism records a kind of painful if not agonizing reappraisal, and the poem itself may be seen in small part as a piece of literary criticism and self-criticism, expressing an Olympian distaste for the triviality and pretentiousness of Restoration drama at its worst, a contempt from which Dryden does not spare his own pretensions in the heroic plays (as 'little Maximins' in the Nursery passage shows us). It is written with constant and explicit reference to the tradition of epic poetry, yet it defines itself primarily by contrast to the epic tradition, and it helps not only to illustrate but to explain, perhaps, the way in which epic poetry was unrealizable for Dryden. *Mac Flecknoe* is by no stretch of the imagination 'Dryden's practice', for this remains too various to allow for any synecdoche or even epitome. And yet *Mac Flecknoe* itself is a various poem, an example of Dryden's brilliant ability to choreograph diverse materials, to contain different tones and styles in a single but loose and flexible mode (far more successfully than the heroic play, certainly); and in so doing, to turn the conditions of one kind of failure into an indubitable success of a different kind.

The poem begins much like a heroic poem. 'All human things are subject to decay,/And when fate summons, monarchs must obey.'[8] Though some of the epic conventions that one might expect are lacking, the tone is appropriately elevated, a solemn assertion of a basic human truth, no less and perhaps more dignified for being obvious. The couplet informs, it presents knowledge of the kind Dryden requires from an epic poet, 'the knowledge of the liberal arts and sciences, and particularly moral philosophy'. (ii. 36; see also ii. 156) The moral philosophy can be called stoic in a loose sense that is clarified by the rest of the passage. Decay may be inevitable, but because it is only part of reality, subsumed under the ordinance of a providential fate that is ultimately benevolent and productive, it may be apprehended calmly. The same fate that now claims Flecknoe in his age had called him to empire in his youth and blest him with peace, prosperity and family, one of whom is presently available, 'To settle the succession of the State'. Settling the succession, continuing the line, is the ostensible subject, and it is this subject that makes *Mac Flecknoe* seem closest to the heroic tradition, particularly to Virgil and Cowley, the epic poets that most immediately influence the poem's expressive details. For the *Aeneid* is about loss and gain under the aegis of fate, the founding of a new city after the destruction of the old. Cowley's epic, too, centers on the succession of a kingly line, with the addition that it conflates Christian with classical materials. In the *Davideis* our expectation is directed towards the new city of Jerusalem, and towards God's throne; as Cowley reminds us constantly, his hero is 'the best and mightiest of that Royal Race from whence *Christ* himself disdained not to descend'.[9] Dryden's poem also conflates Christian and classical materials, and he adopts the same framework of Christian typology, alluding to Cowley or Cowley's sources, Old Testament prophecies, New

Testament fulfillments, in order to suggest the final victory of the Word, sung by the poet, taught by the priest, predicted by the prophets, and embodied in the King of kings.

From these epic heights, dignified by tradition and sacred in their implications, Dryden's poem *falls*, over and over again, deeper and deeper, in an astonishing variety of ingenious ways. Bathos is central to its statement, to its vision of experience; the poem's art is 'the art of sinking in verse'. The most obvious sort of bathos is achieved by Dryden's introduction into the poem's epic formulas of specific contemporary details of the most inappropriately sleazy kind.

> Heywood and Shirley were but types of thee,
> Thou last great prophet of tautology.
> Even I, a dunce of more renown than they,
> Was sent before but to prepare thy way.
> And, coarsely clad in Norwich drugget, came
> To teach the nations in thy greater name.

The Biblical formulas remind us of the most striking instance of Old Testament prophecy, Isaiah's 'new message' ('the voice of him that crieth in the wilderness', 40:2), and its fulfillment in John the Baptist (Matthew 3:1–4). But the details strike exactly the wrong note. Unlike the meaningful simplicity of John's dress ('And the same John had his raiment of camel's hair and a leathern girdle about his loins; and his meat was locusts and wild honey'), Flecknoe's coarse drugget evokes the meaningless impoverishment of Grub Street; Norwich, moreover, whether or not it is an allusion to Shadwell's birth place, emphasizes how far we are removed from 'the wilderness of Judaea' where John 'in those days came...preaching'. The names of the persons, obviously, jar as well. By no stretch of the imagination can either Heywood or Shirley be cast in the rôle of John the Baptist; and Shadwell himself is blasphemously grotesque as Christ.

So much for Christian epic; other details elsewhere deflate the tone of classical epic. When Dryden plucks 'Empress Fame' out of Book IV of the *Aeneid* to announce Shadwell's coronation, he suggests a heroic context, but this is immediately localized and trivialized. 'Rous'd by report of Fame, the nations meet,/ From near Bunhill, and distant Watling Street.' Bunhill and Watling Street again strike the wrong note – low, mean, small.

The point is emphasized in the antithesis between near Bunhill and distant Watling Street (an antithesis blurred in the pirated version's 'near Bunhill *to* distant Watling Street'). Watling Street may be further removed than Bunhill from the site of Shadwell's coronation, but the poetic effect is of minute degrees of distance. It is the smallness of this particularized environment that gives the lie to the heroic pretensions of 'nations'. 'Nations' might be appropriate for the *Aeneid*, concerned as it is with Troy, Carthage and Rome – the whole known world. But *these* nations are the neighborhood rabble, 'suburbian' citizens – no more. Or if they do qualify as nations when we see them gathered to witness Shadwell's coronation, it is only in the least dignified sense, that of physical mass:

> Rous'd by report of Fame, the nations meet,
> From near Bunhill, and distant Watling Street.
> No Persian carpets spread th'imperial way,
> But scatter'd limbs of mangled poets lay;
> From dusty shops neglected authors come,
> Martyrs of pies, and relics of the bum.
> Much Heywood, Shirley, Ogleby there lay,
> But loads of Sh—— almost chok'd the way.
> Bilk'd stationers for yeomen stood prepar'd,
> And Herringman was captain of the guard.

'Nations' here, along with 'much', 'loads' and 'chok'd' (and, for sound, 'bilk'd') later, suggests an enormous crowd stuffed into a circumscribed area. A mob, in short; this is an astonishingly prescient view of the new bourgeois culture, a literary market place in which unsold manuscripts are products, constrained to realize *some* commercial value for the entrepreneurs ('Herringman', 'bilk'd stationers'), even if they are not put to the uses for which they were originally intended ('martyrs of pies, and relics of the bum').

The poem's informing assumption is the distance between old and new, the immense discrepancy between the values of the heroic tradition (the epic formulas, the dignified old meanings) and the egregious valuelessness of contemporary experience (Bunhill and Watling Street, to say nothing of Pissing Alley). *Mac Flecknoe* is predicated upon historical decay, upon ruin, and in the poem's central passage (central in both senses), the description of the Nursery as the site of the new king's coronation, this ruin is described as absolute and all-inclusive:

> *Close* to the walls which fair Augusta bind,
> (The fair Augusta much to fears inclin'd,)
> An ancient fabric rais'd t'inform the sight,
> *There stood* of yore, and Barbican it hight:
> A watchtower once; but now, so fate ordains,
> Of all the pile an empty name remains.
> From its old ruins brothel-houses rise,
> Scenes of lewd loves, and of polluted joys,
> *Where* their vast courts the mother-strumpets keep,
> And, undisturb'd by watch, in silence sleep.
> *Near* these a Nursery erects its head,
> *Where* queens are form'd, and future heroes bred;
> *Where* unfledg'd actors learn to laugh and cry,
> *Where* infant punks their tender voices try,
> And little Maximins the gods defy.
> Great Fletcher never treads in buskins *here*,
> Nor greater Jonson dares in socks appear;
> But gentle Simkin just reception finds
> *Amidst this* monument of vanish'd minds:
> Pure clinches the suburbian Muse affords,
> And Panton waging harmless war with words.
> *Here* Flecknoe, as a *place* to fame well known,
> Ambitiously design'd his Sh——'s throne.

This passage is a sustained development, the emphasized words combining with the syntax to suggest a single movement, progressively more exact in locating the site of Shadwell's throne. But the actual development turns out to be far different – temporal rather than spatial. In placing the ruins of Barbican 'close to the walls' of the city, Dryden notes in passing the historical process of decay by which they became ruins: the '*ancient* fabric' that 'stood *of yore*', 'a watchtower *once*; but *now*...' One is willing at first to take this as a subordinate development, a bit of local color incidental to the primary descriptive purpose, which apparently remains spatial, but as the passage continues this historical vision assumes increasing significance. The brothel-houses rising from the *ruins* of Barbican (a locale, a place) seem to be the direct consequence of the *ruination* of Barbican (a process, historical decay). The new 'court' could not apparently exist but for the decline of the old, and the implication of causality is confirmed by the verbal echo describing the mother-strumpets' peaceful sleep: They are 'undisturb'd by watch' because the 'watchtower', the emblem of legitimate authority, has disintegrated. (Now, in retrospect, we can see the city's anxiety – 'The fair Augusta much to fears inclin'd' – as far more than an aside: Her 'binding walls' are crumbling.) The Nursery is a further manifestation of decay or, better, a manifestation of further decay. While it may be located '*near* these ruins', it is seen even more significantly as yet another consequence of the ruination, still more significantly as a projection of this ruination into the future. The perverted nurture accorded its inhabitants is the kind of maternal care one might expect from 'mother-strumpets'. The future heroes bred there, rather than being trained to preserve order, are taught to defy the gods. The queens who are formed there are such as are fit to inherit their mother-strumpets' courts – that is, queens in the other sense, whores raised by whores. This is great uncreating anti-nature at work, as it is in the father-son relationship at the center of the poem ('Mature in dulness from his tender years'; 'Trust nature, do not labor to be dull.') As the repository and breeding ground of all that is *un*natural, the Nursery has to be defined finally by negations. This is the place where Fletcher and Jonson are not, a 'monument of vanish'd minds'. The actual inhabitants, punning Simkin and Panton, simply confirm the negations until the culminatory 'Here' at last places Shadwell's throne not so much in any particular place (for where is 'an empty name?') as in the center of a concept, historical decay, annihilation, absolute ruin.

This passage has a mythic resonance in the absoluteness of the divorce that it asserts to exist between past and present. Everything that is past is now irrelevant, not just the heroic monuments of antiquity, but the immediate traditions of the recent past: Waller and, by implication, the cavalier strain of royalist verse are annihilated by allusion in Flecknoe's song to King John of Portugal;[10] Cowley's College of Prophets and Davenant's House of Astragon realize their fate in echoes in the Nursery passage itself.

> Midst a large *Wood* that joyns fair *Ramahs* Town
> (The neighborhood fair Rama's chief renown)
> A college stands, where at great *Prophets feet*

The *Prophets sons* with silent dili'gence meet.[11]
This to a structure led, long known to Fame,
And call'd THE MONUMENT OF VANISH'D MINDES.[12]

Both Cowley and Davenant are working in a convention of seventeenth-century verse which describes and eulogizes a great public monument for its embodiment and continuation of tradition.[13] The Nursery, however, Shadwell's coronation place, is a different sort of monument altogether, and its difference is located brilliantly in Dryden's turn on '*of* vanish'd minds'. Here what is institutionalized is not the minds of the absent, the collective traditional wisdom of mankind, but rather the absence of mind. The dream of the new science, sprung from Bacon's progressivist hopes, turns here into nightmare. Rather than legitimately extending tradition by refining it, the Nursery represents a radical alienation from all the values of the past, rendering the Imperial Palace and the House of Astragon effectively equal in their absolute irrelevance to the new order; bathing Jonson and Fletcher in nostalgia no less than Augustus and Ascanius. All are part of an 'ancient [cultural] fabric' that 'stood of yore' (the archaisms, 'of yore' and 'it hight' suggest Spenser's nostalgic diction more than his heroic scope), that continued to stand for an indeterminate period of time, but that has ended *now*, in the moment of the poem. The near-contemporaneity of Jonson and Fletcher offers no relief. In this poem's myth-like historical structure, there is no 'recent past' as middle ground; everything of value is non-contemporary.

By the same kind of inexorable logic, everything contemporary is non-valuable. I have noted how filled the poem is with details of contemporary life of the most inappropriately sleazy kind. One might reasonably suppose that Dryden carefully selected such details, rigorously excluding nobler locales (the court, say) or more appropriate candidates for the rôle of contemporary hero (the king, say, or even Etherege), but the poem's historical view denies that any sublime contemporary options really exist. Pissing Alley and Shadwell truly figure forth a contemporary experience which is, in *all* of its details, sleazily inappropriate to the heroic tradition. What is more, the king and the court do in fact find their way into Dryden's poem, at least by allusion, for Shadwell's musical procession down the Thames is specified to pass 'before the royal barge'. This detail might be taken as a kind of reassurance that all, or that anything, is well, but in a poem so resolutely committed to a vision of decay, such an interpretation is hard to justify, especially in view of the facts that Charles founded the Nursery and that Charles's own 'court' was, as a matter of common knowledge, 'vastly' intimate with 'lewd loves' and 'polluted joys'. The king's presence, in every sense of the word, remains impenetrably vague, but if one wants to endow it with significance, it seems to me legitimate to speculate as follows: first, that *King Charles is on the barge* and (though what he is doing there and to whom I do not choose to guess) second, that *King Charles is enjoying Shadwell's music*. Etherege alone escapes debasement, implied or otherwise, shining for a brief moment like a good deed in a naughty world: 'Let gentle George in triumph tread the stage...' Before long, however, even this suggestion becomes remote as, speaking about Jonson, Flecknoe asks his son, 'When did his Muse from Fletcher scenes purloin,/As thou whole Eth'rege dost transfuse to thine?' Etherege is still available in the present tense in this last line, but only passively available, only to be perverted by Shadwell. By virtue especially of the syntactic parallelism, he is relegated in effect to the same ambience as Fletcher inhabits, the same golden age, the same not-here and not-now.[14]

We are left, then, here and now, alone with Shadwell, a portentous negation of the epic tradition – which is to say, by virtue of a synecdoche typical of Dryden, the negation of all tradition. If the epic tradition is progressive in spirit, as epitomized by the ritual of succession announced in the opening lines, Shadwell and his new order embody regression into nil. From their uncreating nature nothing is produced but waste. The environment is polluted ('the morning toast that floats along the Thames', for example; relevance mongers might well choose this poem to begin an ecology collection), and the poem is filled to the point of Swiftian obsessiveness with references to excrement, excremental piles and their sources which become increasingly insistent and significant: 'Pissing Alley...Aston Hall...brothel-houses rise...that in this pile...Bunhill... relics of the bum...loads of Sh—— almost chok'd the way' – until we reach the following picture of the new king: 'The hoary prince in majesty appear'd,/High on a throne of his own labors rear'd'. Like Satan's throne to which the passage alludes (*Paradise Lost*, II. 1–10), Shadwell's throne is a monument to perverted love, lewd (the *whorey* prince), self-centered ('his own labors'[15]), and immature in that it is not directed towards succession, the production of offspring. In this couplet the scatalogical 'innuendo' combines with the Miltonic 'allusion' (in Wilding's terminology) to characterize the anti-heroic uncreativeness of the new order. In love with his own labors, his poems and his feces (which, of course, are impossible to distinguish), he remains fixated in the anal stage, a resounding unsuccess.

The pun in this last word is Dryden's, for what Flecknoe teaches his son – 'Success let others teach, learn thou from me/Pangs without birth, and fruitless industry' – is not only failure but unsuccess. Recalling the crucial line, 'To settle the succession of the State', this pun is yet another way of informing us that frustration and not development is what Shadwell's coronation celebrates. The pun is Miltonic in particular ('by success untaught', *Paradise Lost*, II. 9) and epic in general; but whereas in Milton's poem every success was a success, every loss would ultimately be regained through providence, the providence manifested in Dryden's poem is of a contrary sort: 'so fate ordains/Of all the pile an empty name remains'. The compensatory Rome for this lost Troy, 'From its old ruins brothel-houses rise', is no compensation at all. The rising of bordellos from the fallen watchtower is just a further falling, or a rising in the sense made clear just after: 'Near these a Nursery erects its head.' The summoning fate at the opening of the poem may have seemed ultimately productive and benevolent in providing a new son-prince to replace the old father-king, but Shadwell for Flecknoe, though literally just, is grim compensation indeed. *Mac Flecknoe's* first line turns out to be not simply a part of the picture but the picture itself, the sum total of reality as it is viewed in this poem: 'All human things are subject to decay.'

The satiric point of *Mac Flecknoe* is made with Dryden's characteristic lucidity; one would have to be Shadwell himself to miss it (as in fact Shadwell did). The constant allusions to classical and Christian epic create a perspective of enduring value which puts this Restoration poetaster in his provincial place. This is true enough, but the poem's grim view of absolute ruin furnishes a contrary assertion as well. It is Shadwell who in a horrible sort of way puts the tradition in its place. Its availability in this poem for judging Shadwell is, so to speak, its death rattle, the last manifestation of its vitality in history. It dies *here* and *now*, condemned to irrelevance by virtue of the new king's coronation, no longer able to endure against the force of Shadwell's uncreative word.

It is primarily in terms of his word, his poetry, that Shadwell's destructive rôle is realized. The poetry is consistently described as dull and nonsensical, appropriate words which we are required to understand literally, devoid of light and sense. Although Dryden furnishes no example, one would imagine this poetry to sound like Scriblerus's illustration of 'THE INANITY, or NOTHINGNESS': 'The Sun himself shall rise – by break of Day'. Or 'THE TAUTOLOGY': '*Divide* – and *part* – the *sever'd* world – in *two*.'[16] Yet such examples are necessarily inadequate, mere incarnations of the idea, shadows of the substance, or rather of the non-substance, the idea-lessness; this is the problem. Because the quality of Shadwell's verse is a non-quality, it remains essentially indefinable. The *genuinely* and *absolutely* non-entitous nature of Shadwell's productions (or better, Mac Flecknoe's productions, because one can always dig up a copy of *Psyche* in the rare book room of a decent library) is metaphorical, beyond or beneath exemplification. One might say that Dryden has bitten off less than he can chew, and yet telling us what Shadwell's verse is like is central to the poem's sense of things, to proving its historical thesis, so to speak. This is not just a technical problem in literary criticism, for Shadwell's bad poetry is more than bad poetry; it is the epitome of all that is bad in contemporary experience. Bad poetry one can always relegate to the garbage heap, but Shadwell's bad poetry has to be shown as effectively relegating the collective wisdom of the ages into the garbage heap.

And this is what we are made to understand in Flecknoe's first speech, the extended contemplation of Shadwell's fitness to inherit the crown.

> Heywood and Shirley were but types of thee,
> Thou last great prophet of tautology.
> Even I, a dunce of more renown than they,

Was sent before but to prepare thy way;
And, coarsely clad in Norwich drugget, came
To teach the nations in thy greater name.
My warbling lute, the lute I whilom strung,
When to King John of Portugal I sung,
Was but the prelude to that glorious day,
When thou on Silver Thames didst cut thy way,
With well-tim'd oars before the royal barge,
Swell'd with the pride of thy celestial charge;
And big with hymn, commander of a host,
The like was ne'er in Epsom blankets toss'd.

Like the system of Christian typology to which it constantly alludes, this passage is anticipatory, directed towards a future fulfillment. Heywood and Shirley suggest this fulfillment only distantly ('were but types'); Flecknoe, too, is only a type, but in his greater fame ('of more renown than they') he moves closer to the promised end, and in its description of Flecknoe's musical entertainment to the King of Portugal, the passage, by offering a concrete action to suggest more specifically the nature of the revelation, conveys the sense of still closer approach. In Shadwell's own musical procession down the Thames '*that* glorious day', we seem to reach the very moment of culmination, and we are encouraged to believe that the quality of the revelation is on the verge of being specified. The 'well-tim'd oars before the royal barge', an apparently neutral descriptive bit, effectively keeps us suspended on the verge. The reiterated birth metaphors with their resonant echoes (it was a famous birth, after all, that the prophets had predicted) focus all of our expectations on Shadwell's hymn, the content of his Word, until at last...

At last ellipsis marks, nothing. The predicative Word is never uttered; what Shadwell did or sang that day is lost for eternity. Instead the passage disintegrates into an irrelevant simile describing Shadwell's colleagues – 'a host/The like was ne'er in Epsom blankets toss'd'. And what is more, or what is less, a simile inadequate even as a description of peripheral matters: 'The like was *ne'er* in Epsom blankets toss'd'. All of Dryden's rhetorical ingenuity in the passage has been devoted to encouraging an expectation in order that he might frustrate it. The sense of developing realization has been illusory, a movement towards nothing, a journey nowhere. Going nowhere –

this, of course, is the point. Shadwell is a 'prophet of *tautology*', and Dryden's verse brilliantly gives this name a local habitation. Not that Dryden's verse is itself tautological. The Epsom blankets simile is not really irrelevant or inadequate itself; rather, it conveys Shadwell's irrelevance and inadequacy. Having the effect of preterition or *occupatio*, it conveys information perfectly satisfactorily even while it pretends to be withholding it, and in this case the information conveyed is particularly damning. The blanket-tossing is a device from one of Shadwell's own plays, an example of his own creation. His Word, thus, is uttered after all, and it is a cheap kind of farcical trick, the dramatic equivalent of the cheapest kind of verbal artifice, a pun, an empty name. This is the hymn that is born, far different from Him that was born in Bethlehem, and in this difference the passage becomes much more than literary criticism. Shadwell's static tautology denies the concept of healthy development that is basic to the very typological framework of Christian epic.

At the end of Flecknoe's opening speech it is the classical rather than the Christian heroic tradition which is in the background.

> Sometimes, as prince of thy harmonious band,
> Thou wield'st thy papers in thy threshing hand.
> St. André's feet ne'er kept more equal time,
> Not ev'n the feet of thy own *Psyche's* rhyme;
> Tho' they in number as in sense excel:
> So just, so like tautology, they fell,
> That, pale with envy, Singleton forswore
> The lute and sword, which he in triumph bore,
> And vow'd he ne'er would act Villerius more.

Flecknoe is still, *toujours*, describing Shadwell's musical extravaganza on the Thames. The focus, ever diminishing, is now on Shadwell's rhythm as conductor. The opening couplet furnishes the image; the remaining lines illustrate it with a series of amplifications – St André's dancing which, by the pun on feet, suggests the further analogue of *Psyche*'s meter, the evenness of which in turn may be hinted at by its dramatic effect on Singleton's acting career. Like the Epsom blankets simile, these comparisons are self-pronouncedly inadequate ('ne'er', 'Not ev'n'), but the negativity is not so immediately bathetic, not such a let down here. In part this is because there are several similes, not just one, and because these similes are medially rather than terminally located in the passage as a whole. They are not the last word and thus may be seen as part of an ongoing process, a movement ever closer to some at least potentially meaningful end. The *Psyche* analogue seems to be less of a failure than the St André analogue. Like the appearance of Flecknoe after Heywood and Shirley in the earlier part of the speech, it approaches more nearly to the truth. 'Not ev'n the feet of thy own *Psyche's* rhyme;/Tho' they in number as in sense excel.' In this sense even if the series ultimately fails, even if the last term in the development remains less than fully adequate to figure forth its subject, we are encouraged to expect a kind of success in the process of developmental succession itself. This expectation is based in large part upon the convention of the epic simile after which Dryden conspicuously patterns his passage, in which the breathless piling up of even insufficient comparisons can manage to suggest the incredible grandeur of the original subject: *As even as all that!* we are invited to utter in wonder at Shadwell's sublime regularity.

However, these analogues to Shadwell's directorial cadence are simply not conducive to wonder. The name St André is not inherently bathetic (he was a dancer much admired in Dryden's time), but at the same time it fails to elevate. St André is an exemplar of the elaborate musical machinery of Restoration drama; thus, comparing his performance in the dance to Shadwell's in musical direction is to tell us very little – as if one were to pronounce in all solemnity that William Inge's crispness of dialogue, say, is unsurpassed by Neil Simon's. This is not comparing great to small, but same to same, and indeed, in the next line's mention of *Psyche*, we rest even more resolutely in a static similarity, for *Psyche* is not only Shadwell's own play, but his most musically extravagant and machine-ridden *opus*. (Is his entourage perhaps rehearsing *Psyche* here on the Thames? in which case, then: Inge's dialogue is 'not ev'n' surpassed by Inge's dialogue.) Singleton and Villerius furnish yet more of the same. Singleton is 'a musical performer of some eminence', and Villerius is 'a principal character in Davenant's *Siege of Rhodes*, where a great part of the dialogue is in a sort of lyrical recitative'.[17] Since Davenant's *Siege* is usually credited with starting the vogue for the kind of play that *Psyche* exemplifies (as it is by Dryden himself, I. 150), these names keep us firmly in the niche, or the rut, where we began. And we remain equally securely in the place of this vacuous enterprise, in the Restoration theater, for we are made to see Singleton in a full complement of the elaborate regalia that he is forswearing, making a melodramatic exit appropriate to the quality of the contemporary heroic play. (Compare Bayes's exit at the end of *The Rehearsal*.) The passage's static quality, moreover, is confirmed by its pictorial effects. The motion of Shadwell's 'threshing hand', resonating suggestions earlier in the 'well-tim'd oars' (not a neutral bit after all) and the blanket-tossing, merges with St André's feet and is finally clinched by the heavy tautological fall of *Psyche*'s meter: The image is of standing still in place, marking time.

Once again the passage's inactivity is a reflection of its subject, Shadwell's absolutely tautological nonsense, here localized in his metrical (or directorial) regularity. In purporting to locate degrees of regularity on an ascending scale, the lines are doomed to tautology. 'St. André's feet ne'er kept *more equal* time', we are told; but of course not; they couldn't. Nothing is more equal than equality, for equality is an absolute, comparable only to itself; St André's yielding to Shadwell himself as the next analogue in the succession is, given the subject, inevitable. A succession starting from equality has to go back to its original, has to go nowhere. We readers, thus, have to reject the inference that Dryden had seduced us into drawing about *Psyche*'s feet:

> St. André's feet n'er kept more equal time,
> Not ev'n the feet of thy own *Psyche's* rhyme;
> Tho' they in number as in sense excel.

The last line does not, as we were made to think, make the ridiculous assertion that *Psyche*'s equality excels St André's. It says only that *Psyche* is equally excellent in both number and sense (a perfect unity of content and form, saying nothing in a metrical stasis). If there is a comparative aspect to the line, it is purely self-contained, a tautological comparison; as Shadwell's conducting had to be compared to Shadwell's poetry, so Shadwell's poetry in one aspect can be compared only with

Shadwell's poetry in another aspect – both aspects being the same, excellently equal, as 'like tautology' as is tautology itself. We are dealing here with the real distinguished nothing, *absolute* nonsense; Shadwell is a paragon, a non-pareil. All attempts to compare, to contrast, to exercise imagination or reason or the moral sense, to structure values in a hierarchy – all these are preposterous in the face of Shadwell's unique stupidity. Not only, then, does the form of the epic simile disintegrate; with it the sustaining concept of the heroic tradition, meaningful development, becomes an irrelevant illusion.

The last lines of Flecknoe's speech, however, are truly climactic, more than more of the same in defining the quality of Shadwell's nonsense.

> So just, so like tautology, they fell,
> That, pale with envy, Singleton forswore
> The lute and sword, which he in triumph bore,
> And vow'd he ne'er would act Villerius more.

Most obviously the lines are conclusive because they are Flecknoe's last words, and because they are a triplet at the end of a long sequence of couplets. Moreover, in describing a consequence of Shadwell's regularity ('*so* just . . . / *That* Singleton forswore') instead of yet another analogue to it, they mark a significant syntactic shift, implying a new kind of descriptive accuracy consistent with a conclusion. The analogues were perforce inadequate, but Singleton's precipitous termination of his career appears to be a measure truly appropriate to the occasion, a genuinely precise index to the Shadwellian dullness, at least if one may infer the quality of a cause from its result. As an action, moreover, it apparently objectifies this elusive non-being. And it *is* finally adequate – in its silliness, its melodrama, its sameness and, above all, its essentially negative unproductiveness. Singleton turns 'pale with envy' (conceivably a humors reference here: he suddenly becomes void of blood, the essential to life; such is the force of Shadwell's uncreation), and he quits the stage, an action which suggests the abrupt cessation not only of a rehearsal of *The Siege of Rhodes*, but the termination of Restoration drama itself. Shadwell is so exquisitely dull that his effect is to destroy at once all traditional value and the very enterprise in which his dullness expresses itself. What more appropriate triumph for this annihilating force than self-defeat?

Reading *Mac Flecknoe* is an experience in frustration. Unsuccess is central not only to its subject but to its strategy, its action upon the reader. Like its anti-hero who promises plays and dwindles into farce, the poem delivers relentlessly less than its apparent commitment. If the auspicious beginning leads us to anticipate what Dryden and his contemporaries regarded as the essential prerequisite of epic, a great and unified action, or at least a great ceremonial act, the rest of the poem serves almost exclusively to violate this expectation. *Nothing happens.* What we get instead of action is talk, Flecknoe-orating in a variety of endlessly interruptive ways for over half the poem's length.

What is worse, the paternal discourse increases in its frustrating power as the old sire goes on, the second of his long orations managing to surpass the first in its capacity to disappoint our expectations. The major transition is articulated at the beginning:

> 'Heavens bless my son, from Ireland let him reign
> To far Barbadoes on the western main;
> Of his dominion may no end be known,
> And greater than his father's be his throne;
> Beyond *Love's Kingdom* let him stretch his pen!'
> He paus'd, and all the people cried, 'Amen.'
> Then thus continued he: 'My son, advance
> Still in new impudence, new ignorance.
> Success let others teach, learn thou from me
> Pangs without birth, and fruitless industry.'

The lines before the pause are stylistically similar to Flecknoe's earlier speech; the turn on *Love's Kingdom* tells us that we were wrong in assuming the passage to describe an ever increasing physical magnitude, for the pen can hardly extend to more than inches over the manuscript. Indeed, we are not dealing with space at all, for the substance of the realm is only the nominal emptiness of a pun, and in retrospect the important terms in the preceding lines are revealed to be empty of all the dignity they had seemed to possess, and the apparent development of the passage is revealed to have been an illusory one.[18] These opening lines, then, promise, or threaten, that Flecknoe's new speech will simply repeat the pattern of the old, will consist of yet more (and in this sense 'new') manifestations of what is 'still' (continuously) the same old stupidity: an 'advance/Still in new impudence, new ignorance'. But as the second speech goes on, even these expectations, bad as they are, must be discarded for worse. For the last couplet quoted above turns out to establish a genuinely different pattern, a formula in which father exhorts son to what are, from his point of view, greater triumphs. A few examples will suffice.

> And when false flowers of rhetoric thou wouldst cull,
> Trust nature, do not labor to be dull.
> Thou art my blood, where Jonson has no part:
> What share have we in nature, or in art?

The pattern is repeated constantly; the hortatory 'let', for example, occurs no fewer than ten times in the course of forty-seven lines, and the imperative mood dominates throughout. Even the flurry of questions in the middle of the speech (ll. 176–83), because the questions are rhetorical, suggests the same certainty in Flecknoe's mind. He will, one is made to feel, go on forever, like Chaucer's Monk or, closer, like some bad eighteenth-century poets, in a series of unmodulated (or seemingly unmodulated[19]) couplets that deprive us of even the specious sense of development conveyed by the earlier speech. Flecknoe's discourse settles like cement into a kind of repetitiousness that is, we discover, genuinely new, not just more of the same. ('Still' is seen in retrospect to modify 'new' rather than 'advance'; it develops an adjectival force too, modifying Shadwell.) The impudence and ignorance are indeed worse than anything we were led to expect.

Worse and worse, less and less; the poem astonishes in its ability to sink even lower than the nadir it has apparently reached. In this it defies all logic. Flecknoe's long-windedness, for instance, may frustrate our expectations, but since these are bad expectations (we quickly enough perceive the act of Shadwell's coronation as meaningless, as in fact opposed to all meaning), the principle of the double negative might be invoked as a means to locate real value in the sire's discourse: Flecknoe's long-windedness is *good* in *preventing* a *bad* thing. But in this poem negatives confirm and corroborate rather than qualify each other, and we find ourselves disappointed in being deprived of even devoutly unwished for consummations. Fleck-noe's pauses are experienced according to the same kind of perverse non-logic. As interrupting a discourse that is itself essentially interruptive, the 'silent raptures' at the end of the first long speech might seem to indicate that we are getting somewhere: 'Here stopp'd the good old sire, and wept for joy/In silent raptures of the hopeful boy.' But this is not the sense rendered. Flecknoe's silence would be meaningful only if he had finished talking, only as the consequence of his having made his point. But Flecknoe has no point to make, and we know he will begin again. If there is any positive quality to Flecknoe's silence it is only, coming after Singleton's exit with all its portentous implications, in extending the negative context: a real step backwards. The pause at the beginning of the second speech – ' "Beyond *Love's Kingdom* let him stretch his pen!"/He paus'd, and all the people cried, "Amen." ' – is even more conspicuous, coming in mid-couplet where, despite the apparent allusion to Nehemiah 8:6, the sense is not of the completion of a public ritual, but of an anxious ejaculation intended to fill the empti-ness of an embarrassed silence. Flecknoe, having run out of ideas, now has nothing more to say; or rather, since Flecknoe never had any ideas to begin with, he now *doesn't even have* nothing more to say. We are blocked at every turn, frozen in stasis. The discourse manages to seem at once too long and not long enough; it realizes Dryden's pun on 'no end', for any dis-course that lacks purpose must seem endless. Even at the literal end, when Flecknoe sinks into eternal silence and the mantle finally ascends (rather than descends) upon the son's shoulders, we have the sense of anti-climax, for when the bard drops he is '*yet* declaiming'.

Like Flecknoe's discourse, the poem's imagery develops ac-cording to an incessant diminuendo. Its words are gradually stripped of the value they were thought to possess until only the least desirable of their nuances remain relevant to our under-standing of Shadwell's new world. The poem can be seen as a grimly expansive clarification of one early couplet: 'This aged prince, now flourishing in peace,/And blest with issue of a large increase'. The epic *pax Flecknovana* realizes its true significance in 'some peaceful province in acrostic land', the doped somnolescent unconsciousness of the filial dullness. What flourishes, it turns out, are 'poppies', 'fruitless industry', 'false flowers of rhetoric'. The concept of abundance achieves its fruition in the mob scene when 'the nations meet' ('loads', 'chok'd'). 'Large increase' becomes 'spread in solemn state', 'mountain belly', 'a tun of man in thy large bulk' – meaning, with inexorably increasing clarity, not the blessing of many offspring but the curse of a fat child.

As good words become no good, so neutral words, 'well-tim'd oars' for instance, are revealed in time to be bad, and bad words, 'advance/Still in new impudence, new ignorance', to be worse than we had supposed. Sometimes our awareness develops slowly, as in the delicately articulated process, sustained over fifty lines, by which the epic 'pile' ('lofty mass of buildings', *OED*) of Barbican becomes the particularly un-epic pile of Shadwell's throne. Sometimes the process is much swifter as in the extremely compressed passage just before Flecknoe's second speech.

> The sire then shook the honors of his head,
> And from his brows damps of oblivion shed
> Full on the filial dulness.

The diction and figures here are conspicuously classical and noble. 'Honors' is a favorite trope of Latin poets and of epic poets in both ancient and modern classical times.[20] It is epic in its implications, the value of healthy organic growth through time, a natural order of providence in which aging is productive of dignity, beauty, grace. The Latinate resonance of 'damps of oblivion' is consistent with this, but the phrase denotes rather a meaningless natural process, wasteful rather than productive and stripped of all dignity – sweating not anointing. The de-metaphorizing significance of sweat is thus a de-mythologizing significance as well, but the full joke resides in the complementary 'filial dulness' instead of dull son, another Latinate trope,[21] which re-metaphorizes and re-mythologizes the passage by endowing nullity with substantive existence. From value, then, to valuelessness, to the establishment of a new value system precisely on the concept of valuelessness – an epitome of the poem in under three lines.

The monarch oak passage is an example of a different kind of developmental momentum.

178

Besides, his goodly fabric fills the eye,
And seems design'd for thoughtless majesty;
Thoughtless as monarch oaks that shade the plain,
And, spread in solemn state, supinely reign.

We are invited at first to take the words in their most elevated
and spiritual senses, but these nuances grow increasingly
dubious until 'supinely reign' forces us to a complete redefini-
tion, systematically and absolutely voiding each of the important preceding terms of potential value.[22] Here the momentum
is both slow and sudden, like the passage I glanced at earlier
purporting to describe the magnitude of Shadwell's realm, and
this is perhaps the most characteristic pace of development in
the poem. But whatever the different paces in these passages,
they all have this in common: Our understanding develops
through the fullness, or better, as this poem has it, the *emptiness*
of time. The effect is to confirm *Mac Flecknoe*'s major assumption, historical decay; for it is decay experienced through
language that is impressed upon the reader during the course of
his brief historical engagement with the poem.

I am wrong, then, in saying that nothing happens in *Mac
Flecknoe*; a lot happens, but it happens in the mind of the reader.
The poem is concerned with a negativity – the emptiness of
sense, the absence of value – that is absolute. Essential negativity, in other words, and though this concept may be nonsense
since only being has essence, it is a nonsense that is the central
trope of the poem – the genuine night that admits no ray. The
poem as a whole develops in a series of increasingly perfect
stases (the solecism can't be helped) in order to reach this
quality of absolute zero at the end.

He said: but his last words were scarcely heard;
For Bruce and Longvil had a trap prepar'd,
And down they sent the yet declaiming bard.
Sinking he left his drugget robe behind,
Borne upwards by a subterranean wind.
The mantle fell to the young prophet's part,
With double portion of his father's art.

Flecknoe's saying nothing (at least that we can hear) is only one
of the metaphors of negativity which becomes literally actual-
ized here. The trap door, for instance, is yet another bit of

Shadwellian dramaturgy. But unlike the Epsom blankets allusion, an allusion only suggesting non-productiveness by its form, or Singleton's exit, an action but only peripheral to the poem's subject, the trap door is central and, moreover, fully definitive of essential negativity – a truly climactic anti-climax. Here is straight *down* (the stress in the final line of the triplet is unavoidable), not an ambiguous up-and-down. Here, in the father's destruction by the son's creation is the full significance of the self-defeating 'success' described by the poem. The Christian tradition, earlier denied only implicitly by the undeveloping style of the 'Norwich drugget' passage, is now explicitly annihilated in the action by which the 'drugget robe' arrives upon the 'young prophet's' shoulders. The allusion is to II Kings 2 where, after Elisha's request of Elijah to let 'a double portion of thy Spirit be upon me...there *appeared* a chariot of fire, and parted them both asunder; and Elijah went up by a whirlwind into heaven'. In going down rather than up Flecknoe is obedient to the particular providence of this poem's world which, contrary to the promise of Christian typology, dwindles to its last things in the realms of the lost. Even the scatalogical innuendo with *its* negative implications is concretized in the very action at the end, for the 'subterranean wind' that bears aloft the drugget robe is not the whirlwind of the divine spirit, the ultimate source of all creation, but rather, as the broken pattern of alliteration deftly suggests – '*p*rophet's *p*art...*f*ather's art' – an act of waste. In our developing awareness of the last word's true significance, the poem's meaning is brutally confirmed: Everything has turned to shit.

Mac Flecknoe's historical sense is the poem's most conspicuous feature, and it deserves some further consideration. It provides the given not only for this particular poem but, in suggesting general qualities of sensibility, it describes the conditions within which Dryden's poetic endeavor as a whole was produced. It sheds light, I believe, on the question of the unwritten epic, among others raised by Dryden's criticism.

At first glance, however, the poem's grim view of decay is likely to strike us as an oddity. Dryden's criticism and other poetry furnishes evidence that his views were progressive.[23] 'The world to Bacon does not only owe/Its present knowledge but its future too', Dryden writes to Charleton. The apostrophe to the Royal Society in *Annus Mirabilis* is well enough known, and the optimistic tone of Neander, with at least its implication that poetry can advance to perfection hand in hand with philosophical discovery – this is a fairly constant presence throughout Dryden's criticism. *Mac Flecknoe*, though, isn't unique or even anomalous. Neander's tone is balanced by Crites's, equally pervasive, a nostalgia for lost and last ages, the great epics of antiquity, the transcendent achievements of Shakespearean drama. These views are not incoherent; they oppose but do not contradict each other. A belief in progress or regress is the function of differing perspectives, but one crucial assumption is common to both, namely, a sense of the discontinuity or at least significant changes that separate past and present. 'Movement and change in time', René Wellek writes, was 'the main concept that made literary history possible'.[24] History itself, one might add, and in this sense, *Mac Flecknoe* is built upon the assumptions of a modern historical consciousness.

This makes *Mac Flecknoe* a new thing. To be sure, the development of an historical sense in England is usually located in a much earlier period, in the endeavor of the Tudor humanists to regain the ancient past from the supposed interpositions of decadent scholasticism.[25] For the medieval mind, history was as Augustine described it, the unfolding of a providence whose universal applicability made discriminations between places and times irrelevant, perhaps even misleading. Wellek's main concept, movement and change in time, becomes meaningful only as the result of 'an increasing willingness to see in the concrete and tangible an area of experience susceptible of analysis in terms of its own observable characteristics, without necessary reference to the transcendental factors inherent in the Divine Plan.'[26] Yet, so many years after Burckhardt, we have learned to recognize that the early sixteenth century did not constitute an immediate 'historical revolution'. The new learning was not conceived to be a denial of orthodoxy; quite the reverse, 'Humanism was committed to a holy alliance with Christianity.'[27] The full implications of secularization were, in general, exceedingly slow in being realized, as painstakingly gradual as the development of methods of historical research by Stow, Camden and the others. Bacon himself seems not to be disingenuous (the Jamesian contortion is deliberate, for Bacon defies certainty) in dividing his renderings between faith and philosophy.

Moreover, imaginative literature, typically conservative, showed even greater resistance to new ways of understanding history. Major Renaissance poems, especially epic or quasi-epic poems, remain fundamentally medieval in their historical assumptions. In *The Faerie Queene* and Shakespeare's histories or Roman plays, singularity and diversity of historical experience is consistently ignored or relegated to a pattern that is outside of history. In *Paradise Lost* an historical sense of development is shown over and over to be an illusion, or at best a lower order of truth, the fragmentary view of a process that is whole. Even 'sceptical' Donne, supposedly so responsive to the 'New Philosophy', is no exception.

> Some moneths she hath been dead (but being dead,
> Measures of times are all determined)
> But long shee'ath beene away, long, long...

Critics used to try fixing the meaning of the *Anniversaries* historically, identifying who she (or 'shee') is and specifying just how long 'shee'ath beene away'. But Donne doesn't perceive experience historically. The literal and the specific, the here-and-there or now-and-then, are deliberately conflated to reveal, or intimate, an archetypal pattern whose ceaseless repetition constitutes reality. *Plus ça change, plus c'est la même chose* – this is crucial to the poem's imaginative structure, and a strong qualification, at the very least, to Donne's much-bruited 'Jacobean melancholy', his presumed sense of historical decay.

It is not until the mid-seventeenth century that Fussner sees the 'historical revolution' as completed; it is in the same period that Wellek locates the birth of literary history. And in literary criticism the evidence of the new view is everywhere, in Dryden and his contemporaries: in the ambivalence of the ancients-moderns controversy, an internalized ambivalence dividing individuals as well as separating men; in the reawakened interest in historical relativism as an evaluative consideration, and in cultural relativism as well, for changes in place become as important as changes in era once the focus sharpens to the particular; in the prevalence of translation on recognizably modern principles, respecting the individual proprieties of one's native tongue. These are not wholly new developments by any means, but their intensity and aggregate force is new, indicating a self-conscious assimilation of the new historical consciousness into fully working critical assumptions.

In poetry too the crucial change occurs around mid-century, in Marvell, for example, Dryden's near contemporary, the other 'transitional figure' of the period-course curriculum. *Upon Appleton House* is a signal poetic document, especially when compared with the *Anniversaries* which it superficially resembles in some respects. Though Marvell's poem begins with a secure assertion of the availability of providential design in the affairs of men, as it develops it plunges us ever deeper into the anxiety of historical fact, the chaos of the civil wars, in the face of whose specificity the typological structures of myth, the traditional means of perceiving order, become increasingly irrelevant. The old paradise within becomes a specious dream, no longer accessible or no longer sustainable when confronted with the tangible chaos of armageddon without. Despite the vision of transcendence, the leap of faith associated with the young girl near the end of the poem, Mary Fairfax alive can offer less hope than Elizabeth Drury dead. The poem comes finally to rest in an ironic view of the human condition in which rationality, the ordering capacity of consciousness, no longer constitutes a clear qualitative distinction between man and beast: 'How *Tortoise* like, but not so slow,/These rational *Amphibii* go.'

In this context the historical sense in *Mac Flecknoe* is the culmination of a major transformation of sensibility. It is coterminous with, or an aspect of, the new empiricism; as mind disengages from external reality, so myth disengages from history. And this perhaps helps to explain why 'the right time never came' for Dryden to write his epic. (I indulge myself here in 'pure' speculation; I don't mean to deny the importance of Dryden's own reasons, lack of encouragement and money.) Traditional epic as Dryden conceived it was predicated upon a sense of the continuity of history. For Virgil and Milton, historical experience in all of its manifestations, individual, familial, communal, political and cosmic, is perceived to be unified by reference to a providential design emanating from outside history. An epic, Dryden wrote, cannot be 'tied too severely to the laws of history'. No doubt Milton would have disagreed; no doubt Milton believed that *Paradise Lost* was consistent with historical process.[28] Yet for Dryden, unlike Milton, the laws of history were derived empirically, from distinguishing the differences and discontinuities and particularities manifest in the tangible actuality of this age and ages past. Or again, Dryden (if we may attach more meaning to his words than he himself intended): 'No heroic poem can be writ on the Epicurean principles.'

We might offer a speculative corollary here, that no heroic poem can be written in heroic couplets. The couplet as Dryden and his successors used it may be seen as a particularly appropriate vehicle of expression for the new sensibility. As a closed structure it lends itself naturally to internal balancing. When the balance becomes antithesis, when the parallel syntax is made to contain elements that should not be paralleled, the couplet is especially accommodated to express the ironic awareness of satire ('To reign, and wage immortal war with wit', 'Dost sometimes Counsel take – and sometimes *Tea*'). By means of its discrete syntactic units, the closed couplet tends to discriminate between isolated parts; its rhetoric is of the judgment, the distinguishing faculty, the observing faculty. It roots us in a richly circumstantialized world of social or natural process. Unlike tragedy and epic, the domains of fancy, in which experience is elevated to a metaphysical level, the couplet tends to articulate a comic or a descriptive mode, in which particulars may be specified, but in which the over-arching and containing unity of these particulars remains distant, as removed as Locke's mixed modes from his primary ideas.[29]

In a brilliant recent article describing 'The Augustan Mode in English Poetry', Ralph Cohen has noted the tendency of Augustan poets to use other meters in a way that reminds us of the couplet. 'The couplet, in the Augustan mode, tends to be end-stopped, and it can, perhaps, be interpreted as a completed fragment containing harmonies and contrasts of the known world. The blank verse of the mode with its phrasal balance and emphatic verbs and participles also tends towards end-stopping for the same reason'.[30] In this context it might be pointed out that some of Dryden's blank verse seems to be exploiting the same set of rhetorical possibilities as his couplets. I am thinking of *All for Love*, in particular the famous scene of charged repartee between Antony and Ventidius (I. i. 244–56) which Dryden felt was the best thing in the play. The 'spruce finality' of its echoed last words – 'leave me...love you...leave you...leave me' – creates an ambience that scarcely conveys the Shakespearean scope in *Antony and Cleopatra*, where the environment o'erflows the measure of observable nature. In fact Dryden's self-congratulatory comment in the play's *Preface* makes no claim for having surpassed or even reproduced Shakespeare's scale; only that, by imitating Shakespeare, 'I have excelled *myself*... I prefer the scene...to anything which *I* have written *in this kind*.' (I. 201; my emphases) Dryden's praise for Davenant's 'excellent contrivance' in their cooperative adaptation of *The Tempest* is another example, here in terms of general dramatic structure. Davenant 'designed the counterpart to Shakespeare's plot, namely that of a man who had never seen a woman, that by this means those two characters of innocence and love might the more illustrate and commend each other'. (Watson, I. 135) The two characters 'illustrate and commend each other' like the balanced clauses of a couplet. The encounter between Ferdinand and Miranda, with its implications in Shakespeare of the regenerative power of innocence and grace, becomes the occasion, in effect, for a witty dramatic chiasmus: girl unknown by boy, boy by girl unknown.

Dryden, of course, wasn't unique among writers during his time in sensing the difficulty of writing a contemporary epic. It was already an old debate by the time *Mac Flecknoe* was written, and would continue to be a live issue well into the eighteenth century. The problem in the particular form that was relevant to Dryden is perhaps first clearly stated in English criticism in the Preface to *Gondibert*. (1650) The old masters of the epic, Davenant complains, are no longer as useful as they are supposed to be in furnishing models for contemporary poems; the need is to bring the traditional epic closer to the common concerns of life, the 'easy' and the 'familiar'. There was much in Davenant's program with which Dryden was fundamentally sympathetic. Dryden's insistence upon naturalness as a pragmatic and mimetic goal, both lucidity of style and faithfulness to the actuality of experience, his interest also during the early years in rendering epic in the more available form of drama –

these indicate a similar sort of emphasis in Dryden upon a proximity to the common apprehension.

Yet in *An Essay of Heroic Plays* Dryden vigorously opposes Davenant and his program, insisting upon elevation of fancy and 'those enthusiastic parts of poetry, which compose the most noble parts' of epic writing. By implication *Mac Flecknoe* too opposes Davenant's program: If Shadwell and his new order represent the quality of common life, then bringing the concerns of heroic verse down to its level would be a betrayal rather than a modification of the epic tradition. Many of Dryden's successors chose to follow this path indicated by Davenant or by Marvell – 'While with slow Eyes we these survey/And on each pleasant footstep stay' – though it was *Cooper's Hill* that most clearly suggested the new direction in poetry. 'And now', 'I pass', 'I see', are the articulating phrases of the perhaps dominant mode of early eighteenth-century poetry, the Georgic-descriptive mode, a temporal and spatial journey whose effect and often intention was precisely to locate the muse closer to contemporary actuality. Such poems do not betray so much as ignore the epic tradition, but when their authors feel responsible to it, absurdity results. I am thinking of John Dyer, whose *Fleece* (1757) attempted to generate a heroic poem on the British wool industry. As Dr Johnson put it, 'The meanness naturally adhering, and the irreverence habitually annexed to trade and manufacture, sink him under insuperable oppression'.[31] For Dryden the Renaissance tradition was too immediate a presence to allow for ignoring the demands of the epic; for him to ignore it *would have been* a betrayal, a mockery. This may suggest why 'mock-epic' is completely unsatisfactory as a term for *Mac Flecknoe*. It is Mac Flecknoe who represents a mockery of the epic, but *Mac Flecknoe* mocks him, and in so doing it appeals for its ironic effects precisely to the values of the epic tradition: growth, creativity, order; nature and art. Far more than Etherege or any other casual allusion within the poem to a worthy contemporary, it is the poem itself, in the brilliant lucidity of its wit, that affirms the continuing health and vitality of tradition.

At the same time Dryden was too much of the new sensibility not to realize the need to modify the inheritance of the past. If he opposed Davenant's program, he also recognized the danger on the other extreme, a kind of purist fidelity to the traditionally heroic that would result in sublime indifference to the conditions of contemporary life. *Prince Arthur* (1695), Blackmore's much-flogged dead horse, is an obvious example; Pope's *Brutus* would probably not have been much better. Dryden's own heroic plays furnish examples in their heroes' rant, more loud than great in the true heroic sense. The names themselves of these heroes – Almanzor, Maximin, Aureng-Zebe – suggest their remoteness from the Restoration context, and to pass from one of these plays to the epilogue with its deliberately 'easy' and 'familiar' style, the immediate here-and-now of direct address between actor-author and audience, all of whom share an abundantly particularized though quite un-heroic cultural milieu – this indeed gives one a sudden sense of the exotic irrelevance to contemporary conditions of such elevated posturing. Or again, Dyer's *Fleece*: 'The care of Sheep, the labors of the Loom,/The arts of Trade, I sing.' There is nothing inherently absurd in writing a poem about the wool industry, if only Dyer hadn't deemed it necessary to parade out the traditional heroic formulas. In this sense, it is not the meanness of the subject that betrays the epic form so much as it is the epic form, with its here-indecorous elevation, that betrays the subject. Of course, though, Johnson's way of putting it is right also; opposite extremes of bad poetry tend to resemble one another.

Characteristically, Dryden tried to chart a mediating course in order not only to avoid the dangers he sensed on both extremes, but also to realize the virtues that each extreme, if only pervertedly, could suggest. *Mac Flecknoe* may be seen in the light of Dryden's consistent critical endeavor to find a comprehensive mode in which epic grandeur and naturalness could coexist. It is a various poem, reflecting the variety of Dryden's criticism, responsive to his multifarious awareness. Though there is surprisingly little in his criticism devoted to this kind of poem as such, his description of Boileau's *Lutrin* in the *Discourse Concerning...Satire* is certainly to the point.

He writes it in the French heroic verse, and calls it an heroic poem; his subject is trivial, but his verse is noble. I doubt not but he had Virgil in his eye, for we find many admirable imitations of him, and some parodies;...And, as Virgil in his fourth Georgic, of the Bees, perpetually raises the lowness of his subject, by the loftiness of his words, and ennobles it by comparisons drawn from empires, and from monarchs...we see Boileau pursuing him in the same flights, and scarcely yielding to his master. This, I think, my Lord, to be the most beautiful, and most noble kind of satire. Here is the majesty of the heroic, finely mixed with the venom of the other; and raising the delight which otherwise would be flat and vulgar, by the sublimity of the expression. (II. 107–8)

Dryden's description of Boileau's formal openness ('the majesty of the heroic, *finely mixed with* the venom of *the other*') suggests that he knew exactly what he was doing in *Mac Flecknoe*, for his poem too is an admixture in which incompatible elements, insoluble into synthesis, are held together by the loose structure of irony.

'Heroi-comical', Pope's term for *The Rape of the Lock*, is appropriate for *Mac Flecknoe*. Unlike 'mock-epic', it specifies the heroic as one positive component in a mixed mode. 'Heroi-comical' may serve to suggest also the compound historical nature of Dryden's poetic achievement, at once traditionalist in looking back to the epic, and innovative in reflecting the new literary taste for the immediate, the literally real, the comic. Dryden *invented* the heroi-comical mode in both senses of the word, and the final advantage in using Pope's term to name it is to suggest how fruitful Dryden's invention was in showing a path for his successors, of whom Pope is only the most obvious example, to follow.

CONCLUSION:

DRYDEN'S VARIETY AND CLASSICISM

Absalom and Achitophel is Dryden's greatest poem, and it deserves at least a smile in passing here, especially because its success is in large measure, like *Mac Flecknoe*'s, in its admixture of contemporary and traditional materials. It is firmly rooted in the exclusion crisis, yet its use of the Old Testament and its frequency of Miltonic allusion give the poem a wide-ranging relevance. *What is the poem's center?* is the question on which the continuing critical discussion about *Absalom* is predicated; or, *what kind of poem is it?*[1] Is it a piece of royalist propaganda, prompted by the king himself, or 'like...*Paradise Lost*...an attempt to recreate imaginatively the simultaneity of all history, from the Creation to the Second Coming, as symbolically implicit within Genesis?'[2] It is, simply, neither. For all its Miltonisms, the poem is distinctly un-Miltonic in its priorities; as Guilhamet points out, Dryden exploits the Biblical story for his own political purposes, making the king himself the ultimate source of authority in an Erastian apotheosis of secular power. On the other hand, as the king's apologist Dryden chooses to admit some curious evidence right from the beginning. The poem's opening lines have received lavish praise and ingenious commentary as an example of the virtue that Dryden could make of necessity. The lines do indeed manage to present Charles's promiscuity (which of course had to be confronted) in a way that will later be seen as a reason for supporting him. But Dryden doesn't stop there, as he might have; instead, the next lines, in their description of Absalom's easy indulgence and the Jews' giddiness – the variously imparted vigorous warmth becoming the warm excesses that purg'd by boiling o'er and finally the raging fevers that boil the blood (ll. 8, 37–8, 136) – tell us that David gets the rebellious son and subjects that he deserves, all of them united in a hot-blooded body politic knowing no restraint. No wonder the Jebusites 'rak'd for converts even the court and stews'.

No wonder, also, the surprise so many readers since Johnson have felt at the end of the poem in the face of the sudden *deus ex machina*. We may well by this point be prepared to accept David as the only reasonable alternative, but we know too much to be able to view him in any superhuman capacity. Mrs Ferry writes cogently about the ending: Because, unlike *Paradise Lost*, the poem does not really affirm the myth of the fall as the archetype of reality, it cannot really restore order through a Christ-like figure; David's last speech does not transcend the corruptions and biases of the power struggle, but we accept the king's statement because the poem's speaker offers it as acceptable, and *his* voice we have learned to trust. As the repository of common sense, wit and intelligence, it offers us the only firm basis for understanding. In its ironic poise and honesty, its ability to see all, to create a single framework within which the intricacies of Restoration politics can coexist with Hebrew history and the Roman heroic tradition, the speaker's voice is the true center of the poem. To name the poem, though, to designate its kind, this other issue of critical debate is much harder to resolve. All of the suggested names, epyllion, historical satire, political poem, are inadequate, for the poem refuses, consistently or as a whole, to stay within any of their prescribed areas. (Schilling's 'poem' evades the issue, perhaps wisely.) Yet virtually all of the critics have responded appreciatively to this very variety of the poem, to the way it brilliantly overflows the bounds by which we try to define its success. Paul Ramsey puts it well: 'In almost all ways, the poem does satisfy and does cohere. As occasional, as polemic, as historical, as satirical, as providential, it stands...The poem might have achieved a greater formal unity and coherence if it were a different, and lesser, sort of poem. But it is what it is: imperfect, fascinating, brilliant, profound.'[3]

If the speaker's voice is the center of the poem, then *Absalom* is an accomplishment of style. Or better, styles, for here too we are made to appreciate a variety, ranging from versions of

Miltonic and Virgilian heroic to an easy conversational tone;
from the prophetic declamation of 'O foolish Israel! never
warn'd by ill!' or 'Barzillai, crown'd with honor and with
years...' to the no-nonsense familiarity of 'What shall we
think! Can people give away...?' The poem's adaptations of
epic styles have been warmly appreciated, and deservedly so,
but what makes the poem as a whole work is the 'lower' tone,
the controlling ease with which the speaker directly addresses
us as an audience only slightly less sophisticated than himself,
a deficiency correctable, we are made to believe, if we only
listen to him, only let his reason work. The 'powerful defense, in
his proper person, of the truth', (Ramsey's words) to which
I alluded earlier ('What shall we think!') is the obvious example
of this sort of tone; the passage convinces us that it is the truth
because of this sort of tone. But it is only one among many such
passages, perhaps the most important of which is the brisk
natural history of religion (85 ff.) which lumps all sects of clergy
together in a shared greed and fanaticism that seems to be the
whole cause of the crisis. The passage works by insinuation and
ellipsis, and it would wither under analysis; but like the conversational style of Dryden's prose, an easy flow 'in which it is
not necessary that every point should be deliberated', it convinces us, before we have the time to consider or debate, that
religiosity and blind destructive zeal are coterminous, that
priestcraft and piety really are inherently contradictory.

Sometimes too much consideration or debate, failing to *hear* the
poem as it was intended to be heard, has led critics to confusion
or over-ingenuity. Verrall takes the hemistich on the Jebusites,
'And theirs the native right...' (l. 87) as an assertion of the
unquestionable authority of the Roman Church, but (the possible Virgilian allusion notwithstanding) it is simply an off-hand
recognition of an historical fact, deliberately truncated it seems
to me in order to avoid the complicated issue of apostolic
purity. *We have all seen the hideous consequences when such issues are
debated*, the poem's tone as a whole suggests. King on the other
hand defends 'swallow'd in the mass, unchew'd and crude' later
in the passage (l. 113) against the charge of bad taste (no pun
intended) by arguing, Robertsonianly, that this is one of many
references to gluttony in the poem. The references are there and
significant enough in the poem's overall view, but hardly im-

portant to this particular passage. If the passage works (and I think it does), it is funny in the way some ethnic jokes are funny today. It is written to an audience of moderate Protestants – again, the tone of direct address – which, like any community, finds willful outsiders laughable. Perhaps this is bigotry, but if so it is directed against those who in their religious zeal would, it was felt, convert all to their way or die fighting. Catholics wouldn't laugh, of course, and neither would dissenters at other parts of the poem. *They* wouldn't be convinced by the speaker of the poem, but he isn't talking to them; they aren't part of the communal audience. Bunyan would hear the tone of Mr Worldly-Wiseman in the poem and from his point of view would be right. Dryden would have considered Bunyan uncivilized and a bad artist, and he too from his point of view would have been right.

Absalom and Achitophel is probably the closest Dryden ever came to sustaining an epic note in his original poetry, yet the style which makes *Absalom* such a success Dryden must have mastered primarily in the prologues and epilogues, poems that were written apparently in splendid obliviousness to the demands of 'A HEROIC POEM, truly such'. The prologues and epilogues treat a wide variety of subjects, the play at hand, plays in general, contemporary taste and fashion, contemporary news and politics;[4] and they vary widely in the voices they adopt. Sometimes Dryden speaks frankly *in propria persona*, sometimes in an anonymous public voice, sometimes even in the person of one of the play's characters, as in the famous epilogue to *Tyrannic Love* in which Nell Gwyn, in the part of Valeria, having been killed at the end of the action, detains those who would bear her from the stage: 'Hold, are you mad? you damn'd confounded Dog,/I am to rise, and speak the Epilogue.'[5] Yet amidst these changes in subject and in voice, what remains constant in these poems is their immediacy, the tone of direct address, the conversational tone.

Dryden writes throughout his criticism about the sophisticated wit and refined conversation of gentlemen; the gathering together of an audience of such gentlemen within the walls of the theater created the perfect situation for Dryden to illustrate what he meant. What must have made the situation even more pregnant with possibilities, the refined gentlemen gathered at the theater, if they did not bring their refined lady friends with them, would sometimes seek to establish at the theater itself friendship with less refined ladies. That prostitutes and theaters asked the same fee in recompense for the entertainment they provided gave Dryden the opportunity, with a variety of puns, to combine literary and social criticism, the two subjects which in the broadest senses are the most often treated in the pro-logues and epilogues. As literary criticism, the prologues and epilogues run a course parallel to the essays in many ways. They deplore farce's appeal to the fancy, they rail generally against contemporary taste, and in the late seventies they reveal Dryden's genuine unhappiness with his own dramatic produc-tions. However, the prologues and epilogues are not intended primarily as literary criticism. Even those given over to criti-cism cannot take the time to sustain an argument and tend to limit the number of literary topics considered to the ones that suited the situation of direct address, primarily the diatribe against contemporary taste. These diatribes seem to be sub-ordinated to, or are an aspect of, the social criticism. Looking out from the stage, one might observe Restoration society in all of its gaiety and lewdness: punks, gentry, pimps, fops, gamblers, roaring boys, royalty. If they are not *sui generis*, the genre to which the prologues and epilogues belong is satire; they observe mankind's vices, make them apparent in verse and, perhaps, try to correct them.

'Perhaps', because no exaggerated claims should be made for the power or intention of the prologues and epilogues to stir amendment in their auditors. For all of their declamation and raillery, the genial Horace is more nearly than the righteous Juvenal in the background. Though we remember Dryden's statement of preference for Juvenal's elevated tone in the *Discourse Concerning...Satire*, the prologues and epilogues em-ploy, masterfully, the Horatian *sermo pedestris* as well as feminine rhymes, neither of which Dryden would countenance when deferring to the demands of the high style; thus, complaining of the noisiness of the pit, he singles out the prostitute drumming up business:

> But stay: methinks some Vizard Masque I see,
> Cast out her Lure from the mid Gallery:
> About her all the flutt'ring Sparks are rang'd;

> The Noise continues though the Scene is chang'd:
> Now growling, sputtring, wauling, such a clutter,
> 'Tis just like Puss defendant in a Gutter.[6]

And like Horace, unlike the aloof Juvenal, Dryden participates in the vices of the society he satirizes. Although Dryden once, in The Prologue to *The Assignation*, facetiously compared prologues to church bells, they sound very little like sermons. Although they are delivered from the stage down to the audience, accusatorily as it were, the tone rarely approaches the superiority of indignant innocence. To reverse the Byronic phrase, the typical stance in relation to the pit is 'of them but not among them'. In the Epilogue to Fletcher's *The Pilgrim*, Dryden admits unrepentantly to participation, at least poetically, in the lewdness of the age:

> Perhaps the Parson stretch'd a point too far,
> When with our *Theatres* he wag'd a War.
> He tells you, That this very Moral Age
> Receiv'd the first Infection from the Stage.
> But sure, a banisht Court, with Lewdness fraught,
> The Seeds of open Vice returning brought.
> Thus Lodg'd, (as Vice by great Example thrives)
> It first debauch'd the Daughters and the Wives.
> *London*, a fruitful Soil, yet never bore
> So plentiful a Crop of Horns before.
> The *Poets*, who must live by Courts or starve,
> Were proud, so good a Government to serve;
> And mixing with Buffoons and Pimps profain,
> Tainted the Stage, for some small Snip of Gain.
> For they, like *Harlots* under *Bawds* profest,
> Took all th'ungodly pains, and got the least.
> Thus did the thriving Malady prevail,
> The Court, it's Head, the *Poets* but the Tail.[7]

Though Dryden is rarely so explicit, the prologues and epilogues in general adopt this tone of complicity; the direct address is based on shared assumptions and on similarity in tastes if not equality of taste. This tone is one explanation for the fact that these poems were so immensely popular with the very audiences they appeared to abuse;[8] this tone, and the fact that even to be abused with such wit and intelligence could only be construed as in some way a compliment.

The prologues and epilogues are among the most readable poems in the language. Though filled with topical allusions that seem to require elucidation, they are supremely capable of standing on their own, for their allusions as well as their metaphors, rhythms and ironies, are emphatically functional, subordinated to and confirming the poetic statement.[9] Even more than the conversational style in prose, the conversational style in verse was largely a matter of Dryden's invention, and it was an invention of far-reaching significance. For Dryden himself it furnished countless new possibilities extending beyond the prologues and epilogues themselves. One is, with a slight elevation in dignity, the middle style, arguing in verse, as in *Religio Laici* and certain parts of *Absalom*. Another is irony, heroi-comical or otherwise, generated by the juxtaposition of this new style against the more traditional and more elevated. Dryden at times exploits this possibility in the prologues and epilogues themselves, as in the discrepant effects of Latinity and feminine rhyme of 'Puss defendant in a Gutter'. Beyond Dryden there were new possibilities for Pope. Without Dryden Pope would not so easily have recognized the path from 'The wooden guardian of our privacy/Quick on its axle turn' to 'Shut, shut the door, good John! fatigued, I said,/Tie up the knocker, say I'm sick, I'm dead'. And beyond Pope, Byron.

> Most epic poets plunge '*in medias res*'
>   (Horace makes this the heroic turnpike road),
> And then your hero tells, whene'er you please,
>   What went before – by way of episode,
> While seated after dinner at his ease,
>   Beside his mistress in some soft abode,
> Palace, or garden, paradise, or cavern,
> Which serves the happy couple for a tavern.

But it is not a question merely of Pope and Byron, the conspicuous followers in this tradition. Every poet who followed Dryden had available to him an alternative of style that was not clearly available before, and this alternative had its effect on poetic significances even if it was rejected, because such rejection itself now represented a significant poetic choice. It is difficult to imagine what English poetry would have been like without this alternative.

The conversational and epic styles, the prologues and the

Aeneid, these are the poles of Dryden's creation. Between is the vast middle range I mentioned earlier, occupied by song, satire, verse epistle, heroi-comical poem, elegy, historical poem, *Absalom and Achitophel* (the unnameable). In the face of Dryden's diversity we tend naturally to divide his career into kinds of achievement, but we should not rely too heavily on these divisions. High and low are separable but not rigorously separated aspects of Dryden's poetry, different but contemporary. 'O foolish Israel!' and 'What shall we think!' are only five lines apart; no transition is felt to be necessary any more than between play and prologue or epilogue. The prologues and epilogues are rarely united in any thematic or tonal way to the plays, not fused into an esthetic integrity. Nothing is more distinguishable than the rant of *Tyrannic Love* from the ease of its Epilogue ('Hold, are you mad?...'), yet in actual presentation they were part of the same experience, prologue–play–epilogue, a striking example of Dryden's characteristic ability to allow difference to coexist in his art.

In the same way we should not allow our reductive impulses as literary historians to diminish our sense of Dryden's career as a whole and the large scope that it comprehended. We tend to remember Johnson's last words about Dryden's effect on English poetry, that 'he found it brick, and he left it marble', as if they were a summary-formula for the whole; Johnson's main point, however, is that 'perhaps no nation ever produced a writer that enriched his language with such variety of models'.[10] Though there is obvious usefulness in treating Dryden's 'tuning of our numbers' as a linear development from the contorted metaphysical verse of the Hastings elegy to the easy and assured mastery of *To My Honor'd Kinsman, John Driden*, the multifariousness and richness of a poetic career cannot be reduced to its major effect upon literary history. 'Line of development' is a metaphor, and if we suppose that we can literally fix upon a point in Dryden's career at which metaphysical conceits are at last effectively removed from his sense of poetic possibility, we drastically simplify the complexity of his situation and achievement. As late as 1692 in *Eleonora* Dryden was writing as fully as he ever had in 'the Donne tradition'. Though obviously a more immediate possibility at the beginning, the metaphysical style must have been a constant possibility for Dryden, and his

196

'reforms' of English poetry must have been effected continually, with each poem, with each line that he wrote, the exercise of a choice among a variety of alternatives to which his mind was always open.

Dryden's *variety*: The keynote was suggested first by Samuel Johnson, and it has been echoed by Dryden's most responsive critics to our own time. Dryden is various within particular modes of poetry, as in *Absalom*, various among his many modes of poetry, and various in his non-poetic endeavors as well, as critic and – the phrase in unavoidable – man of his times, intensely responsive to the social, political, religious and intellectual currents of the late seventeenth century. In all of these aspects the variety of Dryden's interests seems to be the consequence of an intelligence singularly reluctant to limit the area of possibility and remarkably open to different ideas. I have tried to suggest in this book that this is a *classical* quality of mind.

Dryden's classicism is not pluralism; his open-mindedness is not an end in itself. There remains always a control at the center, the balance of the golden mean, a gravitational core around which the various values can revolve. Dryden's classicism is, to use one of his own favorite concepts, an ordered variety. It allows for and even insists upon the diversity of old and new, high and low, French and English, metaphysical and Augustan, Virgilian and Ovidian, Juvenalian and Horatian; but notwithstanding, it maintains control,

just as they say the orb of the fixed stars, and those of the planets, though they have motions of their own, are whirled about by the motion of the *Primum Mobile*, in which they are contained.

It is this mixture of freedom and restraint that invites oversimplifying views: on the one hand that Dryden didn't really care about control, that he 'let the rules take care of themselves'; on the other that Dryden's Catholicism, Royalism and Traditionalism were somehow inhibitive, as William Carlos Williams implies in 'A Point for American Criticism': 'Within the tradition lies "perfection," the Sacred Grove, a study of Dryden. Outside is imperfection and formative chaos.' Williams and Saintsbury are wrong in the same way, in seeing order and freedom as contraries, mutually exclusive. Their claims oppose, of course, and in this respect they can never be related without certain tensions. But in Dryden's flexible articulations, the tensions are largely unrealized; opposite becomes different, and different various. What Dryden makes us aware of is how much freedom can thrive within control, how 'formative' control itself can be. This makes 'a study of Dryden' – that is, a responsive attention paid to the sound of his voice in prose and poetry – a richly rewarding experience.

ABBREVIATIONS

ECS	*Eighteenth-century studies*
ELH	[*Journal of English Literary History*]
HLB	*Huntington Library Bulletin*
HLQ	*Huntington Library Quarterly*
JEGP	*Journal of English and Germanic Philology*
MLN	*Modern Languages Notes*
MP	*Modern Philology*
N&Q	*Notes and Queries*
PLL	*Papers on Language and Literature*
PMLA	[*Publications of the Modern Language Association of America*]
PQ	*Philological Quarterly*
RES	*Review of English Studies*
SEL	*Studies in English Literature 1500–1900*
SP	*Studies in Philology*

NOTES

INTRODUCTION

1 (Nashville, 1963). Or comparable, for that matter, to H. James Jensen's *Glossary of John Dryden's Critical Terms* (Minneapolis, 1969).

2 Samuel Johnson, *Lives of the English Poets*, edited by George Birkbeck Hill (3 vols.; New York, 1967), I. p. 410. Johnson's point is that Dryden 'first taught us to determine upon principles the merit of composition', the emphasis on principle, Dryden having substituted rational evaluation for blind appreciation.

3 (Ithaca, 1970).

4 *The Idea of the Humanities* (2 vols.; Chicago, 1967), II. pp. 157–75, p. 164.

5 *Lives, op. cit.*, I. p. 418.

CHAPTER I

1 *Style and Proportion* (Boston, 1967), p. 128.

2 E. B. O. Borgerhoff has demonstrated it as a vital element in all the major French classical theorists in *The Freedom of French Classicism* (Princeton, 1950).

3 See Emerson R. Marks, *Relativist and Absolutist: The Early Neoclassical Debate in England* (New Brunswick, 1955); and Thomas A. Hanzo, *Latitude and Restoration Criticism* (Copenhagen, 1961).

4 For 'paradox', see Irving Ribner, 'Dryden's Shakespearean Criticism and the Neo-classical Paradox', *The Shakespeare Association Bulletin*, XXI (1946), pp. 168–71. For 'dilemma', see Hanzo's chapter on Dryden, *Latitude and Restoration Criticism, op. cit.*, pp. 84–117, especially p. 87 and p. 110. For 'antagonism' and 'collision', see Dean Tolle Mace 'Dryden's Dialogue on Drama', *Journal of the Warburg and Courtauld Institutes*, IV (1962), pp. 87–112, p. 89 and p. 112.

5 On this point see Emerson R. Marks's excellent chapter, 'Ends and Means', in *Relativist and Absolutist, op. cit.*

6 The list is long and impressive of critics, French and English, seventeenth- and eighteenth-century, who insisted that the rules were founded upon the practical experience of pleasure. See Francis Galloway, *Reason, Rule and*

Revolt in English Classicism (New York, 1965; original edition, 1940), pp. 197–200. As for the common recognition of graces beyond the reach of art, see *ibid.*, p. 295.

7 *A History of Criticism and Literary Taste in Europe* (3 vols.; London, 1922), II. p. 389.

8 As it does in George Watson's 'Introduction', I. xiii. There is a venerable tradition of inconsistency-finding among Dryden's commentators dating back to his own day.

9 *Dryden's Criticism* (Ithaca, 1970), pp. 187–230.

10 *JEGP*, LXVIII (1969), pp. 432–40.

11 *MP*, XLIV (1946), pp. 84–96, p. 87 and p. 92.

12 John C. Sherwood compiles a list of such comparisons prior to Dryden's in 'Dryden and the Rules: The Preface to the *Fables*', *JEGP*, LII (1953), pp. 12–26.

13 Such cultural relativism Marks (*Relativist and Absolutist, op. cit.*, especially chapter four) and Hanzo (*Latitude, op. cit.*, especially chapters one and two) have shown to be a major aspect of the latitudinarianism not only of Dryden but of many of his contemporaries as well.

14 John Aden has made this point in 'Dryden and the Imagination: The First Phase', *PMLA*, LXXIV (1959), pp. 28–40, p. 34. Dryden's emphasis on propriety, adopted for the first time in 1677, is maintained in later discussions of wit. See I. 258, 1685 and I. 270, 1685.

15 'Pope on Wit: The *Essay on Criticism*', reprinted in *Eighteenth Century English Literature: Modern Essays in Criticism*, edited by James L. Clifford (New York, 1959), p. 53.

16 He had anticipated exactly this conclusion seven years earlier. Horace's 'Satires...are incomparably beyond Juvenal's, (if to laugh and rally is to be preferred to railing and declaiming)'. (I. 266) *Is to be* functions as subjunctive in the clause and the same doubt is implied here as in the other *if* clauses we have examined. Though the emphasis has changed, there is no inconsistency between these two statements.

17 Compare his objection in the *Dedication of the Examen Poeticum* of the same year to the false critics of the 'present age'. ' 'Tis not with an ultimate intention to pay reverence to the *Manes* of Shakespeare, Fletcher, and Ben Johnson, that they commend their writings, but to throw dirt on the writers of this age.' (II. 4).

18 Dryden almost certainly knew some or all of Jonson's critical prefaces – to *Sejanus* (1605), *Volpone* (1607), *Catiline* (1611), *The Alchemist* (1612) and *The New Inn* (1631). His knowledge of Corneille's *examens* of his plays, which were written for the 1660 edition of his *Oeuvres* is, of course, a certainty. For Dryden's own not very trustworthy comments about his sources for the form, see II. 255 and Watson, I. 133.

19 See I. 116. See also Johnson's *Lives of the English Poets*, edited by George Birkbeck Hill (3 vols.; New York, 1967), I. p. 397.

20 *John Dryden, A Study of His Poetry* (Bloomington, 1960), p. x. Some recent studies of Dryden's prose: J. Soderlind, *Verb Syntax in John Dryden's Prose* (Uppsala, 1951); Janet M. Bately, 'Dryden's Revisions in the *Essay of Dramatic Poesy*', *RES*, XV (1964), pp. 268–82 and 'Dryden and Branded

Words', *N & Q*, ccx (1965), pp. 134–39; D. D. Brown, 'John Tillotson's
Revisions and Dryden's "Talent for English Prose" ', *RES*, xii (1961),
pp. 24–39; Irène Simon, 'Dryden's Revision of the *Essay of Dramatic Poesy*',
RES, xiv (1963), pp. 132–41 and 'Dryden's Prose Style', *Revue des Langues
Vivantes*, xxxi (1965), pp. 506–28.

    Since writing this chapter I have read K. G. Hamilton's splendid essay,
'Dryden and Seventeenth-Century Prose Style', in Earl Miner, editor, *John
Dryden* (Writers and Their Background; London, 1972), pp. 297–324.

21 'Dryden's Prose Style', *op. cit.*, p. 525.

22 *Lives*, *op. cit.*, i. p. 418.

23 *Ibid.*, ii. pp. 242–3. Dryden himself could write fairly effective Johnsonese, as
in his comparison of Plutarch and Seneca (Watson, ii. 11–13). That Dryden
could write Johnsonese at all should caution the reader that my description
of 'Dryden's style' is really a description of only one of Dryden's styles, but
the typical one, as I think.

24 See William Kurtz Wimsatt, Jr, *The Prose Style of Samuel Johnson* (New
Haven, 1963), pp. 15–49.

25 For Johnson's jerkiness, see *ibid.*, pp. 46–7. Wimsatt suggests the internal
structure of the couplet as an antecedent to Johnson's prose style, pp. 124–8.

CHAPTER 2

1 A number of works have contributed towards suggesting or clarifying or
confirming my ideas about Dryden's *Essay* expressed in this chapter. All of
the following seem to me helpful: F. L. Huntley, *On 'Dryden's Essay of
Dramatic Poesy'* (Ann Arbor, 1951); Thomas A. Hanzo, *Latitude and Restoration Criticism* (Copenhagen, 1961), chapter three; Dean Tolle Mace, 'Dryden's Dialogue on Drama', *Journal of the Warburg and Courtauld Institutes*, iv
(1962), pp. 87–112; Mary Thale, 'Dryden's Critical Vocabulary: The
Imitation of Nature', *PLL*, ii (1966), pp. 315–26; and Robert Hume,
Dryden's Criticism (Ithaca, 1970), pp. 188–203.

2 See George R. Noyes, ' "Crites" in Dryden's *Essay of Dramatic Poesy*', *MLN*,
xxxviii (1923), pp. 333–7; Cecil V. Deane, *Dramatic Theory and the Rhymed
Heroic Play* (Oxford, 1931), pp. 102–3; F. L. Huntley, 'On the Persons in
Dryden's *Essay of Dramatic Poesy*', *MLN*, lxiii (1948), pp. 88–95; Charles E.
Ward, *The Life of John Dryden* (Chapel Hill, 1961), p. 61 and pp. 343–4; and
Stanley Archer, 'The Persons in *An Essay of Dramatic Poesy*', *PPL* ii (1966),
pp. 305–14.

3 The relevant documents have been collected by D. D. Arundell in *Dryden and
Howard, 1664–1668* (Cambridge, 1929).

4 Harth's understanding of the *Essay*, though, differs radically from mine. See
Contexts of Dryden's Thought (Chicago, 1968), pp. 34–5. Contrast also Richard
V. LeClercq, 'The Academic Nature of the Whole Discourse of *An Essay of
Dramatic Poesy*', *PLL*, viii (1972), pp. 27–38.

5 See George Williamson, 'The Occasion of *An Essay of Dramatic Poesy*', *MP*,
xliv (1946), pp. 1–9. See (sceptically) Mary Thale, 'The Framework of *An
Essay of Dramatic Poesy*', *PLL*, viii (1972), pp. 362–9.

6 Others have seen Dryden's criticism generally in terms of the *Essay*, though not always with enough awareness of the difficulties inherent in such an attempt. See F. L. Huntley, *The Unity of John Dryden's Dramatic Criticism: The Preface to 'Troilus and Cressida'* (Chicago, 1944) and *On Dryden's 'Essay'*, *op. cit.*, chapter four, especially pp. 70–1; and Hanzo, *Latitude*, *op. cit.*, chapter three.

7 A vast amount of material has intervened between Aristotle's *Poetics* – which (along with Horace's *Ars Poetica*) Crites cites as the sources from which 'the famous rules' have been 'extracted' (I. 38) – and Dryden's *Essay*, but I postpone until the fourth chapter discussing the pressure of critical traditions upon Dryden's formulations.

8 See the Preface to the *Duke of Lerma* in Dryden and Howard, *op. cit.* A. W. Verrall offered the same sort of interpretation in *Lectures on Dryden* (Cambridge, 1914), chapter five, *passim*, especially p. 134.

9 As does, for example, the unambiguous statement in *A Parallel*: ' 'Tis one great end of Poetry to please the mind...The means of this pleasure is by deceit'. (II. 128)

10 Compare, 'Observation is an effect of the judgment'. (I. 138).

11 Compare Dryden's defense of unity of action in the *Preface to Troilus and Cressida* (1679): 'The natural reason of this rule is plain; for two different independent actions distract the attention and concernment of the audience.' (I. 208)

12 See I. 121, II. 37 and II. 81. Note also the criticism of Fletcher whose luxuriant fancy made all his characters sound alike (I. 166 and 172), and of the painter whose portraits all looked like him rather than their originals in nature. (I. 254)

13 'The Dialectical Foundations of Critical Pluralism', in *A Symposium on Formalist Criticism*, edited by William J. Handy (Austin, 1965), pp. 49–50.

14 At certain times a just and at other times a lively imitation are emphasized as pleasurable. For the former emphasis, note I. 121 ('half-satisfied when there is not truth'); I. 234 ('cloys...instead of satisfying'); II. 161 ('Nothing but Nature can give a sincere pleasure.'). For the latter emphasis, note I. 2 ('so many various intrigues, as the labouring audience...may rest satisfied'); and II. 84 ('gives me as much pleasure as I can bear').

15 'Dryden's Critical Vocabulary', *op. cit.*

16 This metaphor seems fairly unambiguously to place the augmentation in the process (imitation) rather than the source (nature) and thus might be construed as a retrospective resolution of the ambiguity in the earlier metaphor. I tend, though, not to be sure of this in view of the consistent ambiguity through Dryden's criticism on this issue. Note his statement, for example, in *A parallel* that poetry and painting 'are not only true imitations of Nature, but of the best Nature, of that which is wrought up to a nobler pitch'. (II. 137)

17 Compare the subordination in Dryden's Neander-like defense of metaphors in *The Author's Apology* (1677): 'The boldest strokes of poetry, when they are managed artfully, are those which most delight the reader.' (I. 183)

18 Perhaps this sheds some light on Dryden's reluctance to insist upon his preference for tragedy to comedy or, more generally, for epic to theater – see *ante.*, pp. 21–2 – lest it be construed as his endorsement of fancy *rather*

than judgment, or his endorsement of heightening *at the expense* of faithful imitation.

19 'Dryden's Dialogue on Drama', *op. cit.*, p. 89.

20 Compare I. 152, I. 222, I. 255, II. 85, II. 149 and II. 201.

21 Note I. 238, II. 148–9 (quoted shortly) and II. 201.

22 *Theory of Prosody in Eighteenth-Century England* (Connecticut College Monograph No. 5; New London, 1954), p. 43.

23 *Purity of Diction in English Verse* (London, 1967), p. 5.

24 'Dramatic Poetry: Dryden's Conversation Piece', *Cambridge Journal*, V (1952), pp. 553–61, p. 553.

25 *Dryden's Criticism, op. cit.*, p. 190. Actually Hume is describing what the *Essay* must be like if one follows Mary Thale; I hope this chapter, which has followed Thale, suggests otherwise.

26 Bohn's article was the only systematic attempt, and some good reasons for its failure are listed by Hume, *ibid.*, pp. 226–8.

27 See John Aden, 'Dryden and the Imagination: The First Phase', *PMLA*, LXXIV (1959), pp. 28–40; and *Dryden's Criticism, op. cit.*, pp. 204–16.

28 On this point, see Hoyt Trowbridge, 'Dryden's *Essay on the Dramatic Poetry of the Last Age*', *PQ*, XXII (1943), pp. 240–50; and John C. Sherwood, 'Precept and Practice in Dryden's Criticism', *JEGP*, LXVIII (1969), pp. 432–40, especially p. 434.

CHAPTER 3

1 'Dryden and the Classics: With a Look at His "Aeneis" ', in Earl Miner, editor, *John Dryden* (Writers and Their Background; London, 1972), pp. 267–96. Frost's notes constitute in effect a comprehensive bibliography of recent work in this area.

2 'The Augustan Mode in English Poetry', *ECS*, I (1967), pp. 3–32, p. 3.

3 Josephine Miles, *Eras and Modes* (Berkeley, 1964), p. viii.

4 See James W. Johnson, *The Formation of English Neo-Classical Thought* (Princeton, 1967), pp. 3–30; Bertrand H. Bronson, 'When was Neoclassicism?' in Howard Anderson and John S. Shea, editors, *Studies in Criticism and Aesthetics, Essays in Honor of Samuel Holt Monk* (Minneapolis, 1967), pp. 13–25; Roland N. Stromberg, 'Lovejoy's "Parallel" Reconsidered', *ECS*, I (1968), pp. 381–95; Louis O. Mink, 'Change and Causality in the History of Ideas', *ECS*, II (1968), pp. 7–25; and Robert Hume, *Dryden's Criticism* (Ithaca, 1970), pp. 150–86.

5 *Nichomachean Ethics*, translated and edited by Martin Ostwald (New York, 1962), 1106ᵃ. All references will be to this edition.

6 *The Greeks* (Chicago, 1951), p. 252. See also C. M. Bowra, *The Greek Experience* (New York, 1957), pp. 34–7.

7 Aristotle's discussion is recapitulated in Aquinas's *Ethics*, II. 8–9. A convenient table of the virtues with their excesses and defects may be found in Millard Pierce Binyon's study, *The Virtues: A Methodological Study in Thomistic Ethics* (Chicago, 1948), p. 27.

8 Ostwald, *op. cit.*, glossary, p. 314.

9 *The Lives of the Noble Grecians and Romans* ('Dryden translation'; Modern Library), p. 1073. All references are to this edition.

10 See 1406ª for a particularly interesting example.

11 *Ars Poetica*, ll. 25 ff. Blakeney translation as modified by Allan H. Gilbert in his edition of *Literary Criticism, Plato to Dryden* (Detroit, 1940).

12 Longinus, *On Great Writing*, translated and edited by G. M. A. Grube (New York, 1957), chapters 3 and 5.

13 *Ibid.*, Introduction, pp. xii–xiii.

14 Ll. 63–74, Françoise Escal's edition of Boileau's *Oeuvres Complètes* (Paris, 1966).

15 Bouhours has a dialogue devoted to *le bel esprit* in his *Entretiens d'Ariste et d'Eugène*. Bouhours, who was a Jesuit priest, composed his *Entretiens* sometime in the 1660s and published them in 1671. There are six dialogues in all, widely ranging in subject matter, of which the three most significant for students of literature, concerning *la langue française*, *le bel esprit* and *le je ne sais quoi*, are conveniently available in René Radouant's edition (Paris, 1920), from which all my quotations are taken.

16 *The Art of Poetry, Written in French by the Sieur de Boileau, Made English*, ll. 75–6. Quoted from George R. Noyes's edition of *The Poems of John Dryden* (Cambridge, 1950).

17 *Critical Essays of the Seventeenth Century*, edited by J. E. Springarn (3 vols.; Oxford, 1908), I. pp. 20–1.

18 See the material gathered by Donald Davie in *Purity of Diction in English Verse* (London, 1967), pp. 205–12.

19 *An Essay on Criticism*, ll. 360–1; *To Augustus*, ll. 268–70.

20 Note his definition of what wit is not in the *Preface to Annus Mirabilis* (I. 14–15) or his descriptions of false wit with particular reference to heroic poetry in his criticisms of Lucan (I. 152) and Tasso (II. 27). The whole of the *Defence of the Epilogue* is in effect such a negative definition.

21 *The Works of John Dryden*, edited by Sir Walter Scott and George Saintsbury (Edinburgh, 1882–93), XVII. p. 41. Compare Neander's urging of the mean in the *Essay*, I. 75.

22 'A Talk on Dante', quoted by Paul Fussell in *op. cit.*, p. 53.

23 'A Change in the Language of Literature', *ECS*, II (1968), pp. 35–44, p. 35.

24 Mazzeo, 'St. Augustine's Rhetoric of Silence: Truth vs. Eloquence and Things vs. Signs', in *Renaissance and Seventeenth-Century Studies* (New York, 1964), pp. 1–28; Robertson, *A Preface to Chaucer* (Princeton, 1962), chapters one and two; Fish, *Self-Consuming Artifacts, The Experience of Seventeenth-Century Literature* (Berkeley, 1972), chapter one.

25 Edited and translated by John Jay Parry (New York, 1941), p. 142.

26 *Summa Theologica*, I. ii. q. 18, a. 6, Modern Library edition, edited by Anton C. Pegis (New York, 1948), p. 530.

27 Hamilton, *Plutarch's Alexander, A Commentary* (Oxford, 1969), p. xxxviii.

28 This is far different in tone and texture from what I prefer to call (following Pope) the 'heroi-comical' mode in the Restoration and eighteenth century. (see p. 186).

29 See J. C. Kamerbeek, *The Plays of Sophocles: Commentaries* (Leiden, 1952), Part II. p. 32.

30 Quoted in the Variorum *Hamlet*, edited by H. H. Furness (two vols.; New York, 1963), I. p. 440.

31 See R. H. Barrow, *Plutarch and His Times* (London, 1967), p. 57; and (for a very sensible discussion) C. P. Jones, *Plutarch and Rome* (Oxford, 1971), chapter xi.

32 *Shakespeare's Tragic Frontier* (Berkeley, 1963), p. 217. Later Farnham quotations are from p. 208 and p. 211. See also (though with some scepticism) Roy Battenhouse's chapter, 'The Reshaped Meaning of Coriolanus', in *Shakespearean Tragedy, Its Art and Its Christian Premises* (Bloomington, 1969).

33 Schiller is quoted by Auerbach in *Mimesis* (Garden City, Anchor edition), p. 3.

34 Barrow, *Plutarch, op. cit.*, p. 53.

35 This kind of comparison is not limited to Dryden and Plutarch. Rapin's comparisons work the same way, and we might want to call this a classical technique. Note, in his comparison of Demosthenes with Cicero, Rapin's deliberate reluctance 'in deciding, to which the Precedence is to be given'. (I. p. 4) Note Rapin's cultural relativism in attributing Cicero's 'great Advantages' to his 'living in a more cultivated age', with the result that 'we cannot from hence Rationally infer that he deserv'd to be Prefer'd before' Demosthenes. (I. p. 54) Note especially Rapin's defense of variety and multiplicity of tastes in his conclusion: 'For every Perfection may have in its kind, different Degrees and be of a large Extent'. (I. p. 89) It is not surprising that Rapin names Plutarch as his model in the prefatory 'Design of the Work'. (I. b4) Rapin's work first appeared in France in 1671 and was translated by Basil Kennet and included in *The Whole Critical Works of Monsieur Rapin* (2 vols.; London, 1705). All my quotations are taken from the second edition, 1716.

36 R. R. Bolgar, *The Classical Heritage and Its Beneficiaries* (Cambridge, 1963).

37 The sense of Samuel Johnson's definition: 'An author of the first rank: usually taken for ancient authors'. Quoted by J. W. Johnson, *The Formation, op. cit.*, p. 11; and see J. W. Johnson's fifth chapter, *passim*.

We may speculate as to the reasons for such a broad-minded view in the late seventeenth and early eighteenth centuries; it may be related among other things to a tendency away from religiosity, a reaction to the Civil Wars, to the developing empiricism; and some of these will be my concern in the fifth chapter of this book. But whatever the reasons, it might be argued that this view itself, in its tolerance, the ample room it allows for classical and Christian views to exist in harmony, suggests the kind of flexibility and responsiveness to variety by which I have tried to characterize a classical response to experience.

38 *Eras and Modes, op. cit.*, pp. 146–7.

39 *Ibid.*, p. 47.

CHAPTER 4

1 Quoted by A. F. B. Clark in *Boileau and the French Classical Critics in England (1660–1830)* (Paris, 1925), p. 242, from the anonymous poem, *The Hind and the Panther Transvers'd*. That surly contemporary of Dryden, Gerard Langbaine, put forward the idea that Dryden borrowed from others because

he was incapable of original thought in *An Account of the English Dramatic Poets* (Oxford, 1691), p. 148. F. L. Huntley remarks that, 'Accusations of plagiarism are so rife in Drydeniana that they must be looked upon with... skepticism.' *On Dryden's 'Essay of Dramatic Poesy'* (Ann Arbor, 1951), p. 3.

2 'The Rise of English Classicism: Study in Methodology', *Comparative Literature*, II (1950), pp. 253–68, p. 267.

3 *La Pratique du Théâtre*, Edited by Pierre Martino (Paris, 1927).

4 The major documents have been collected by Armand Gasté, *La Querelle du Cid, Pièces et Pamphlets* (Paris, 1898).

5 See H. T. Barnwell's edition of Corneille's *Writings on the Theatre* (Oxford, 1965), p. 80.

6 See René Bray, *La Formation de la Doctrine Classique en France* (Paris, 1963), p. 207 and p. 257; Humphrey House, *Aristotle's Poetics* (London, 1956), p. 66. It was common knowledge for Corneille and Dryden as well. Corneille comments about the unity of place, 'Je n'en trouve aucun précepte ni dans Aristote ni dans Horace.' *Trois Discours sur le Poème Dramatique* (*Texte de 1660*), edited by Louis Forestier (Paris, 1963). All the Corneille references will be to this edition. Dryden quotes this comment in the *Essay*, I. 48.

7 Bray, *La Formation, op. cit.*, p. 227.

8 *Ibid.*, p. 242. See also Joel Elias Spingarn, *A History of Literary Criticism in the Renaissance* (New York, 1963), p. 62.

9 Dryden translates this and adds, 'That is not for every mile a verse'. (I. 48) Corneille might well have conceived this last barb, but he would never have uttered it.

10 *La Pratique, op. cit.*, p. 123. See also Barnwell's translation of Castelvetro on this point, *op. cit.*, p. 239. As Dryden puts it, 'The time of the feigned action ...should be proportioned as near as can be to the duration of that time in which it is represented.' (I. 39) Dryden, *nota bene*, adopts the notion of proportion rather than equality.

11 D'Aubignac had taken this hard line. See Bray's paraphrase, *La Formation, op. cit.*, p. 283. As Dryden says, 'The stage...being but one and the same place, it is unnatural to conceive it many.' (I. 40) But this, as we remember, is not the only perspective the *Essay* offers on this issue.

12 *Writings, op. cit.*, p. 240.

13 J. Schérer, *La Dramaturgie Classique en France* (Paris, 1950), p. 86.

14 *Préface de l'Adonis* (1623), quoted by Barnwell, *Writings, op. cit.*, pp. xvi–xvii.

15 See Bray, *La Formation, op. cit.*, p. 207.

16 There is a discussion of what Corneille intended by 'le beau sujet' in *Les Conceptions dramatiques de Corneille*, by Marie-Odile Sweetser (Paris, 1962), pp. 114 and ff.

17 Barnwell, *Writings, op. cit.*, p. xviii.

18 Corneille himself seems to recognize that his disjunction between these concepts (*le vraisemblable* ou *le nécessaire*) is not consistent with the *Poetics* where the terms are generally used as synonyms. See especially 1451^a of the *Poetics* and House's discussion under 'Probability and Necessity', *Aristotle's Poetics, op. cit.*, pp. 58–62.

19 See Moore's discussion in *French Classical Literature* (Oxford, 1961), pp. 63–5.

20 *Writings, op. cit.*, p. xxvii.

21 *La Formation, op. cit.*, p. 282 (my emphasis).
22 'Dryden, Corneille, and the *Essay of Dramatic Poesy*', *RES*, VI (1955), pp. 147–56, p. 147. The following works are also useful: Pierre Legouis, 'Corneille and Dryden as Dramatic Critics', *Seventeenth Century Studies Presented to Sir Herbert Grierson* (Oxford, 1938), pp. 269–91; Huntley, *On Dryden's 'Essay,' op. cit.* (including references to other studies); Phyllis Hartnoll, 'Corneille in England', *Theatre Research*, I (1958), pp. 14–16; and (the best, I think) R. V. Le Clercq, 'Corneille and *An Essay of Dramatic Poesy*', *Comparative Literature*, XXII (1970), pp. 319–27.
23 *Boileau...in England, op. cit.*, p. 242.
24 *La Pratique, op. cit.*, p. 72. The concept is discussed by Bray, *La Formation, op. cit.*, pp. 224–30.
25 For Atkins, see R. S. Crane's devastating footnote in *The Idea of the Humanities* (2 vols.; Chicago, 1967), II. p. 162, which shows that Rapin anticipated practically all the liberating assumptions of English critics. For healthy correctives to Clark, see F. L. Huntley, 'Dryden's Discovery of Boileau', *MP*, LXIV (1947), pp. 112–17; and John Aden, 'Dryden and Boileau: The Question of Critical Influence', *SP*, I (1953), pp. 490–509.
26 James Sutherland, *English Literature of the Late Seventeenth Century* (Oxford, 1969), p. 397 (my emphasis).
27 *Dryden's Criticism* (Ithaca, 1970), p. 159.

CHAPTER 5

1 The following is a selective list, in roughly chronological order of original publication, though specifying conveniently available modern reprints where appropriate: Morris W. Croll, *Style, Rhetoric and Rhythm*, edited by J. Max Patrick, *et al.* (Princeton, 1966); T. S. Eliot, 'Metaphysical Poetry', reprinted in the various editions of *Selected Essays;* R. F. Jones, *et al.*, *The Seventeenth Century: Studies in the History of English Thought and Literature from Bacon to Pope* (Stanford, 1951); George Williamson, 'The Restoration Revolt Against Enthusiasm', *SP*, XXX (1933), pp. 571–603; Basil Willey, *The Seventeenth Century Background* (Garden City, 1953); Donald F. Bond, ' "Distrust" of Imagination in English Neo-Classicism', *PQ*, XIV (1935), pp. 54–69, and 'The Neo-Classical Psychology of the Imagination', *ELH*, IV (1937), pp. 245–64; R. L. Sharp, *From Donne to Dryden* (Chapel Hill, 1940); George Williamson, *The Senecan Amble* (Chicago, 1951); G. Walton, *Metaphysical to Augustan* (London, 1955); Frank Kermode, 'Dissociation of Sensibility', *Kenyon Review*, XIX (1957), pp. 169–94; Walter J. Ong, *Ramus, Method and the Decay of Dialogue* (Cambridge, Mass., 1958); P. Cruttwell, *The Shakespearean Moment* (New York, 1960); Ernest Tuveson, *The Imagination as a Means of Grace* (Berkeley, 1960); K. G. Hamilton, *The Two Harmonies* (Oxford, 1963); William Youngren, 'Generality, Science and Poetic Language in the Restoration', *ELH*, XXXV (1968), pp. 158–87.
2 I do not think that I misrepresent Addison's position, but for a more sympathetic view of Addison on his own terms, the reader should consult

Tuveson's classic study, *op. cit.*, especially chapter five. My conclusions often differ from his, but they are the result of my different focus and are not intended in any way to contradict his.

3 See Aristotle, *Rhetoric*, 1405[a]; Cicero, *De Oratore*, xxx, xl. 162; the *Rhetorica ad Herennium*, IV. xxxiv. 45. Note Puttenham's insistence on the poet's need for 'measure and just proportion' in his use of the 'colours' in *The Arte of English Poesie*, edited by Gladys Doidge Willcock and Alice Walker (Cambridge, 1936), p. 138. (All subsequent references to Puttenham are to this edition.) See also Tuve's *Elizabethan and Metaphysical Imagery*, (Chicago, 1947), especially chapter ix.

4 *Rhetorica ad Herennium* in Harry Caplan's translation (London, 1934), IV. xxxii. 43.

5 The translation is Fairclough's in the Loeb Classical Library edition.

6 The transference is, if we want a name for it, closest to 'anthimeria, the substitution of one part of speech for another', discussed by Sister Miriam Joseph in *Shakespeare's Use of the Arts of Language* (New York, 1947), p. 62. All my examples are taken from Dryden's three major illustrated discussions of figurative language, which are distributed throughout the range of his criticism: one in the *Essay* (1665, I. 52–3); another in *The Author's Apology* (1677, I. 184–8); and one in *A Parallel of Poetry and Painting* (1695, II. 150–3). Seventeen figurative passages are quoted, of which four are praised explicitly for their softness. Of the remaining thirteen that are praised for their proper boldness *per se*, nine are characterized by the devices described above.

  The sources of the figures offer passing statistical confirmation of a fact that has long been recognized, Dryden's reliance on Latin poetry in general and Virgil in particular as models. Only five of the seventeen examples are drawn from English poetry, one from Dryden and two each from Cowley and Cleveland. Eight of the remaining twelve are taken from Virgil, with two from Ovid and one each from Horace and Statius. Neither device, of course, is exclusively 'Latinate', but the grammatical shift of anthimeria is an especially likely potentiality in an inflected language – as Puttenham notes (with regard to the related grammatical scheme of 'Enallage, or the Figure of exchange'), 'more observable to the Greeks and Latines...for the multiplicitie of their Grammatic accidents'. (p. 171)

7 *Purity of Diction in English Verse* (London, 1967), pp. 35–6 and p. 38.

8 Three aspects, of course, for Dryden talks of the qualities of the poet's soul that produce this kind of discourse. But this is not much elsewhere his concern, and it may be here simply because it was part of Longinus's definition.

9 See Aristotle, *Rhetoric*, 1405[b] and *Poetics*, 1458[a]. My interpretations of Renaissance attitudes towards metaphor in the following pages are heavily indebted to Rosemond Tuve's study, *op. cit.*

10 *De Oratore*, translated by H. Rackham (London, 1960), III. xl. 160.

11 See Cicero, *De Oratore*, III. xxxviii. 155; and Quintilian, *Institutio Oratoria*, VIII. vi. 5.

12 Edited by Hoyt H. Hudson (Princeton, 1935), p. 29. All further references will be to this edition. Compare Puttenham on catachresis, in which 'for lacke of naturall and proper terme or worde we take another, neither

naturall nor proper and do untruly applie it to the thing which we would seeme to expresse'. (p. 180).

13 *An Apology for Poetry*, edited by Geoffrey Shephard (London, 1965), p. 100. All further references will be to this edition.

14 Sidney's nearly romantic position seems to be unique in this period. See the material gathered by William Rossky, 'Imagination in the English Renaissance: Psychology and Poetic', *Studies in the Renaissance*, V (1958), pp. 49–73; and Donald M. Friedman, 'Wyatt and the Ambiguities of Fancy', *JEGP*, LXVII (1968), pp. 32–48.

15 Both Sidney and Puttenham emphasize the inventive rather than representational skills of the poet. See the *Apology*, p. 102 ('the meaner sort of painters...') and the *Arte*, p. 307 ('not as the painter to counterfaite the natural...'). See also Chapman's rejection of the simple ability 'onely to make knowne who it represents', quoted by Tuve, *op. cit.*, p. 31.

16 *The Garden of Eloquence, Containing the Most Excellent Ornaments*, augmented (London, 1593), p. 27.

17 *Of the Dignity and Advancement of Learning*, VI. iii; *The Works of Francis Bacon*, edited by Spedding, *et al.* (Boston, 1864), Vol. IX, pp. 132–3.

18 Wilbur S. Howell in *Logic and Rhetoric in England, 1500–1700* (New York, 1961) shows how common it was for Ramists and Ciceronians to overlap. Most modern scholarship has admitted the difficulty of drawing too sharp distinctions between any of these styles. See the excellent summary by John M. Wallace in *Style, Rhetoric and Rhythm, op. cit.*, pp. 45–50.

19 I am agreeing here with Fish's epilogue in *Self Consuming Artifacts* (Berkeley, 1972), that the dominance of 'the plain style' in the late seventeenth century is most usefully explained as the result of 'an epistemological shift that cuts across party lines'. (p. 380).

20 Part I. Chapter i; *The English Works of Thomas Hobbes*, edited by Sir William Molesworth (London, 1839; reprinted 1966), Vol. III. p. 1. Page references to this edition will henceforth be interpolated parenthetically into the text along with Part and Chapter numerals, the volume specified only when other than Vol. III.

21 I have taken the liberty of repunctuating this crucial sentence. The rhetorical punctuation in Molesworth can be misleading at first: 'All...qualities, called *sensible*, are in the object, that causeth them, but...'

22 *An Essay Concerning Human Understanding* (2 vols.; London, 1968; Everyman edition), III. x. 15. All references are to this edition.

23 I have been helped greatly in the following discussion by the essays of Jackson, Barnes and Bennett reprinted in *Locke and Berkeley, A Collection of Critical Essays*, edited by C. B. Martin and D. M. Armstrong (Garden City, 1968), pp. 53–125; by John W. Yolton, *John Locke and the Way of Ideas* (Oxford, 1956); and by James Gibson, *Locke's Theory of Knowledge* (Cambridge, 1960).

24 Note the 'mist before people's eyes' in III. x. 6 and the 'mists' of words 'employed to darken truth' in III. x. 13. See also the famous 'closet simile' (II. xi. 17) and consult Tuveson, *The Imagination as a Means of Grace, op. cit.*, p. 21.

25 Nos. 411–21. All quotations are taken from Donald Bond's four-volume

edition of *The Spectator* (Oxford, 1965). Unless otherwise indicated, page references are to the third volume and will subsequently be interpolated parenthetically into the text.

26 In the following discussion I substantially follow, Robert L. Morris, 'Addison's *Mixt Wit*', *MLN*, LVII (1942), pp. 666–8.

27 Note the relative values of 'understanding' and 'imagination' in Addison; this represents a complete reversal from Renaissance usages. But of course, the concept of the real (and therefore of the true, trustworthy, valuable) has been changed radically.

28 These lines occur in the manuscript only of *Spectator* No. 417. They are quoted by Bond in his notes, pp. 563–4.

29 Father Walter J. Ong notes a connection between Lockean psychology and the disappearance of these traditional critical terms in 'Psyche and the Geometers', *MP*, LXIX (1951), pp. 16–27, p. 22.

30 While the word can have the usual modern meaning of 'natural scene' in the period (Addison uses it in this sense in the long quotation on page 138), Addison's context here makes it clear that he means 'landscape painting', which was the usual contemporary meaning according to the *OED*.

31 This famous reference to the *camera obscura* experiment, 'very common in Opticks', should remind us of the contemporary context of Newtonian ideas, the influence of which upon Addison cooperates with and confirms that of Locke. See Marjorie Hope Nicolson, *Newton Demands the Muse* (Princeton, 1946).

32 *History of the Royal Society*, edited by Jackson I. Cope and Harold Whitmore Jones (St Louis, 1959), p. 26.

33 Hobbes makes the same distinction in two other places, *Elements of Philosophy* (IV. xxv. 8) and *Leviathan* (I. viii). See Molesworth, Vol. I. p. 399 and Vol. III. p. 57. W. Lee Ustick and Hoyt H. Hudson cite passages in Boyle's *Occasional Reflections* (1665) and Temple's *Of Poetry* (1690) in 'Wit, "Mixt Wit", and the Bee in Amber', *HLB*, VIII (1935), pp. 103–30, pp. 111–12 and pp. 114–15. George Williamson cites passages from Henry More's *Enthusiasmus Triumphatus* (1656) and Parker's *A Free and Impartial Censure of the Platonick Philosophy* (1666) in 'The Restoration Revolt', *op. cit.*, p. 588 and pp. 592–3. The distinction that Locke makes in the *Essay* (II. xi. 2) is quoted by Addison at the beginning of *Spectator* No. 62. Pope can assume his readers to have assimilated this distinction by the time he writes *An Essay on Criticism*, ll. 80–7.

34 Quoted by Williamson in 'The Restoration Revolt', *op. cit.*, pp. 586–7.

35 See R. S. Crane's review of one of Jones's essays in *PQ*, X (1931) pp. 185–6, and Youngren's 'Generality', *op. cit.*, pp. 160–3.

36 *The Poems of John Dryden*, edited by James Kinsley (4 vols.; Oxford, 1958), I. 311.

37 It was Hobbes's endeavor also. The passage from Hobbes distinguishing between fancy and judgment which I quoted only in part continues in viewing both these faculties as combining cooperatively to define 'that *quick ranging of mind*' which is the contrary to dullness. On this point, see Clarence DeWitt Thorpe, *The Aesthetic Theory of Thomas Hobbes* (Ann Arbor, 1940). Pope attempted to make the same kind of suggestion of cooperative combination; see my discussion above, pp. 26–7.

38 Once we start thinking in practical terms, the argument is an example of the nonsense Dryden is driven into in his efforts to justify an untenable position. Is it really true, as Dryden claims, that if Act I is set in one room, Act II is more plausible if it is set in the next room than if it is set in a room in another house? If Act I is set in London, would it be twice as easy for us to accept that Act II is set in New York as for us to accept that it is set in Los Angeles?

39 See Robert Hoopes, *Right Reason in the English Renaissance* (Cambridge, 1962). In 'Psyche and the Geometers', *op. cit.*, Father Ong notes the limitation of reason in the eighteenth century to Locke's 'primary sensibles', commenting that, 'In this milieu, the much commended "reason" tended to be an intellect manqué – circumscribed...by a mathematic horizon.' (p. 27).

40 Thorpe emphasizes 'the psychological approach' in Hobbes, *Aesthetic Theory*, *op. cit.*

41 With Dryden's discussion of the wheel-of-fortune figure, compare Goldsmith's handling of hard metaphors in *Hamlet* in 'On the Use of Metaphors', reprinted in *Hamlet, Enter Critic*, edited by Claire Sacks and Edgar Whan (New York, 1960). As for Johnson's narrower limits, his criticism of Gray for adapting a figure from Dryden ('Gray drove it a little more beyond common apprehension') might be cited, but my point cannot be easily documented by means of specific examples. See *Lives of the English Poets*, edited by George Birkbeck Hill (3 vols.; New York, 1967), III. p. 435.

42 See Howell, *Logic and Rhetoric, op. cit.*, pp. 247–81 and pp. 318–41.

43 'Dramatic Poetry: Dryden's Conversation Piece', *Cambridge Journal*, V (1952), pp. 553–61, p. 561.

CHAPTER 6

1 See *The Life of John Dryden* by Charles E. Ward (Chapel Hill, 1961), chapter five.

2 D. W. Jefferson, 'The Significance of Dryden's Heroic Plays', *Proceedings of the Leeds Philosophical and Literary Society*, V (1940), pp. 125–39, and 'Aspects of Dryden's Imagery', *Essays in Criticism*, IV (1954), pp. 20–41; Bruce King, *Dryden's Major Plays* (Edinburgh, 1966).

3 See Cloris's parody in *The Rehearsal*, II. iii of Almanzor's rhetoric in I *Conquest of Granada*, V. iii. Dryden's own good-natured jest at his own expense may be found on I. 224.

4 *The Prologues and Epilogues of John Dryden*, edited by William Bradford Gardiner (New York, 1951), p. 68.

5 Especially in the *Preface to Ovid's Epistles* (1680), *Preface to the Sylvae* (1685), *Dedication of the Examen Poeticum* (1693), *The Life of Lucian* (c. 1696), *Dedication of the Aeneis* (1697) and *Preface to the Fables* (1700).

6 H. T. Swedenberg, Jr, 'Dryden's Obsessive Concern with the Heroic', *Essays in English Literature of the Classical Period Presented to Dougald MacMillan*, edited by Daniel W. Patterson and Albrecht B. Strauss, *SP*, extra series, no. 4 (1967), pp. 12–26.

7 Besides Swedenberg see Ker again in *Form and Style in Poetry* (London, 1928),

pp. 103–4; Reuben Brower, 'Dryden's Epic Manner and Virgil', *PMLA*, LV (1940), pp. 119–38; and Mary Thale, 'Dryden's Unwritten Epic', *PPL*, V (1969), pp. 423–33.

8 Unless otherwise indicated, all quotations of Dryden's poetry are taken from George R. Noyes's edition of *The Poetical Works of John Dryden* (Cambridge, Mass., 1950; original edition, 1909). In discussing the poem, I have drawn freely upon Noyes's notes as well as upon James Kinsley's in his edition of *The Poems of John Dryden* (4 vols.; Oxford, 1958), and on the following: Brower, 'Dryden's Epic Manner', *op. cit.*; A. L. Korn, '*Mac Flecknoe* and Cowley's *Davideis*', *HLQ*, XIV (1951), pp. 99–127; and Michael Wilding, 'Allusion and Innuendo in *Mac Flecknoe*', *Essays in Criticism*, XIX (1969), pp. 355–70. The following are also worth noting (though I didn't get to them until after I'd written this chapter): Jerome J. Donnelly, 'Movement and Meaning in Dryden's *Mac Flecknoe*', *Texas Studies in Language and Literature*, XII (1970), pp. 569–82; Robert F. Willson, Jr, 'The Fecal Vision in *Mac Flecknoe*', *Satire Newsletter*, VIII (1970), pp. 1–4; and John R. Clark, 'Dryden's "Mac Flecknoe", 48', *Explicator*, XXIX (1971), item 56.

9 *The Poems of Abraham Cowley*, edited by A. R. Waller (Cambridge, 1905), p. 12.

10 Noyes prints the passages from Waller's poem, 'Of the Danger of His Majesty Escaped in the Road at Saint Andrews', that are explicitly parodied in ll. 38–46 of *Mac Flecknoe*.

11 *Davideis*, 1; Cowley's *Poems*, *op. cit.*, p. 258. The Nursery passage as a whole is patterned on Cowley's description of hell earlier in Book 1 (*ibid.*, p. 244), and this is not without significance.

12 *Gondibert*, V. 36. The quotation is taken from a reissue of the 1673 edition of Davenant's *Works* by Benjamin Blom (New York, 1968), p. 112.

13 To Korn's list of such poems in '*Mac Flecknoe*'. *op. cit.*, one might add the following, in whole or part: Jonson's 'To Penshurst', Waller's 'Upon Her Majesty's New Buildings at Somerset House', Carew's 'To Saxham' and 'To My Friend G. N. from Wrest', Marvell's *Upon Appleton House* and Pope's 'Epistle to Bathurst'.

14 Anyone offended at my ignoring Sedley (l. 166) is welcome to build up whatever case he might wish on this tenuous basis.

15 The self-centered quality was implied earlier in the poem in the suggestion that Shadwell was conducting his own work (I discuss this on p. 172 above) and later confirmed in 'Set thy own songs, and sing them to thy lute'. This last line, in conjunction with 'There thou may'st wings display and altars raise', is seen by F. E. Hutchinson as proof that Dryden is attacking Herbert: 'the reference to Herbert is...certain', *The Works of George Herbert* (Oxford, 1964), p. xlv. Wings and altars, however, were common to the *type* of poetry that Herbert wrote; thus Hobbes's disparagement of the generic 'he that contrived Verses into the formes of an Organ, a Hatchet, an Egg, an Altar, and a paire of Wings' in his 'Answer to Davenant', Spingarn's edition of *Critical Essays of the Seventeenth Century* (3 vols.; Oxford, 1908), II. 55. The setting and singing *may* point specifically to Herbert, with his musical interests, but it is the idea of self-absorption which makes the line part of a consistent pattern of meaning in the poem and not just an isolated pot shot.

16 *The Art of Sinking in Poetry*, edited by Edna Leake Steeves (New York, 1968; original edition, 1952), Chapter XI, p. 57, p. 58 and p. 59.

17 Noyes's notes, *op. cit.*, p. 968, quoting Scott.

18 'Ireland' is thus revealed to be less a place than a quality of mind, or rather mindlessness, barbarity, and to reign from Ireland to the Barbadoes is simply to extend Shadwell's soporific ruin from one bastion of non-civilization to another. 'No end' denotes purposelessness and long-windedness rather than the physical or temporal boundaries of the realm, and the son's throne is 'greater than his father's' only in its refinement upon the paternal vacuity.

19 This is only the effect of Flecknoe's speech, not the quality of Dryden's verse which is no more dully static here than it was earlier tautological. Rather, it is brilliantly diverse 'in number as in sense'. In sense it is ingenious in the changes it rings on the original formula; in number, though the passage consists entirely of couplets, the closed rhetorical units vary in length from two to ten lines, resulting in an engaging counterpoint. At the same time, the irony and varied wit are effectively removed from Flecknoe himself, making the speech seem endlessly redundant and dull even when the passage isn't.

20 See Virgil, *Georgics*, II. 404, *Aeneid*, I. 591 and X. 172; Horace, *Epodes*, XI. 6 and XVII. 8; Cowley, *op. cit.*, p. 284 and p. 306; and Pope's *Odyssey*, XI. 235 and XVIII. 182.

21 The reversal certainly sounds Latinate, but I have been unable to find examples in Latin poetry or rhetoric. 'Horror Plum'd' instead of a horrible plume in *Paradise Lost*, IV. 989 might be cited as another example.

22 Like 'damps of oblivion', the pivot occurs because of a discrepancy between sound and sense. 'Supinely' sounds dignified, and probably for this reason both Dryden and Pope use it in their translations from classical epics. (See Dryden's *Ceyx and Alcyone*, ll. 294–5, and Pope's *Iliad*, IV. 603.) But sound aside, the physical posture denoted by the word is unmistakably demeaning. It makes Dryden's adverbial usage ironically inappropriate, since one can't *do* very much supinely, the more ironically inappropriate because the word is made to modify the most active of all verbs, 'reign'. In retrospect, then, we see that though the oak may be a traditional symbol of royalty, the real similarity between Shadwell and the oak is that they both lack consciousness, they are literally 'thoughtless'. And, of course, both Shadwell and the oak are huge. Shadwell is eye-filling not in some spiritual and quasi-metaphorical sense of strikingly graceful, but literally because of his enormous girth, his 'goodly...spread'. The values suggested by the epic vocabulary gradually disintegrate under the inert weight of fact: the man is fat and dull.

23 See Earl Miner, 'Dryden and the Issue of Human Progress', *PQ*, XL (1961), pp. 120–9.

24 *The Rise of English Literary History* (Chapel Hill, 1941), p. 26.

25 For my discussion in the next few pages the following works may be cited: J. B. Bury, *The Idea of Progress* (London, 1928); Douglas Bush, *The Renaissance and English Humanism* (Toronto, 1939); Wallace K. Ferguson, *The Renaissance* (New York, 1940); R. G. Collingwood, *The Idea of History* (Oxford, 1946); Wallace K. Ferguson, *Renaissance Historical Thought* (Boston, 1948); Patrick Gardiner, editor, *Theories of History* (The Free Press of Glencoe, 1959); Harry Elmer Barnes, *A History of Historical Writing* (New

York, 1962); F. Smith Fussner, *The Historical Revolution* (London, 1962);
Arthur B. Ferguson, *The Articulate Citizen and the English Renaissance* (Durham,
N.C., 1965); F. J. Levy, *Tudor Historical Thought* (San Marino, 1967); and
Peter Burke, *The Renaissance Sense of the Past* (London, 1969).

26 Ferguson, *The Articulate Citizen, op. cit.*, p. xiv.
27 Fussner, *The Historical Revolution, op. cit.*, p. 9.
28 See French R. Fogle, 'Milton as Historian', in *Milton and Clarendon, Two Papers on 17th Century English Historiography* (Los Angeles, 1965).
29 It would be tempting to suppose that Dryden himself came to some such realization in falling out of love with rhyme, as he says in the Prologue to *Aureng-Zebe*. One might even speculate that his work in 'tagging' *Paradise Lost* (1674?) had contributed to such an awareness, or that his experience in adapting *Antony and Cleopatra* the year before writing *Mac Flecknoe* tended to confirm it. But certainly Dryden didn't think in these terms, either of '*the couplet*' as a single fixed stylistic ideal, or of an inevitable connection between meter and sensibility.

Dryden's relation to Milton, though, remains a fascinating area for speculation. See the following: Bonamy Dobrée, 'Milton and Dryden: A Comparison and Contrast in Poetic Ideas and Poetic Method', *ELH*, III (1936), pp. 83–100; Morris Freedman, 'Milton and Dryden on Rhyme', *HLQ*, XXIV (1961), pp. 337–44; George McFadden, 'Dryden's "Most Barren Period" – and Milton', *HLQ*, XXIV (1961), pp. 233–96; and Anne D. Ferry, *Milton and the Miltonic Dryden* (Cambridge, Mass., 1968).
30 *ECS*, I (1967), pp. 3–32, p. 22.
31 *Lives of the English Poets*, edited by George Birkbeck Hill (3 vols.; Oxford, 1905), III. p. 346.

CONCLUSION

1 The criticism on *Absalom and Achitophel* is particularly good, a secondary index to the poem's success. The following works offer interesting and informative commentary: Samuel Johnson, *Lives of the English Poets*, edited by George Birkbeck Hill (3 vols.; Oxford, 1905), I. pp. 436–7; A. W. Verrall, *Lectures on Dryden* (Cambridge, 1914); R. F. Jones, 'The Originality of *Absalom and Achitophel*', *MLN*, XLVI (1931), pp. 211–18; Ruth C. Wallerstein, 'To Madness Near Allide: Shaftesbury and His Place in the Design and Thought of *Absalom and Achitophel*', *HLQ*, VI (1943), pp. 445–71; Godfrey Davies, 'The Conclusion of Dryden's *Absalom and Achitophel*', *HLQ*, X (1946), pp. 69–82; Ian Jack, *Augustan Satire* (Oxford, 1952); Morris Freedman, 'Dryden's Miniature Epic', *JEGP*, LVII (1958), pp. 211–19; A. B. Chambers, '*Absalom and Achitophel*: Christ and Satan', *MLN*, LXXIV (1959), pp. 592–6; Bernard N. Schilling, *Dryden and the Conservative Myth, A Reading of 'Absalom and Achitophel'* (New Haven, 1961); Arthur W. Hoffman, *John Dryden's Imagery* (Gainesville, 1962); Alan Roper, *Dryden's Poetic Kingdoms* (London, 1965); Earl Miner, *Dryden's Poetry* (Bloomington, 1967); Anne D. Ferry, *Milton and the Miltonic Dryden* (Cambridge, 1968); George R. Levine, 'Dryden's "Inarticulate Poesy"', *ECS*, I (1968), pp. 291–312; Leonora Leet

Brodwin, 'Miltonic Allusion in *Absalom and Achitophel*: Its Function in the Political Satire', *JEGP*, LXI (1969), pp. 24–44; Léon M. Guilhamet, 'Dryden's Debasement of Scripture in *Absalom and Achitophel*', *SEL*, IX (1969), pp. 395–413; Bruce King, '*Absalom and Achitophel*: A Revaluation', in *Dryden's Mind and Art*, edited by Bruce King (Edinburgh, 1969), pp. 65–83; and Paul Ramsey, *The Art of John Dryden* (Lexington, 1969).

2 King, '*Absalom and Achitophel*: A Revaluation', *op. cit.*, p. 68.

3 Ramsey, *The Art of John Dryden, op. cit.*, pp. 124–5.

4 See Mark Van Doren's more extensive list, *John Dryden, A Study of His Poetry* (Bloomington, 1960), pp. 134–9.

5 *The Prologues and Epilogues of John Dryden*, edited by William Bradford Gardiner (New York, 1951), p. 29.

6 *Ibid.*, p. 131.

7 *Ibid.*, p. 182.

8 Dryden plays interestingly and amusingly on this apparent incongruity in his Prologue to *The Disappointment, ibid.*, p. 142.

9 See K. G. Hamilton, *John Dryden and the Poetry of Statement* (East Lansing, 1969).

10 Johnson's *Lives, op. cit.*, I. p. 469.

INDEX

Abbreviation used: D for Dryden